THE AMERICAN WAY OF LIFE

by

THE CITY LIBRARY ASSOCIATION
SPRINGFIELD, MASSACHUSETTS

THE
AMERICAN WAY
OF LIFE

by Ashley Montagu

G. P. PUTNAM'S SONS

NEW YORK

Fourth Impression

Library of Congress Catalog Card Number: 66–27680

Five of the essays in these pages have appeared in slightly different form in
other places. For permission to reprint I am grateful to the following: "Television and the New Image of Man," Columbia Broadcasting System, New
York, and Holt, Rinehart and Winston, New York, from *The Eighth Art*,
1962, pp. 125–134; "Life, Liberty, and Homeostasis," *Archives of Environmental Health*," vol. 9, 1964, pp. 403–407; "Clothes and Behavior," *Profiles*,
vol. 2, 1964, pp. 9–11; "The American Woman," *Saturday Review*, vol. 41,
1958, pp. 13ff.; "The Masculine Expression of Emotion," *The New York
Times Magazine*, May 26, 1957, pp. 17–18.

PRINTED IN THE UNITED STATES OF AMERICA
BY AMERICAN BOOK–STRATFORD PRESS, INC.

To
ROSALIND GREENE

Contents

[7

Preface

OF AMERICA, however critically one speaks, one can only do so with love, for America, as Scott Fitzgerald said, is a willingness of the heart. Is there another land of which this can be said as profoundly as it can of America? If in this book I write of America as one would of a winsome peccant child or of a generous and gifted friend who is living his life neither wisely nor well, it is not from dislike or despair, but from deep affection and the hope that wisdom and a decent regard for the welfare of others may yet prevail in this magical land. For it *is* a magical land, in which almost anything can happen—and usually does. And this is the promise of America, that it is so vitally alive and so full of promises. Many of these promises have already been realized; others are in process of being achieved. But there are also many to whom these promises have never been kept, to whom these promises have been broken, millions who have remained impoverished and unfulfilled. Great injustices, cruelties, and overwhelming follies have been committed in this land of ours and visited upon its natural beauties. The rape and pillage continue. All these things need to be underscored, and the remedies, wherever possible, suggested. There are also many little things that require attention. And, finally, there are certain special qualities and virtues, characteristically American, which bear remarking.

If the unexamined life is not worth living, so is that of the unexamined society. America has not wanted for examiners. Perhaps it has wanted for a sufficient number of self-examiners. In any event, I can only express the hope that my desultory thoughts on the Great Experiment, which may yet turn into the Great Society, will be received in the spirit in which they are offered.

The title of this book requires an explanation, and perhaps also an apology. The book is in no sense intended as a study in depth of either America or the American character. It pretends to be no more than a series of animadversions on various aspects of the American scene that have exercised my interest and, I hope, may similarly exercise that of the reader. To describe the burden of ideas which the book so lightly bears, it was decided, after much discussion, to call the book *The American Way of Life,* for that is what it is about. If the title suggests a systematic study in depth, as well it may, I regret if it shall have misled some readers. That was not the intention.

ASHLEY MONTAGU

Princeton, New Jersey
25 October 1966

The New Yahoos

THEY LOOK like human beings. They dress like human beings. They make sounds like human beings. They have been to school and even to college, and they are as kind to their women and children as most other parents, and yet while they must be fully acknowledged as members of the species man, they are essentially antihuman. They stand opposed to virtually everything that humanity has triumphantly achieved in the course of two million years of evolution. The rule of law, political equality, justice, truth, reason, beauty, excellence, the enduring values of Western civilization—these are empty and meaningless shibboleths to these antihuman men and women. Worst of all, they not only do not believe in these values, but also consider them evil, dangerous, subversive, Communist, liberal, radical, and, at any cost, to be abolished. These are the New Yahoos, conspicuously represented—only because they were so prominent —by Mr. Barry Goldwater of Arizona and Mr. William Miller of New York.

It is an appalling reflection that in the second half of the twentieth century anyone could have considered these two men seriously for any governmental office whatever. But the dreadful fact is that millions not only did so, but also voted

[13

for the one as President and for the other as Vice-President of
the United States. Not only were millions of Americans
shocked into the realization that their country had fallen into
a frightening state, but so was the greater part of the rest of
the world.

Something very clearly had gone wrong. That there could
have been so many Americans who were unable to see what
was wrong with a Goldwater and a Miller, and who thought
as they did—if what they were engaged in could have been
said to have been thinking at all—would in itself have been a
disheartening thought, were it not for the consideration that
by virtue of the fact that these people belong to the species
man, their children, if not they themselves, are capable of
being taught to use their minds critically; to distinguish right
from wrong and good from evil; to weigh the evidence for
themselves; to be able to distinguish prejudices for what they
are, not alone in themselves but also in others; and not to
deny them when they recognize them, but to admit them
freely and do what is necessary to control them.

It is not that our schools have failed, but they have never
begun to do what they were presumably created for—namely,
to educate. We instruct. We do not educate. Instruction is
the training in the three R's, in practical skills and techniques. These have their place and their importance, but
only in the secondary service of by far the most important
skill: the ability to relate oneself warmly, cooperatively, and
creatively to other human beings. This entails not only the
cultivation of the human spirit, of *humanitas,* but also the
training in the ability to think, to use one's mind as a finely
critical instrument. It is principally because this has not been
done in our schools, as well as outside them, that the New
Yahoos are so many among us.

What are the marks of the New Yahoo? *One,* he is unable

to use his mind to weigh, judge, and evaluate evidence critically for himself. *Two,* he is uninterested in discovering what the facts are and is concerned only with pushing his prejudices, his prejudgments, which serve him for truth enough. *Three,* he functions by rationalizations, stereotypes, clichés, shibboleths, unexamined evidence, and wish fulfillment. *Four,* he is a true believer—that is, he believes that what he believes must be right because he believes it and is therefore quite unwilling to admit that he may be wrong. He speaks, therefore, ex cathedra, with the conviction of infallibility, and even though this means that he is infallibly wrong, his defenses are such that he is quite incapable of ever becoming aware of the fact. Like the pupil of the eye, the more light one exposes him to, the narrower he becomes. *Five,* he speaks with great glibness and is wholly unaware of the fact that his eloquence obscures a virtually complete absence of ideas. The "facts" and the "ideas" that constitute his currency are usually wholly spurious, but this does not faze him a bit, because he can always rationalize his original statements. This is, of course, never thought of by him as rationalization. It is an "explanation." Should the "explanation" be torpedoed, there then follows an "explanation" to "explain" the "explanation." His stock-in-trade, therefore, is a profusion, or rather a confusion, of pseudological rationalizations based on a muddlement of unexamined wish fulfillments. The trouble with the New Yahoo is that he is unable to distinguish a fact from a fancy and, what is worse, doesn't want to. *Six,* he is, of course, a passionate patriot and regularly displays the flag on the proper and even the improper occasions. He is likely to be, if he is old enough, a member of such august organizations as the American Legion and the Veterans of Foreign Wars. He loves to sing the national anthem, to salute the flag, to place his hand over his spleen, his sternum, or the apex of his left lung—under the impression that his heart is in one or another of these places—and pledge allegiance to the flag of the United States of America, one nation under God, indivisible, with liberty and justice for all—and then to oppose the civil rights bill, discriminate against whoever he believes ought to be discriminated against, maintain the *status quo* which terrorizes Negroes into submission, declare white murderers of Negroes and civil rights workers not guilty of the crimes everyone knows they committed, and be doggedly opposed to every measure that would ensure liberty and justice for anyone other than the members of his own group. He is a joiner, for being essentially a weak character himself, he draws his strength from the group. Since there are others like himself everywhere, he never wants for a group to join. *Seven,* he does not read books, except an occasional lurid novel, or a short political tract, and, of course, the reactionary newspaper or periodical which feeds him all he wants to know and supports him in his beliefs. *Eight,* he is not much of a churchgoer, but he firmly believes in religion. If not a pillar, he is at least a flying buttress of the Church. He knows that if he looks after God, God will look after him. In God he trusts. It never occurs to him that to the kind of man he is and to what he stands for, virtually all religions, especially the religion represented by the teachings of Jesus, are opposed—at least by the book, if not in practice. *Nine,* he believes in the Constitution of the United States of America— that is, after it has been privately amended to meet his special requirements. After all, that document was put together by a lot of revolutionaries, some of whom like Thomas Jefferson, were out-and-out radicals. The Constitution has needed revision for a long time, and he and his friends are the ones to do it. And *ten* (to round out our arbitrary number), he identifies national welfare with self-interest; hence, he is opposed to anything designed to minister to the welfare of others, since he is afraid it will cost him money and lead to all sorts of "Socialistic" changes—"Socialistic" being merely his euphemism for "Communistic." He is therefore opposed to any form of federal support of medical care or individual or community welfare. As Mr. Goldwater has said, the poor have no one to blame for their poverty but themselves, and it is *they*, not the government, who ought to do something about their lot. Anything approaching the welfare state is Socialism, which everyone knows is "the back door to Communism." That Sweden and England have been welfare states for many years and continue to be in every way antipathetic and utterly opposed to Communism is a fact which they wholly ignore, since it does not suit their book, if one assumes, of course, that they have in some cases taken the trouble to acquaint themselves with the facts. In the majority of cases they are wholly ignorant of the facts, since their ignorance of other peoples is equaled only by their ignorance of their own.

The highest frequency of Yahoos undoubtedly occurs in the South, with California running a close second. All John Birchers qualify, as well as Ku Klux Klanners and, of course, the larger proportion of the members of other extreme right groups. The New Yahoos are to be found in all walks of life, and the thought of their ubiquity constitutes genuine cause for alarm. Their number has increased, and so, I suspect, have their proportions. They have become more vocal and more influential than ever before. Since their views are in essence and in fact antihuman, it would be worth the effort to prevent even a single individual from exposure to the contagious disease which the Yahoos constitute. Millions of Americans are infected and transmit the virus to their children. What is so alarming about this is not merely that damage is done to so many Americans, but that because of the great power that America wields in the affairs of the world, the New Yahoos are frequently in a position to influence, unfavorably, the lives of millions of other people throughout the world. This is why the proceedings at the Republican convention in 1964 and its culmination in the nominations of such candidates as Messrs. Goldwater and Miller had such a disquieting effect abroad.

What most frightened the peoples of the world was the fact that there were in America a large enough number of people who were enough like Goldwater* and Miller to want to see them in the highest and most important offices in the land. It was not so much the thought that these men might be elected that was frightening, as the idea that such men could be nominated for such posts at all. What it meant for them was that Americans must be in a very bad way indeed if they could seriously consider that such men represented the best interests of humanity, even though those interests were limited to the United States. And, indeed, it was a frightening thought to millions of Americans. The only foreign government and press to express approval of the Republican candidates were those of fascist Spain. It figures.

Fortunately, Goldwater was resoundingly beaten. It is best to regard that event not as a victory, but as a grace, a warning not to return to that complacency which will ever again permit the spread of the virus of domestic extremisms of the right, while our attention is focused on the control of foreign-born extremisms of the left.

The dangers we must be alive to from within are not less serious than those we have to be concerned with from without. If anything, the threats to our integrity and well-being

---

* It has been said that the press was very unfair to Goldwater. I believe there can be no doubt of it: the papers printed everything he said.

from within are more dangerous than those from without. Because they are native-grown and because we are so much in the midst of them, there is a tendency to take our domestic extremisms less seriously than those introduced from foreign sources. This is a mistake. We must reflect deeply on the meaning of Goldwater's candidacy and learn from that experience what it is that must be done to make the candidates for high office in both parties worthy of those offices and of their country.

Extremism in defense of liberty *is* a vice, and moderation in the pursuit of justice *is* a virtue. And that is the essence of the meaning of democracy. Those who deny this are the greatest enemies of democracy. They are the New Yahoos.

Generosity

AMERICANS ARE the most generous people in the world. Generosity is one of the happy traits that immediately impress visiting Europeans, and it is an experience in humanity which they never forget. Whether it is the largeness of the land which is responsible for this expansiveness of the American spirit or whether it represents the continuation of the tradition of good-neighborliness of pioneering days, whatever the explanation generosity is an outstanding trait of Americans. And this is so at every level: individual, familial, community, collective, and governmental.

The hospitality of Americans approaches the proverbial. If there isn't such a proverb, then there ought to be: hospitable and generous as an American. This generosity extends from the lowermost to the uppermost classes. Such things as strangers do not exist in America. Even the familiar greeting of the standard Western, "Howdy, stranger," is an invitation to becoming better acquainted and a bid to friendliness. In other parts of the English-speaking world the established attitudes make it mandatory that others remain strangers until they are properly introduced. In America, formalities in general are held to be so much window dressing, and it is considered quite unnecessary to go through the machinery of a formal introduction before speaking to anyone. It is taken for granted that everyone's intentions are the friendliest. Hence, most Americans feel quite unconstrained and free to open a conversation with anyone who may be within earshot.

Finding himself at the side of his newfound friend in a vehicle bound for some distant destination, the average American will before very long take his wallet from his pocket and introduce his companion, by way of photographs, to all the members of the family, naming each one and extolling their individual virtues. This will usually be followed up by an invitation to visit them all if you are ever in the neighborhood. He means this quite honestly and is not merely being polite. Most Americans are not polite. They tend to regard politeness with some suspicion, even as an evidence of insincerity. They themselves tend to be unpolished, but diamonds—even though in the rough—for all that. The President of the United States, Lyndon B. Johnson, was exhibiting this friendliness when he exposed the scar on his upper abdomen following his gallbladder operation. It was a generous gesture, made among friends. If it offended the sensibilities of those who saw the photograph in the newspapers, it was because they thought the gesture lacked the dignity which should be associated with the person holding the office of President of the United States. But following Sterne's remark that dignity is a mysterious carriage of the body calculated to conceal the infirmities of the mind, Mr. Johnson would have none of it. As some wit remarked, it is perhaps a good thing that the operation had not been for hemorrhoids.

American generosity is infectious. Europeans who settle in America quickly lose the constraints that have intimidated and prevented them from being as free and open as Americans. It is a much healthier and pleasanter state in which to be. Human beings are much less islands unto themselves in America than elsewhere in the Western world. Interestingly enough, there are regional differences in the warmth, demonstrativeness, and neighborliness of Americans. Middle Westerners generally complain of the lack of neighborliness they experience in other parts of the country. Indeed, Middle Westerners pining for the human warmth of their own region have been known to relinquish their jobs in the humanly colder climates of the land and return to the balmier environment of the Middle West.

Although in other regions of the country the people tend to be more restrained, they are not less generous. Even in New England, where the frost of the Puritan spirit still holds many of its victims in an emotional deepfreeze, perhaps the most courageous forms of expression of the generous human spirit that exist anywhere in the world are to be found. The possible exception is the Vermonter, laconic, taciturn, and frugal, who could hardly be described as generous. Possibly it is because Vermont has for long been a sort of rural backwater, unwealthy, with a rocky soil and a difficult environment in which to make a living. What is hard to get is difficult to give.

Getting and spending bring us naturally to a highly important aspect of American generosity. It is the belief, and its implementation, that the more generous one is, the greater are likely to be the satisfactions one derives from that generosity. In this belief Americans differ, especially in the business world, very markedly from other peoples. In much of Europe, for example, especially in England, it is the general belief that the more one saves, the more profits one makes. It is the very opposite of the principle by which Americans work—namely, the more one spends, the greater the profits. The prosperity of the United States testifies to the soundness of that principle, while England, beyond all other countries, stands as eloquent testimony to the fact that a penny-pinching, shortsighted economy works nowhere nearly as well. America is not simply the affluent society; it is the opulent society, and it is opulent because it is generously spirited. The meanness and pettiness, the narrowness of vision, the couldn't-care-less attitudes of many Europeans, and the consequent inefficiency simply do not exist in America at any level. American businessmen are not only willing but anxious to spend enormous sums of money investing in ideas that businessmen hardly anywhere else in the world would even venture to consider.

In America there are more foundations by far whose sole purpose it is to give away money than there are in the rest of the world put together. The Ford and the Rockefeller foundations are the best known, but there are literally hundreds of others. The generosity of the great foundations is not limited to America but embraces the entire world. The good these foundations have done in the world is immense. It matters not whether it is appreciated abroad in the lands in which that generosity has done so much good—and this is a measure of the genuine generosity of Americans—for they do what they can to help where help is needed, with no strings attached.

Whatever some may believe concerning the nature of the political motivation behind the gifts, amounting to billions of dollars, which the United States government has made to so many nations, those gifts have been made in the genuine desire to be of help. Never before in the history of international polity has any nation been so bountiful, so humanly concerned for the welfare of less fortunate peoples. The cynic may sneer and point out that our gifts are not altogether disinterested or without certain returns on the investments made in this manner. And that may be true. The American government, unlike many other governments, is *not* disinterested in the welfare of other peoples. It *is* concerned that those peoples shall maintain their independence and not be wracked by the internal disorders which provide opportunities for the imposition of external ideologies. In short, the American government wants to encourage the conditions in which democracy may have a chance to develop rather than stand idly by and see other peoples, for want of the necessary help, fall victim, in desperation, to the siren promises of Communism. Because of its conspiratorial character, Communism is a threat to the continued existence of democracy, and most Americans, rightly I think, believe that democracy is a far superior form of government to Communism, and they react to the threat that Communism constitutes, if not always with wisdom, with behavior calculated to reduce the dimensions of that threat. Government spokesmen have openly and repeatedly avowed this viewpoint, and there is nothing deep, dark, or secret about it.

The American worker

IN POST OFFICE murals and similarly disposed representations one sometimes encounters the work of a perceptive artist paying homage to the American worker, but for the most part the American worker goes pretty much uncelebrated. Like the nose on one's face, the American worker is, I think, too much taken for granted. I want to sing a paean of praise to him.

Comparisons may be odious, but one has only to compare the American worker at every level, especially the laborer, with his English counterpart to be struck by the significant contrast. The English laborer at work is a study in slow motion. In comparison with the American laborer, while working, the Englishman is unemployed about two-thirds of the time. His heart is not in it. He seems to be dispirited; the life appears to have gone out of him. By contrast, the American laborer throws himself into his work wholeheartedly, as if it were something worth doing well, even though it may be anything but that. When he works, he works. He efficiently does the job for which he is paid. The English laborer seems more interested in avoiding work, in slacking on the job, and efficiency is no concern of his. The American worker, on the other hand, is interested in doing a good job; he takes pride in doing a good job, whatever the job may be. The result is a high-quality product, whether it be a road, a bridge, a ditch, plumbing, or planes. And what a difference this makes to an economy—as one may observe by comparing the English with the American economy!

The foundation of every industrial society is its workers. If the workers do not work, the society does not work. If the workers are incompetent and inefficient, the society will suffer. Against such a contingency, American society has a built-in safeguard—the American worker. I don't think his merits are sufficiently recognized or appreciated or celebrated.

Management has the advantage, in America, of being able to rely on a superb working force. American management deserves great credit for utilizing that labor force as intelligently as it does.

The pursuit of happiness

HAPPINESS, IN AMERICA, is a guarantee set out in the Declaration of Independence. It is one of the unalienable rights, the other two being life and liberty. As that distinguished American philosopher the late Fred Allen once remarked, "You only live once. But if you live it right, once is enough." And most Americans are frenetically engaged in attempting to live it right.

Liberty is interpreted as the moral right to get away with as much as one can without being caught or, to put it in the higher English, economic libertinism. Happiness is the biggest business. American parents are dedicated to the proposition that unless their children are a mighty sight happier than they themselves were as children, they have failed as parents. And so, of course, everything must be made easy for the children, and their every need satisfied. Even the bandages with which their scratches are covered must be "ouchless." It is all very well meaning, but brainless, and it does a lot of harm. It is the myth of happiness that is at the root of the trouble, and it is, therefore, worth examining.

The pursuit of happiness in America is perhaps the most misconceived of human endeavors. Life and liberty are indeed necessities, but the pursuit of happiness is a fool's game, a will-o'-the-wisp that eludes all who believe that by making it a goal, they can, by the prescribed or some other means, achieve it. The truth is—and it is not a sad truth—that happiness cannot be pursued and caught like a butterfly in the collector's net. It defies pursuit, and all attempts to contain it are vain. Nor can it be purchased. It is one of the many things that money cannot buy.

Who was it who started this hare, and how long ago? At English dog races there is a mechanical hare that the dogs chase but are never supposed to catch—but sometimes they do make a catch in spite of the men working the machine. The god in the machine who presides over the races that men run sees to it that they seldom catch up with the hare. He knows that permitting them to catch the hare is no way to run a race, thereby exhibiting the wisdom we have a right to expect from an all-seeing and understanding god in possession of all his faculties. Competent gods possess horse sense; this is more than human beings do. And horse sense has been defined as that which enables a horse not to bet on human beings.

The truth is that it is not the purpose of life, of a human being's life, to be happy. Perhaps this is a shocking statement to those who have been conditioned to feel otherwise, but it is nonetheless true for all that. If true, then millions of human beings have misspent and are misspending their lives.

What is happiness? The answer to that question is not a matter of definition, but rather what most people mean by happiness. What is it that they desire for themselves and for others when they think of happiness? Apart from the obvious requirements of health, money, an attractive spouse, gratifying children, a beautiful abode, esteem, prestige, recognition, wit, wisdom, valor, love, and the attainment of whatever one has set one's heart on, what other ingredients should go into this cake? Possibly a good many others, but this will be according to each person's fancy.

My own view is that not one of these conditions is either a necessary or a sufficient condition of happiness, although one or all of them together may give some people for a time a feeling of whatever they consider happiness to be. But such a feeling soon loses its power to please as, in time, one returns to the steadying level of everyday life. I believe with Aristotle that the steadiest and most enduring states of which human beings are capable are states that are characterized by an absence of pain—physical pain and mental pain. Such states of the positive absence of pain are appreciated for the most part only when they are interrupted, as by the experience of illness or a bereavement. It is in the state when one is least conscious of oneself that one is likely to be at one's happiest. What folly it is to believe otherwise! To believe that those occasional peak experiences, those thrilling moments when the goal one has set oneself has been achieved, or it just feels good to be alive, or one receives an unexpected windfall, or one's work is highly praised, are likely to be numerous and prolonged is silly. Such occasions are indeed memorable, but the feelings of euphoria they generate do not endure, nor should they. How unpleasant it would be to be in a constant state of high spirits! Madmen are often so. The healthy-minded are content with occasional elevations of spirit. It is the sick and the depressed who seek to buoy their flagging spirits with drugs and "thrills" that will render them high.

There is a Kentucky hillbilly response to the greeting "How are you?" It is, "So's t' git along." It is enough—perhaps more than enough, but enough. As Lord Morley remarked many years ago, it is enough for a man to be, to do, and to depart gracefully. How ridiculous this cult of happiness is! "So's t' git along." That is what the majority of human beings who live at a subsistence level would be willing to settle for. To have enough to keep body and soul together, a bed to sleep on, a spouse, sexual satisfaction, and children. The rest is gravy. Those who live at a subsistence level are unconcerned with such trivial and unreal matters as happiness. It is only when the standard of living rises that the interest in happiness seems to develop—not, it would appear, because life has in other ways become happier, but largely because under the improved conditions of life the new problems that are created produce the pressures, the need, for their reduction. And one way of counterbalancing, it is thought, the weight of these new problems is the pursuit of happiness. It sounds silly put that way, but it is no less than the truth. And what is no less than the truth is that life will always be difficult. "Life," as E. M. Forster put it, "is a public performance on the violin, in which you must learn the instrument as you go along." It takes a lot of stress and strain to bring off such a performance, and if sometimes we manage a credible few bars, it is as pleasant as it is unexpected. And so it is. The moments of happiness we enjoy take us by surprise. It is not that we seize them, but that they seize us. Walking in a field on a lovely summer day, and suddenly stopping in one's tracks, filled with the beauty of it all, feeling how good it is to be alive—*this* is happiness.

But would the felon in the same field, pursued by his trackers, looking about him and perceiving the same beauty, glad that he was alive, say that at that moment he was happy? I think not. The sudden glory one experiences at such moments, if I interpret it aright, represents the expression, the culmination, the reward for something that has been earned—not by any means something that one has set out to earn, but a by-product of the dedication, the labor, that has been involved. Those who, looking back on their lives, have reflected most deeply on the matter, have independently arrived at the same conclusion—namely, that work is the most dependable of all sources of happiness. As Voltaire put it in

Candide, "Labor preserves us from three great evils—weariness, vice, and want. . . . Let us work without disputing; it is the only way to render life tolerable." Baudelaire wrote, "How many years of fatigue and punishment it takes to learn the simple truth that work, that disagreeable thing, is the only way of not suffering in life, or at all events of suffering less." John Ruskin wrote, "When men are rightly occupied, their amusement grows out of their work, as the colour-petals out of a fruitful flower." Ask yourself whether you are happy, said John Stuart Mill, and you cease to be so. Seek happiness, and it will escape you. Happiness is a by-product of other things and comes by the way, chiefly as a by-product of work.

It is not so much the pursuit of happiness as the happiness of pursuit that is most likely to yield the desired gratifications, and then only occasionally. It is work, work that one delights in, that is the surest guarantor of happiness. But even here it is a work that has to be earned by labor in one's earlier years. One should labor so hard in youth that everything one does subsequently is easy by comparison. In much of America we take the opposite view, and by trying to make things as easy as possible in childhood and youth, we most of the time succeed only in making them difficult later. And this brings us naturally to the subject of work.

Work

Work is doing what one likes to do. Labor is doing what one has to do, and generally something that one does not like to do. It is a very necessary distinction, especially in a land like the United States, in which labor is confused with work. Because work is thought of as something unpleasant, parents and others do everything in their power to help their children do as little as possible of anything resembling work. As

Nathaniel Hawthorne put it, "Labor is the curse of the world, and nobody can meddle with it without becoming proportionately brutified." At least this is the view that many Americans take of work insofar as their children are concerned. This seems to be particularly true of those parents who have themselves had to labor hard in order to establish themselves. With the best intentions they resolve that their children will not have to work as hard as they did, that life will be easier for their children than it was for them.

This apparently well-meaning attitude of American parents toward their children is often a device for enjoying vicariously the freedoms that they themselves were not permitted when they were young. When they make things easy for their children, they are as often as not indulging themselves. To demand work of children seems cruel when after a long day at school they should enjoy their freedom howsoever they please and should be encouraged to do so, especially by their parents. No one speaks of the freedom to work as the greatest of all freedoms, as necessary to health as physical exercise. Work exercises and is necessary to the growth and development of the human faculties. It is the chord of might that gives the human being his essential powers.

"Life, liberty, and the pursuit of happiness" do not imply in any way that work is to be avoided. Indeed, since work is the most dependable source of happiness, the most efficient way of achieving happiness is through work. If parents and all others would understand this and do what is necessary to train their children in habits of work, they would be doing, in the best of all possible ways, what would be most likely to ensure their children's happiness. All studies designed to throw light on the subject agree in showing that those children who have been brought up by strict loving parents who have expected their children to work and who have brooked no laxity are likely to be the healthiest and most accomplished achievers. There is an old German saying, "Work makes life sweet," that in four words comes as near to stating the formula for happiness and success as any has ever done. Work is the solvent for pain and the means to fulfillment. And it is as essential for individual health as it is for the health of the nation.

Children should be trained in regular habits of work from the earliest age, not for work's sake, but for the sake of such happiness as they may through its means be able to achieve.

Conformity

A FRIEND OF MINE, a high-school teacher in one of the Mountain States, was criticized publicly by a powerful local businessman for riding a bicycle to school on the ground that it was unbecoming in a teacher and smacked of subversion. What made the offense even worse was that the bicycle was not American—it was made in England. How un-American could a teacher get!

On more than one occasion I have been criticized for appearing on the lecture platform in a nonwhite shirt. Surely a man capable of wearing a nonwhite shirt on such an occasion would be capable of anything! And I suppose he would.

Such incidents could be dismissed as silly and beneath notice, were it not for the fact that they are anything but. Unfortunately the attitudes reflected by such criticisms indicate a kind of conformism that is widespread in America and is symptomatic of more serious disorders. These disorders mostly add up to a profound feeling of insecurity, one of whose external evidences is a generalized anxiety. This takes the form of a fear of anything that in any way challenges or in the least deviates from the rigid beliefs and practices to which most Americans conform. These rigidified conformists

dare not depart from the straight and narrow path which
they so anxiously follow, for fear that if they did deviate to
the left or right, they would never be able to find their way
back again.

This kind of conformity is produced by the rigid set of
requirements to which children are forced to subscribe by
their parents, teachers, church, peer groups, and other socializing agencies. Under the pressures of such socializing agencies it is difficult for most individuals to escape becoming
anything other than the echo of other people's voices. It is
certainly easier that way. The weak always need to draw
strength from identification with the group, even though the
members of the group may covertly engage in conduct which
is anything but conformist. The important thing is not to
rock the boat. Anyone who does that makes the conformist
feel insecure, and that he finds abhorrent. Any departure
from moral norms and their violation upset him and tend to
elicit his hostility. Because he is different, the conformist sees
the nonconformist as an implied threat to his ego. This is
frightening to the conformist, and therefore, he insists on
conformity or else attempts to destroy the nonconformist
because he sees him as independent, free, strong, mature, and
imaginative—all the things which the conformist is not and
which, often, he would unconsciously like to be.

The psychosclerosis from which the conformist suffers is
one of the most dispiriting things to behold, for it is when the
individual loses his freedom by becoming hardened in his
beliefs and conduct that he becomes most inhuman and in
the name of freedom is likely to commit the most frightful
atrocities. It is for this reason that conformism, no matter in
whom and where it is found, must be viewed as a psychosis
which should generate something more than alarm, for, as
Emerson put it, "Whoso would be a man must be a non-

conformist." Blessed, indeed, is the society which has its proper share of nonconformists, for they are the reshapers and remakers of the world. The conformists tend to be obstructionists, the maintainers of the *status quo,* come weal or woe.

It is doubtful that America breeds more conformists than other countries, and I also doubt that, on the whole, they exercise more power in this country than conformists do in other countries. Certainly extreme forms of conformity, of a kind from which other lands are comparatively free, are encountered in many places in America. For example, American schools, colleges, and universities, unlike their European equivalents, scarcely ever provide a berth for or encourage the eccentric. It is possible to visit one educational institution after another without ever observing an oddball on the faculty. Yet it is the oddballs who, because they choose to be independent in their thinking and conduct, have often been the most significant contributors to the welfare of their fellowmen. One thinks of Newton, Robert Hooke, Voltaire, Immanuel Kant, Rousseau, Heaviside, Veblen, and numerous others who would have had a difficult time, just as Thorstein Veblen did, holding a post in an American educational institution. There are and have been exceptions, but they are quite rare.

Most distressing are the young conformists. Remmers' and Radler's study *The American Teenager* (Indianapolis, Bobbs-Merrill, 1957) and Philip E. Jacob's *Changing Values in College* (New York, Harper, 1958) present a discouraging picture of the conformist young. Remmers and Radler found that 92 percent of teen-agers thought it important to think and act as other people expected them to act! By far the majority in all other respects were out-and-out conformists in their thinking, if not altogether in their conduct. Professor

Jacob's survey showed that American college students tended to think, feel, and believe alike: "To an extraordinary degree, their values are the same wherever they may be studying and whatever the stage of their college careers. The great majority seem turned out of a common mold so far as outlook on life and standards of conduct are concerned."

Could we not begin a change of stance by, for example, rewarding individuality, by teaching the young *how* to think rather than *what* to think?

Hollywood

HOLLYWOOD, THE DREAM FACTORY, situated in the middle of that anticity Los Angeles, beckons to the sun through a perennial blanket of smog, as if light ever affected the pupil of its vulgar eye in any way other than to narrow it. But let us be fair. Hollywood, during the last half century, has made some good movies, but mostly, one may suspect, by accident rather than by design. Having so long been in the hands of the most venal businessmen in the world, it has been the box office that has determined the formula for the successful film. By such a standard, as in the theater, there can be little expectation of any enduring works of art emanating from such a quarter.

The best films produced in America—*The River; David and Lisa; The Lonely One*—were made on a shoestring outside Hollywood. And that is where the best films of the present and the future, one may depend on it, will be made. The best and most gifted directors are making their films abroad. And they are making their films successfully in the only language that Hollywood seems to understand—money.

Why are foreign films so much better than American films? The box office as the principal factor has already been mentioned, but there are other factors. Hollywood reflects the taste and imagination, not so much of its film directors as of the producers and particularly the front-office people who have to justify their salaries. Talent is not wanting in America, as is evidenced by the successes of American producers and directors abroad. Jules Dassin, Richard Lester, and Stanley Kubrick could not have made the films they achieved in Europe in Hollywood. Unimpeded by the ubiquitous producer, the director enjoys the power to do pretty much as he pleases, and the result is a *Tom Jones,* a *Dr. Strangelove, The Mark, The Loneliness of the Long-Distance Runner,* and the like. Most producers ought to be discontinued, laid aside, or altogether abolished. The few who might learn to know their place should be relegated to the minor role of taking care of the husbandry, so to say, the comptrolling details, and that is about all. Whether *they* have taste and imagination is of no importance. What is of importance is that the director is well endowed with these qualities.

Foreign-produced films are better than American-produced films because in the production of foreign films the producer has usually had the good sense to leave the making of the film to the director. In other words, foreign films are better than American films because foreign films have had no producers in the American sense of the misuse of that office. Mere professionalism, of which there is plenty in Hollywood, is not enough.

Hollywood has money, technical competence, and little else. Of course, it has the great public which delights in spectaculars, Abbott and Costello, and similar mindless atrocities. As long as Hollywood caters to the lack of public taste, it will continue to produce mediocre movies. It is, of course, a mistake to think of Hollywood as it is now constituted as anything other than an industry, big business—and big business is interested in money, not in art. With this approach it is painful to observe what Hollywood does with the opportunities available to it. Virtually every subject it lays its rapacious hands on, it treats with such banality as to confer mediocrity on the most promising of themes.

As an industry, Hollywood aims to entertain, to give the public, as the stereotype has it, what it wants. In this aim Hollywood is largely successful. It has no incentive to produce works of art. The businessmen who govern the industry believe it would lose money if their films did something more than entertain. No one can say that they are wrong. But it may be argued that they are not altogether right. In fact, as the European experience proves, it may be argued that Hollywood would make more money were it to make good films rather than bad ones. The films that make most money are not the flash-in-the-pan ephemera, but the long-run films that are continually being revived. One thinks of such classics, produced over a generation ago, as *Grand Illusion, The Cabinet of Dr. Caligari, He Who Gets Slapped, The Informer, Grand Hotel, M,* and, I suppose, there will always be *Gone With the Wind.* There are also the Chaplin films. All of them are repeatedly revived, and although not all of them appeal to the popular taste, they all have earned large sums. Occasionally Hollywood has made an excellent film and has apparently been rather astonished to find that it more than earned its keep!

The unexalted, unelevating, uncourageous, conformist, and utterly antiseptic products of Hollywood, highly lacquered and colorfully prettied up, on the whole successfully manage to avoid any discussion of the basic issues of the day. No one can outdo Hollywood in the egregiousness of its patriotic fervor, guaranteed to please the Daughters of the American Revolution and American Legionnaires alike, or its flatulent reiteration of the eternal platitudes and innocu-

ously treated themes. Conventional, conformist, and cow-
ardly, Hollywood avoids the basic and controversial issues of
our times and cleaves to the safe and the insignificant. The
quality of its vision is murky; 'tis not strained. Most of the
time it takes sides—the sides that its customers are on, for
Hollywood has never failed to remember which side its bread
is buttered on.

Just as the city in which Hollywood has its being is not a
city at all but, as I have said, an anticity, so Hollywood films
are not art but anti-art. They are not even "kitsch," "camp,"
or "op," the striptease, the burlesque, of art. The works of art
that have been produced in Hollywood for the most part lie
buried in the files, in script. There, in the steel sarcophagi,
lie the scripts of such writers as Scott Fitzgerald, Aldous
Huxley, and Richard Aldington. Some of these scripts are the
best of their kind—but not for Hollywood's taste. The writers
were paid well for their work, but they wasted their time—
time which they could have put to more creatively useful
purposes. Hollywood is a bordello which attempts to force its
writers into becoming whorehouse piano players in the back
room. Prostituting its talents so shamelessly, Hollywood's
painted harlotry presents to all the world what amounts to a
perversion of what was once a great and promising medium
of communication.

The image of Americans and of American life that Hollywood presents to Americans and foreigners abroad is comprised of a combination of extreme violence, murder, deceit,
tough men and hard women, impossible children, and values
which are concentrated principally on money and sex. For
Americans it serves as a self-fulfilling prophecy: even if
America is not altogether like that, one tries to make it come
out the way it says it should be in the movies. In the movies,
crime *does* pay, even though justice eventually brings the

criminal to book, but the interim is full of accessible blondes and the blandishments of cash. If the world is full of graft and corruption, it would be foolish and very unprofitable to buck it. With its meretricious values Hollywood serves to communicate to its impressionable public that the crime lies, not in making the prophecy come true, but in getting caught during the process.

Hollywood's strange depersonalization of human beings and the glossy but dehumanized finish it puts on them are reflected in its relations with its personnel, all of whom are shuffled as if they were objects, commodities to be exploited. To this approach the more sensitive and exploited sex seems to be particularly vulnerable, as the many breakdowns and suicides over the years testify. Hollywood—the very name has become a symbol of, a synonym for, the specious, tinsel, and glitter.

Television and the new image of man

THE FIRST MAJOR STEP taken by the order of mammals that eventually led to the emergence of man was the adoption of a way of life which placed a high premium on the experience of the world through vision. Assisted by the sense of hearing, vision has been man's principal means of perception, of endowing the raw sensation with meaning, and of apprehending the dimensions of space and its content. This has constituted the experience of man's primate ancestors for a period extending more than 70,000,000 years, culminating in that most complex development—the visual brain in man.

It is, perhaps, not surprising that the vast world of experience that television presents to the sedentary viewer should have the unprecedented appeal and immediate impact it does. That one picture is worth a thousand words was already fully understood by prehistoric man of the Old Stone Age, for he spent a great deal of his time manipulating the natural and supernatural powers through the agency of his invocational cave paintings and similar devices. Prayer and incantation undoubtedly accompanied the graphic acts of communication, but these were private ritualistic acts. Television is a public communication, in which the pictures are living events brought to the viewer either as they are occuring or as they have occurred, with words and sounds that are the living realities, not merely the counterparts, of those who have uttered or created them. As such, television has conquered and controls both time and space. The whole world of experience is now brought to the viewer seated in his own home before his television set. On the television screen he may observe the living scroll of history unrolling before his eyes at the very time it is being written thousands of miles distant in regions otherwise quite inaccessible to him. Persons and places, events and ideas that he would otherwise never have experienced, are brought to him to see and hear and contemplate.

Television is the magic lantern of our grandparents, with the difference that while the magic lantern projected a static, soundless, motionless image, television brings to the viewer the simultaneous dynamic stimulations of sight, sound, and motion. Indeed, television represents the most vital of all living miracles. And as with most miracles, the theoretical and technical development of television began in the minds of men, in Clerk Maxwell's equations, in Hertz's waves, Nipkow's disk, and in Zworykin's iconoscope, and it is in the minds of men that this great victory of mind over matter can achieve even more consequential miracles, for television has it in its power to be the instrument of far greater good than any other device born of man's ingenuity, not excluding the invention of printing.

Commercial television was authorized in July, 1941. At the end of World War II there were 7,000 television sets in the United States. At the time of writing (1966) there are, in the United States, some 68,000,000 television sets in active use, and almost everyone capable of watching television does. This means, in fact, that in less than a single generation

television has become the most important means of communication in the country. Not only is the extent of its reach
without precedent or parallel, but—what is even more to the
point—so is its influence. Television is capable of moving
men to thought and action as no other medium is, and no
other medium is more fully capable of reifying the maxim
that the meaning of a word is the action it produces.

It is generally agreed that were it not for television, John
F. Kennedy would not have been elected President of the
United States. The television debates between the candidates
for the Presidency placed not only the issues, the skills, and
the knowledge of the principals before the public, but also
their personalities. It is believed that a large number of
individuals who might otherwise have voted for Mr. Nixon
switched their vote to Mr. Kennedy, not only because of the
better total showing that they believed Mr. Kennedy made,
but also because Mr. Nixon's personality did not impress
them as favorably as did Mr. Kennedy's.

Another example of the powerful influence of television is
represented by the McCarthy-Army hearings. No one who
saw those revolting proceedings on television will ever forget
the impact they made, above all, at that heroically dramatic
moment when Mr. Welch administered the ringing rebuke
which it is generally agreed delivered the *coup de grâce* to
the career of the late Senator Joseph McCarthy. If it had not
been for television, much of the impact of those hearings
would have been lost, for the conduct and personalities of the
principals could not have been communicated nearly as well
by any other medium. It was one thing for his colleagues to
experience Mr. McCarthy on the floor of the Senate, but
quite another for those selfsame Senators to experience their
colleague through the pressure of public opinion that television made possible. Without this pressure there would have
been no Senate vote of censure on Mr. McCarthy, and the

latter would impenitently have proceeded on his reckless way. No court of law has ever held the scales of justice more fairly balanced than television did for the judge and jury represented by the viewing public of the McCarthy-Army hearings. Those televised hearings were the beginning of the end of Senator Joseph McCarthy.

The difference that television has made in national elections, by bringing virtually the full proceedings into the home, is incalculable. Participation in the inauguration ceremonies is now possible for every American by way of television. The President and other members of the government now address the people directly so that for the first time in the history of nations the representatives of the people can communicate with them immediately and receive their responses almost as immediately. The fact that this is possible draws attention to an extremely important change which television has brought about. Just as the automobile has produced vast social changes and the airplane has contracted space, so television has accelerated the rate of communication at many very different levels of discourse. There can be not the least doubt that television has it within its power to become the most important of all agencies of social change. And this brings us squarely to the question which this chapter is designed to ask and to answer—namely, what are the uses of television?

No critical examination of the uses of television should, however, leave the question structured in that form. A more realistic form of the question is, what are the uses and abuses of television? Just as the morbid, the pathological, helps us understand better the meaning of healthy functioning, so a brief consideration of the abuses of television may help us understand better what the impediments are to the development of the healthy uses of television.

The principal fault of the networks and the planners of

programs has been the underestimation of the needs of the great varieties of viewers, actual and potential, of television. Too often the television audience has been treated as if it were some conglomerate mass, of low intelligence and of even lower taste, incapable of appreciating the best that is being said, done, and performed in the world. We are told that the average mental age in America is about thirteen years. During the greater part of its history, television has looked as if it were deliberately appealing to an audience of that mental age. After all, the sponsor will pay most for the program that reaches the greatest number of potential purchasing units, and television is in business, and to stay in business, it has to make a profit. Television has never exclusively catered to what it has considered to be the needs of the mass audience, and television can always claim that it gives the public what it wants.

Without our putting too fine a point on it, those who will guide the future development of television require to understand that it is not so much what the public wants as what the people need that should be considered and that what the people want is not incompatible with what the people need. The advertising world has long understood that it is not difficult to persuade people to want what they do not need. It would balance things in the right direction if the mandarins of television would help people to want the things they need. In recent years some progress has been made in this direction, but, alas, too often the viewer seated before his television screen cannot after a while help exclaiming:

" 'But, soft! what light through yonder window breaks?'
It speaks, and yet says nothing."

And often, worse than nothing.

There can be no possible excuse for many of the most popular television programs of the present and past. Take, for example, the Westerns. For the most part, not only are these degrading and debasing, but they also serve to falsify and perpetuate the myth of the savage, American Indian. Apart from the anthropological absurdities that are invariably committed, the American Indian is still mostly presented as a savage, inferior, unfeeling barbarian. Although, here too, there has been some improvement in recent years and some American Indians are presented as relatively acceptable human beings, the James Fenimore Cooper wooden Indian still holds the stage. In these same programs the quanta of evil, treachery, rapine, and murder (not to mention the murder of the language) that are set out for the delectation of the viewer are utterly loathsome and abominable. There can be very little doubt that such programs habituate those who are exposed to them to an easy valuation of life, a not uncongenial view of the place of violence in human relations, and the cultivation of an opportunistic morality. Television can no longer be regarded as a merely passive viewing. It is an experience in which the viewer usually participates and identifies with one or another of the characters or the values he represents. The viewer is influenced, and television cannot evade its responsibility for the consequences by disclaiming any other than a business interest in what it is doing.

But enough on the obvious abuses of television, the principal and worst of which seems to me to be the commercially motivated servitude to erroneous ideas concerning the needs of the masses and the debasement of the image of man to which this leads. The bright speciousness and mindless vulgarity of some of the most popular television programs—programs in which the human experience is neither extended nor enlarged, but impoverished and corrupted—constitute living testimony to the depths to which television can descend. Let us now consider some of the better uses to which television can be put.

If the word "education" is used in its original nonformal sense (*educare,* to nourish and to cause to grow), television potentially constitutes the greatest educational medium of all time. By its very nature television enjoys an unprecedented opportunity to be a power for good in this world, for the enrichment of the lives of men, and for the enlargement of the conception of mankind, such as that which no other medium has ever enjoyed. I am using the term "education" in its broadest sense, but strictly within the limits defined above, as meaning the nourishing and causing to grow of man's potentialities for humanity, for humaneness, for love, and not merely instruction in the three *R*'s. I also use the term in its practical meaning, not in its formal classroom sense, as meaning that anything which is learned contributes either positively or negatively, for better or for worse, to one's education.

Without in the least undervaluing the important future which television has before it in the classroom, it is outside the classroom, in the informal setting of the home, for all the members of the family, but especially for adults, that television can make a major creative contribution in education and reeducation. Man is a mythmaking animal, and the mythmaking faculty assists him to "explain" whatever is in need of explanation. One of the functions of myth is to enable the individual to live comfortably with his beliefs in a fidelity so satisfyingly ritualistic that he eventually comes to identify his prejudices with the laws of nature or the canons of received religion. It is at just this juncture that television can enter as the creative solvent and educate by reeducating.

It is not the function of television to hold up a mirror for man to see himself merely as he is and to maintain himself in that image. On the contrary, it should be the function of television to exhibit the image of man as he can and should be, for man is a growing creature and his birthright is development. For development he requires the stimulation of new experience and new ideas, not the vacuous kind of entertainment he is so often offered. Television is in an unrivaled position to bridge the gap for man between the world of what *is* and the world of *what ought to be,* or rather the gap between what man has made of the world and what man can make of it, what he *ought* to make of it. Every society to a large degree creates itself through the image it holds up for itself to see. Culture—that is, the man-made part of the environment—is never a static thing but always a dynamic process. Television, therefore, will contribute to the individual and the social good to the extent that it projects "good" images. To the extent that it projects the trivial, the meretricious, and the stereotyped, television will contribute to cultural and social shallowness.

Television, then, is an institution of major social importance. It is, therefore, time that television took a good dispassionate look at itself and arrived at some common agreement on what its aims and purposes should be. For too long, television has appeared to resemble the young man in the Italian proverb who, having taken every road that he saw, eventually got nowhere. The concentration on staying in business has been equated with making money, and this has led to the general lack of purpose and directiveness and to the subordination of desirable ends to undesirable means. Expediency appears to be a governing principle of what under healthier conditions one would prefer to think of as a service rather than as an industry.

In spite of itself, television has become one of the most widely influential institutions of all time. Perhaps the meaning of an institution should be defined. An institution is an organization designed to regulate behavior with respect to the values considered essential to group welfare and survival. As *the* most widely influential institution in the land, television has become the god of the common man's idolatry, his oracle, and the principal source of his news and entertainment. By no more than the turn of a knob he can tune in on men and events with an immediacy and impact which he could never otherwise experience. In the face of the viewer's hunger to have the vast spaces of his mind filled, it is a kind of treason, a failure of the viewer in his need, to fill those vacant spaces with the kinds of vacuities with which he is too often presented.

As an institution of unprecedented reach and power, television has not yet taken itself seriously enough. Now and again there are signs that those who preside over the destinies of television would like to make an earnest attempt to define its role in contributing to the welfare of the people, but somehow or other the attempt gets lost in the next spectacular. The responsibility which should accompany the power seems to get dissipated in the fragmentation of the power and the demands of a constantly changing panorama of the slight and the ephemeral. There is an atmosphere of insecurity, of capriciousness, and of opportunism in the television world which appears to grow out of the lack of any clearly defined codification of its own role and significance and of even any clear recognition of the nature of its own power. Hence, without recognition of the responsibility that power entails, the corrupting effect of power inevitably follows, and it is seen in the contaminated programs that supervene so perfunctorily, one upon the other, with an odious disregard for the standards of excellence of which we hear so much.

Television must become alive to its institutional powers

and responsibilities, and invest itself with a form and a being rather more elevating and in keeping with the functions it should perform than those to which it has seemed to aspire in the past. Emancipation from the sterile puerilities which find so congenial a home in the television world is not incompatible with the provision of every variety of entertainment, which will amuse and divert and have no other purpose but to do so. But in the name of nothing more nor less than good taste, let us abate the noisome vulgarity of so much that passes for entertainment today. Vulgarity is *not* what the viewer wants, in spite of what the pundits and pollsters may say, for the simple reason that there is not one kind of television viewer but many different kinds, with different tastes and different standards, all characterized by the common trait of being able to learn to accept what is good, especially when the bad is not offered.

If television will responsibly use the power with which it is endowed, it will not permit itself to have its tastes formed for it by the pressures exerted by majority opinion. The strength of a democracy lies in the possibilities for increasing its orders of freedom without yielding to the pressure of any group, no matter how massive. And as Lord Acton pointed out many years ago, freedom does not consist in the liberty to do what one likes, but in the right to be able to do what one ought. And doing what one ought is not incompatible with liking what one ought to do. Right and wrong, good and bad, are not values that can be determined by a show of hands, but by the measure of universal criteria, which television might well adopt as the standards by which to direct its own activities.

What *ought* to be done is what is *good,* and the good is simply defined as any act or acts which confer survival benefits upon others in a creatively enlarging manner. And this, as the institution it has become, television is so eminently well equipped to do, efficiently and unsanctimoniously.

There is a new image of man emerging in the world, and to that transformation television has made a major contribution. Television has done so by bringing the peoples of every part of the world, in their native habitats and out of them, into the living room of the viewer. Representatives of many of these peoples have been seen in interviews, at the United Nations, on panels, and elsewhere. The personalities of these individuals, the charm, high intelligence, and warm humanity which they frequently exhibit, as they have projected from the television screen, have had the most extraordinary effects upon millions of viewers, who, it is important to note, would have remained largely unaffected by exposure to any other means of communication. The repeated shock of recognition experienced in this way has led to the revelation of the fact that the whole world of mankind is, indeed, kin, and that so-called inferior races are only technologically inferior, and that given adequate opportunities, they are *obviously* capable of producing men and women of high intellectual caliber and of a humanity which can at least compare favorably with our own. The very expression "inferior race" is one that would be considered in bad taste by more people today than would have been thought possible only a few years ago. To this, without any awareness of the fact that it was doing so and without the least propagandistic motivation, television has made a very substantial contribution. While much has been achieved in this enlargement of the image of man, it is nothing compared with what remains to be achieved.

It is not merely the image of mankind that is undergoing a renovation. Equally significant is the revision of the individual's self-image which television is capable of working. The potentialities of man are infinitely varied and exciting. But the image of man and of human potentialities handed down to us by tradition and traditional ways of setting limits to individual development often constrict and imprison what is best in man. Today more than ever he stands in need of the stimulation and direction which will release the "imprison'd splendour" that is within him.

What man stands so critically in need of today are the models, the images, that will be to him the standards on which he can form himself and by means of which he can learn to work on himself to free himself from the errors in which he has been conditioned and the incapacities for thinking in which he has been trained. These are, of course, functions that should be performed in the home and in our educational institutions. The hope is that this will become increasingly possible. Toward such an end television can make and continue to make a major contribution, not by offering viewers programs that will divert them from the main business of life, but by giving them the programs that will help them live as humanely, richly, and effectively as possible. It is to the achievement of such humanistic ends that television should be primarily dedicated—not so much by giving people what they want as by giving them the best it has to give.

To the extent that television contributes to the enhancement of man's understanding, the deepening of his sensibilities and involvement in the welfare of others, and the ability to weigh the evidence critically for himself—to that extent not only will television assist man to fulfill himself, but in this manner, and in this manner alone, will television serve to fulfill itself.

Selling America short

AT AN INTERNATIONAL meeting which I attended some time ago a member of our State Department reported on the views which people of other countries hold concerning America. The picture was not a pretty one. Polls had shown that foreigners think of us as material, technical, and "money-theistic." We were lacking in spirituality, we were arrogant and egocentric, and we were poor sports. A very large number of people didn't like us.

Is not this dislike strange? Why should we be disliked? We who liberated Europe. We who have poured so many millions into Europe and sent grain to India. Where would the French and the English be today had it not been for our gifts and our loans? And yet there are millions of Frenchmen, Englishmen, and others who do not like us. Why?

This attitude toward Americans is not something new in the world. One has but to read Mrs. Trollope, Charles Dickens, Matthew Arnold, and numerous other nineteenth-century writers who visited these shores to realize that the low esteem in which Americans are held abroad is by no means a new phenomenon. What is perhaps new is the greater extension and the increase in the intensity of this dislike.

Although probably largely of English origin, this tradition seems to have been gradually diffused throughout Europe, there to become in the course of time independently confirmed by that unique of all American exports, the American tourist. It was reinforced by numerous eminent visitors to these shores who were adept at both pen and persiflage, who returned to their homelands and there enlightened their countrymen on what the Americans were really like. What these eminent visitors mostly saw were the superficial things, but they also saw some of the deeper sources of American traits, sources which many Americans were not sufficiently distantly removed from themselves to be able to perceive as clearly as their foreign evaluators and critics.

Most people are not able to stand personal criticism of themselves, especially when it emanates from strangers. Criticism of one's country, particularly it appears if one is an American, is even less tolerable than criticism of oneself. Americans, more than any other people, seem to feel that a criticism of any of their country's institutions or ways constitutes a criticism of and an insult to themselves. A psychologist cannot help wondering whether this sensitivity does not betray a rather deep-seated insecurity—individually and collectively—which causes most Americans to respond in this way to such criticisms. This insecurity explains a great many things about Americans which foreigners see but which many Americans are frequently unwilling to face. What looks to the foreigner like arrogance and conceit are simply over-compensatory devices, by means of which the American is trying to compensate for his feeling of inadequacy and show that he is a "success."

America today is the most powerful nation in the world. Most of the remainder of the world's nations are by comparison weak. The relation of America's power to the rest of the

world's weakness constitutes a grave problem not only for America, but even more important, and Americans would be wise to recognize this as quickly as possible—for the whole of the rest of the world. With such great power at its disposal foreigners are today more than ever interested in America and in Americans, and more distrustful of them, for large numbers of them as a result of World War II saw Americans in the flesh for the first time. With all the willingness in the world to like them, most Europeans were sorrowfully forced to conclude that Americans were not likable people.

The chief ambassador from the American people to Europe was the American G.I. The general feeling about the American G.I. in England was summed up in the refrain "Overdecorated, Oversexed, and Over Here." The lack of courtesy, the frequent absence of the ordinary forms of politeness, the general crudity of behavior, the forwardness, and high frequency of criminal behavior among American troops had a devastating effect.

In France, as in England, the French were appalled by the brutishness of so many American soldiers. One of the phrases I heard most frequently applied to the American G.I. by townspeople was "sexual beasts." In mock grudging admiration one would encounter the following kind of remark: "A European soldier, when he steals, will steal a package or even a carton of cigarettes. But Americans—nothing but a whole train with all its contents will do! They will steal a whole train and sell not only its contents, but the train, too! Americans always do things in a big way."

What about the higher-ups? The "liberators" of Europe? As everyone knows, the incoming American forces were greeted throughout the length and breadth of Europe as the liberators of mankind. No foreign army had ever been greeted with a deeper feeling of gratitude and welcome than the Americans. And then what happened? The Americans, instead of removing the Nazis and Fascists and other undesirable elements, astonished the people by maintaining them in office and even dragging many out of hiding and putting them into office over the heads of the men and women who had sacrificed virtually everything to keep the flame of decency alive during the Terror. The Europeans' conclusion is unequivocally that the Americans are on no one's side but their own.

Americans, it is generally believed by Europeans, are so afraid of the Russians that they will do anything to keep that bogey from their door. Europeans in general, rightly or wrongly, believe that the Russians do not want a war, that they want to fight a cold war, not a hot one. It is for this reason, so it is held, that the Americans behave as they do in Europe and elsewhere, and it is this reason which causes so many Europeans to disapprove so violently and fundamentally of American foreign policy and American political conduct in the occupied areas of Europe, Asia, and elsewhere in the world.

All that Europeans can see is that if there is a war between America and Russia, it will be the Americans who will have forced it on the world, for the Russians, they believe, want to avoid war since with the aid of American foreign policy they can make all the gains they wish without war. In such a war, the Europeans feel, they would be crushed beyond recovery. At the best, whoever won, they feel, they would lose.

The most successful propaganda job done by the Russians in India, our State Department tells us, has been to convince the Indians that the Americans are not interested in dealing on a basis of equality with the colored "races" of the world. To support their claims, they print photographs, for those who are unable to read, showing race riots and lynchings in the United States. For those who are able to read, they quote chapter and verse proving that these things actually occur in the United States. Now our tendency, when dealing with foreigners, is to play down or even to deny the faults from which we Americans are alleged to suffer. This tendency is another of our traits which people abroad do not like in us. If we really want to make friends and influence people abroad, we should let them know the whole truth about ourselves. The truth about ourselves will be much more sympathetically received than the unconvincing glosses. Race riots and lynchings have occurred in the United States for many years; we should admit this freely, and we should deplore with all the feeling that is within us the occurrence of such tragic disasters. We should explain to those who are genuinely interested in an explanation the reason for such ghastly occurrences, and we should set out some of the great gains which have been made especially in the recent period, in the realm of race relations, and we should also make clear some of the reasons why greater progress has not been made. We may legitimately point with some satisfaction to the states and towns and villages and institutions which have abolished all discriminatory racial laws and practices and have instituted laws and procedures calculated to make all discrimination on such grounds illegal.

Europeans often feel that not only has Europe become a dependency of the United States, but that the government of the United States is using its money to influence and shape the foreign policies of their own countries. As one European political figure said to me, "We have become a nation of lickspittles. We are told to be quiet, for we must on no account offend the Americans. We need dollars."

In keeping with this policy of quietism, jokes about Americans are discouraged on the stage, and in one case, so I was informed, the management of a private theatrical group running a play which had several jokes about Americans was heavily penalized on the charge that they had admitted a nonmember who paid at the door.

Among many other Europeans there is the strong feeling that America needs Europe vastly more than Europe needs America, and their attitude is: "Certainly we shall be willing to help the Americans with any reasonable request they may make, but they must permit us to run our own affairs our own way. We want to cooperate, but we don't want to be coerced or compelled."

That such views can be held by Europeans suggests that something is somewhere wrong. Whatever the truth may be, it would appear that we have not done a very good job of human relations. The fault may not be altogether our own, but that it is partly so I think there can be little doubt. We have tried to sell ourselves and we've sold ourselves short. We might try giving up the values and the practices of the marketplace and, instead of attempting to sell ourselves, take a good look at ourselves and attempt to see ourselves as others see us, for what we are is not what we think we are but the appearance we present to the world. We might also attempt to take a look at others in terms of *their* needs, as well as our own.

Europeans and other peoples want to like us, and *we* genuinely want to like them. The only way one ever gets to be liked is by liking others. Apparently we have not succeeded in conveying our liking for them to the peoples of the rest of the world, and until we learn how to do so, we shall never be understood by them, and they will continue to think as they do of us.

Liking other peoples consists of making them feel that we are genuinely interested in their welfare and that we are not helping them for exclusively selfish interests of our own. Since much of our motivation is already of this kind this task should not prove too difficult.

The American atmosphere

THERE IS AN ELECTRIC spark in the air. Americans may not be consciously aware of it; nevertheless, they behave as if they were affected by it: they are jumpy, alert, excited, hopping about all over the place like jack-in-the-boxes. All foreigners are aware of it and, if they stay, become as invigorated and enlivened by it as the indigenes. It is one of the many things they like about America. Whether or not there is something in the physical atmosphere that differs from that of other countries I do not know. I am inclined to believe that there may be. Even the winters in America are stimulating. In Europe, at least, winter is a penance to be endured. The dampness of even a cold summer day has to be experienced in order to be shivered at. That dampness literally gets into the marrow of one's bones. It is an extremely unpleasant feeling. Chilblains, those perfidiously itching torments of the skin, caused by the chilling atmosphere, are virtually unknown in America. In Europe the winters are dreary, dull, and depressing. Not so in America, where the winters, even in Minnesota, are exciting, challenging, and stimulating. The air is crisp and electric. The summers are bona fide summers, the kinds of summers the English dream about, not brief intervals between the rain and gloomy unpromising skies, in whose thrall men sit and hear one another groan.

Even more marked than the electricity of the physical atmosphere is the sparkling character of American culture. It is like a high-tension wire free at one end and discharging a continuous stream of dancing multicolored sparks. No other display of fireworks has ever equaled it. It is this liveliness of the social atmosphere that continually replenishes the energies of Americans; their batteries thus recharged, they too take on the characteristics of a high-tension wire. Nothing more American can be said of a man than that "He's a live wire." In fact, Americans aren't interested in anyone who isn't.

The unique vitality of the United States can only be appreciated to its full by one who has been brought up in Europe, has lived for many years in America, and then, at intervals, has returned to Europe and back again to America. The contrast is, was, and I believe largely still is, striking. In comparison, Europe impresses one as almost moribund. It is, of course, anything but—but that is the general overall impression it makes upon one in contrast with America, especially with respect to its inefficiency and outmoded ways of doing many things.

In May, 1948, I recall being asked by an English friend in London how England appeared to me after an absence of nine years. I said that it seemed to me like a very old museum, built long, long ago, once great and distinguished, in which all the curators who had made it what it once was had gradually died, leaving layers of accumulating dust to gather on the desiccated specimens, moth-eaten and decaying, with an old diener left over from an earlier generation, who went about with his feather duster, ineffectually attempting to sweep the accumulated dust and cobwebs from the specimens and cases. He thought the description most apt, and that it applied to all Europe. We both were, of course, exaggerating, but there was enough of truth in the exaggeration to make the point of difference between Europe and America: America was like a young and vigorous youth just finding his oats; Europe, like a decaying old man.

America has all the faults of youth and all its virtues. It may be true that, as Oscar Wilde remarked, America's claim to youth is one of its oldest myths. But then, America isn't very old, and the truth is that America's youthfulness is not a myth at all, but the living experience of everyday existence.

A three-year-old boy once inquired of me why it was that while he was growing, he couldn't hear himself doing so. I suspect that the answer is that no one's hearing is good enough for that, but if the processes of growth could be amplified, they could be heard clearly enough. In America the processes of growth are perennially, and often too noisily, evident. All over America whole towns rise in a matter of months, where the last time one passed that way, only trees and wild flowers grew, and the only sounds one heard were those of the birds and the crickets. Orchards and groves are ruthlessly chopped down and farmlands laid waste in order to make room for housing developments. The population increases by 1.7 percent per annum, and room must be found for its destructive spread. But population growth is no explanation of the vitality of the United States. The population growth of Latin America is 2.8 percent per annum, but far from there being a concomitant growth in cultural vitality, the Latin American population growth has had a depressing effect.

No land has ever before drawn upon so many diverse cultural elements for its population as America, and there can be very little doubt that a great part of the vitality which is so characteristic of the American scene is due to the static generated by so many different cultural charges.

The excitement of America is the excitement of a new country, of a new world. It has all the excitement and passion of a pioneer enterprise. It is not difficult to understand why: America still is, as it has never ceased to be, a country of pioneers. The first and the last of its immigrants have come to America in order to begin a new life. They left the old country for the new country in order to better themselves. Very few of these immigrants were in the least interested in bettering the country they had chosen to make their own. And so it has largely remained. Of the 200,000,000 Americans living at the present time, surely it is fair to say that only a very small proportion are interested in the welfare of their country.

It is this spirit of pioneering, even though it may be pioneering largely in the interest of self, that contributes most to the liveness of Americans. It is a good feeling, even though it is accompanied by a great many side effects that are bad: the gangsters; the robber barons and their contemporary equivalents; the corrupt politicians; the Boss Tweeds, Jimmy Walkers, and Jimmy Hoffas; the graft; the lawlessness; the destruction and desecration of the land; the disfigurement of its natural beauties; and so much else that is repellent and revolting and so much a part of the American scene. This side of America is very hard to take. But America, as Scott Fitzgerald put it, is a willingness of the heart, and there are still a large enough number of Americans left who want to see its promises fulfilled.

Americans want badly to be good, and in spite of all appearances to the contrary, they are doing better all the time.

Life, liberty, and homeostasis

VIRTUALLY EVERY VISITOR arriving in the United States during the winter months is at once struck by the bracing, exhilarating climate outside American buildings and the strikingly debilitating and enervating climate that prevails inside those buildings, domestic and otherwise. Keeping warm in America in winter means insulating oneself from the external atmosphere and elevating the temperature of the internal atmosphere of buildings. Habituated from birth to such overheated interiors, Americans take such temperatures to be normal, even though they are often uncomfortable in them themselves.

I write as an objective observer who has spent many years living in the cold damp climate of England and an equally great number of years in America, mostly on the Atlantic seaboard.

Of the climate of England, there is only this to say in its favor: it is excellent for lawns, vegetable gardens, women's complexions, umbrella and raincoat manufacturers, but for the rest, it is strictly for the birds—that is, for those who can afford their own solar system by flying south. Those who have had any experience of that fourth wonder of the world, English plumbing and devices for raising the temperature (I do not say devices for keeping warm, for this only *appears* to be the intention), will be grossly mistaken if they conclude that it is a lack of know-how that is principally responsible. It is certainly in part that, but it is not all. As an aboriginal of the British Isles, my own interpretation of the facts is that the English have a passion for making themselves uncomfortable. Their plumbing and so-called heating arrangements constitute a self-abnegating defense against spiritual and corporeal pride. This is the basic reason why the English more than willingly put up with inclemencies of the weather and accounts for their lack of enthusiasm for doing anything serious about it indoors.

In passing, it may perhaps be observed that the habit of covering the body in order to keep it reasonably well protected from the cold may have played a role in the genesis of that prudery which, in England at least, has by a peculiar translation become a psychological device for keeping up the erotic temperature in a cold climate.

If the English believe in mortifying the flesh, Americans, being more practical, are inclined to take the view that there is no profit in it and go to the other extreme. In contrast with the English, Americans may be said to have a passion for making themselves comfortable. "Life, liberty, and the pursuit of happiness" seem to be interpreted by most Americans to mean "life, liberty, and homeostasis," or making oneself as physically comfortable as possible. In the furtherance of this end, Americans have dedicated themselves to the proposition that comfortable temperatures within the buildings they occupy in winter and in summer are the birthright of every good citizen over the greater part of the land. Therefore, central heating has been one of the altars before which the good American warms the hands of life, and air conditioning is rapidly becoming so for the other season.

Both central heating and air conditioning are very good things. But all good things can be overdone, and too much of a good thing turns a good thing into a bad one. And this is what Americans have for long been doing with central heating and are beginning to do with air conditioning. In what follows, I shall be concerned with the effects of both these forms of artificial temperature control upon the health of Americans. There is now abundant evidence that both forms, unwisely used as they are by most Americans, exert a deleterious effect upon their health.

Central Heating

An interesting fact which emerged during my inquiry is that nowhere in the United States does there exist a significant body of data on the temperatures prevailing in homes and in public buildings during the winter months, although the authorities consulted agreed that from general observation, they are usually higher than necessary for either health or comfort. During World War II the government attempted to persuade citizens that a temperature of 65 F. was adequate for both health and comfort, in most cases without success. At that time *Fuel and Oil Heat* magazine, on the basis of a considerable sampling of oil heating service departments, found that the average temperature in American homes during the winter months was somewhere between 72 and 73 F.

My own very small sampling among oil heating service firms indicates that average domestic temperature during the winter months in the Middle Atlantic States is about 74 F. In the New England States the domestic temperature varies between 68 and 70 F. In the South Atlantic States the average is about 77 F. In the New England and Middle Atlantic States the housewife—who largely determines the household temperature—appears to be more accustomed to cold than her South Atlantic counterpart. The same would appear to hold true for the Central States; the farther north one goes, the lower the average domestic temperatures. One New York City oil heating authority wrote me, "In my own home we keep the thermostat set at 72 F., but often our visitors are not warm enough, particularly if they come from the south or from the dry climate of the west. For them we set up the thermostat to 75 F."

The American Society of Heating, Refrigerating, and Air Conditioning Engineers in its *Guide and Data Book, 1961,** states that a winter indoor dry-bulb temperature for homes that conform to "good practice" is between 73 and 75 F. One cannot help wondering what "good practice" means here, whether in fact it does not mean the temperatures most frequently found to prevail. According to Yaglou,† for men and women at rest and dressed according to season, the comfortable range of temperatures usually is between 65 and 75 F. in cold weather.

Common experience testifies to the fact that during the winter season, temperatures in American homes are seldom below 70 F. and are often above 80 F. for extended periods of time. Most Americans spend one-third of their lives sleeping in a bedroom which, during the winter season, is tightly sealed against the external atmosphere by storm windows and other insulating devices, with central heating on all through the night. Considerably more than another third of their lives will be spent in buildings and in vehicles which are similarly tightly sealed against the external atmosphere and which, during the winter months, are overheated. But, as everyone knows, it is not the heat, it is the humidity—in our present context, not its presence, but its absence.

* *Ashrae Guide and Data Book, 1961* (New York, American Society of Heating, Refrigerating, and Air Conditioning Engineers, 1961), p. 439.
† C. P. Yaglou, "Indices of Comfort," in *Physiology of Heat Regulation and Science of Clothing,* L. H. Newburg, ed. (Philadelphia, W. B. Saunders Company, 1949), p. 283.

The effect of continuous overheating or drying of air is to reduce its humidity to the vanishing point. The optimal range of relative humidity for normal functioning of the respiratory mucosa is between 40 and 70 percent. These figures are based on an evaluation of conditions for normal noses in a temperature of 70 F. But such conditions of humidity are rare in winter, and normal noses are the exception rather than the rule, especially among individuals suffering from allergies, colds, and an addiction to heavy smoking. In physiological reality, the nose requires air breathed at a humidity higher than 70 percent in order for the air entering the lungs to be adequately moistened.

The mucous secretion of the nasal glands consists of 96 percent water, but it is more viscous than the mucous secretion of any other part of the body. Even slight drying increases the viscosity of the nasal mucus so that ciliary action is impaired. Even in a comparatively humid environment the glands in the nose work very hard. They have to humidify some 500 cubic feet of air every 24 hours so that when the air reaches the lungs, its relative humidity is about 85 percent. This means that the nose has to produce at least a pint of water daily—which is quite a load for any nose, whatever its dimensions. When the outside humidity is low, the nose has to work still harder. With disease or drying inside the nose, the secretory glands cease producing the needed humidification, and the respiratory tract runs into trouble. The mucous membranes of the ear, nose, throat, bronchi, and bronchioles produce secretions from their glands which form a protective investment of the passages over which those secretions move as a continuous blanket. The movement is produced and maintained by the mucous membranes. Dry air rapidly inactivates the ciliary action of the mucosa and may result in death of the ciliated cells.

When the action of the cilia is impaired and infection

occurs, a burning sensation is often experienced upon breathing in. This is because the mucous lining is no longer able to protect the tissues from the air being inhaled.

One reason some individuals have postnasal drip is that their nasal glands have had excessive demands made on them so that they have hypertrophied and continue to produce excessive amounts of mucus, even when it is no longer required.

Like love for the human psyche, excessive humidity is not in the least damaging to the nose, since the latter organ continues to provide the necessary humidification, and no more. It is drying that is damaging.

When the mucosal cilia are inactivated by drying, the dried mucus accumulates in small piles or crusts. These gelatinous heaps of mucus constitute hospitable culture media for bacteria. The highly bacteriolytic enzyme lysozyme, secreted by the glands of the mucous membranes, ceases to be elaborated by the nonfunctioning mucous membrane so that bacteria are now able to multiply in great numbers. The dried mucous membranes become highly permeable so that the multiplying bacteria may now pass freely through them and infection is produced. Disease of the respiratory tract, especially in the form of the common cold, is greatly facilitated in the presence of a dried-out mucous membrane. But every form of disease of the respiratory tract and of the middle ear through the Eustachian tube is probably facilitated by a disabled mucous membrane.

It is probable that the majority of the patients seen by ear, nose, and throat specialists are suffering from diseases which originated in physiological failure of the respiratory mucous membranes induced by excessive drying as a result of artificial temperature control.

In many homes, buildings, and vehicles in America, the

relative humidity is often reduced to 5 percent or lower. The fact is that the air in the average American home in winter is drier than it is in the center of the Sahara Desert! This invariably produces dryness of the mucous membranes, for the immediate effect of dry air is to reduce the water content of mucus and mucous membranes. The astonishing thing about this is that most Americans are aware of the fact that their mucous membranes are dried out, for they experience very definite and frequent discomfort as an accompaniment. The discomfort is so frequent that it comes to be considered normal. Relatively few Americans resort to artificial humidification, by using mechanical humidifiers to counteract the artificial dehumidification they so sedulously produce, or take a daily walk out of doors no matter what the weather may be.

In addition to the deleterious effects of drying on mucous membranes, there are very noticeable effects on the skin. Ever since Europeans began visiting American shores and since Americans have been returning the compliment by visiting Europe, Europeans have been struck by the sallow complexions of Americans, the dried, rather yellowish tinge to the skin compared with the skins of Europeans, which is likely to be more moist and pinkish or, even when the skin is dark, of a generally healthier appearance. It is probable that this difference in the appearance of the skin is due, at least in part, to the dry air in which the skins of Americans must attempt to function so much of the time. Dried skin is very much more likely to age, as well as to be more susceptible to the invasion of bacteria, than skin that is adequately moist.

Air Conditioning

A related abuse is overcooling.

Air conditioning implies cooling of air. Since air cooling is largely practiced during the summer months, when the outside air is likely to have a high relative humidity, such air, when brought inside and cooled, at first increases humidity and may produce chilling. Chilling has much the same effect as drying on the respiratory mucosa, with all the possible sequelae of infection. The relative humidity in air-conditioned rooms should lie in the range from 40 to 50 percent, and the optimum temperature in an air-conditioned room is one which, while producing the desired cooling effect, departs least from that which prevails outside. Even temperatures should be maintained and all drafts avoided in air-conditioned rooms. These conditions are not usually satisfied, and summer respiratory disturbances are becoming very much more frequent than they used to be.

Skin disorders resulting from the misuse of air conditioning identical with the wintertime skin disease known as winter itch (*dermatitis hiemalis*) have now been described in many individuals in summer.* As a consequence of dehydration, the outermost layer of the skin (*stratum corneum*) becomes brittle and chapped or split. The itching results in scratching or rubbing, and this leads to inflammation and edema. In some individuals eczematous plaques appear and these may become moist and exudative and subject to secondary bacterial infection. Clinical recognition of this new disease is essential for its proper treatment, for it has usually been incorrectly diagnosed.

Even when improper air conditioning does not produce disease, it may adversely affect the normal physiological functioning of the skin by derangement of the mechanism of thermoregulatory sweating. Normal sweating assists in the removal of water from the body by means of evaporation from the skin. Cold drafts of air directed upon the skin

---

* M. E. Chernosky, "Pruritic Skin Disease and Summer Air Conditioning," *Journal of the American Medical Association*, Vol. 179 (1962), pp. 1005–1010.

results in a lack of sweating and of moisture on the skin, and this prevents adequate emulsification and distribution of sebum over the skin surface. This may result in a very unpleasant dry-skin syndrome, which may be the forerunner of more serious disorders of the skin.

Summer colds as a result of improper air conditioning are becoming a common thing, and it is not unlikely that air conditioning has played a role in increasing the incidence of other respiratory disorders.

It is certain that the overheating that Americans practice during the winter months and that the overcooling they indulge in during the summer months are each responsible for a much larger share of disabling symptoms than is at present generally recognized or adequately appreciated by physicians. The remedy lies in awareness of the dangers inherent in the abuse of central heating and air conditioning and in the elimination of these abuses by proper humidification of the inside air and the avoidance of turbulence and drafts. The amount of water required to humidify the air rises with the temperature, and the same is true of the human body. All the tissues of the body require a substantial amount of water in order to function adequately. The reduction in the water content of body tissues can have a lethal effect. Sublethal reduction in the water content of tissues can have a damaging effect to the extent of seriously incapacitating the individual and reducing his longevity. The tissues most directly vulnerable to the drying effects of devaporized air are the mucous membranes of the respiratory tract, and next in order of vulnerability, not surprisingly, is the skin.

What the mad American sun worshiper does to his skin by deliberately bathing in the sun is another story.

Psychoanalysis in America

PSYCHOANALYSIS HAS BEEN DEFINED as conversation *ad libido*. An equally appealing definition is the art of living off one patient. In this world of stress and strain, millions of human beings are in need of a parental figure who will listen to their troubles and give them surcease from them. The symbol for this age of anxiety ought to be a giant auricle. People are in search of listeners. I am told that in Los Angeles there are practitioners who call themselves Listeners and that they earn a living solely by listening to the troubles of others, without making or being required to make any comment whatever. The Catholic Church has provided such a service for hundreds of years in the institution of auricular confession. For non-Catholics and for the varieties of unbelievers, psychoanalysis has become the modern equivalent of auricular confession.

Psychoanalysis has provided profound insights into the nature of human behavior, its conditioning, and its pathology. It has had a considerable humanizing effect on the practice of medicine, the treatment of the mentally ill, the understanding of human relations, and much else. No doubt there are some persons who have benefited from psychoanalytic treatment. But it is a question whether those persons

[74

would not have been benefited by other forms of psychotherapy or even without any form of treatment. An individual, whose difficulties have been built up over a lifetime, can sometimes be substantially helped in no more than a few hours' conversation with an understanding counselor. On the other hand, a psychoanalysis extended over many years has often failed to produce any noticeable improvement in the condition of the patient. There are analyses called terminable and others called interminable. Some of the interminable ones might not have been any more successfully handled by any other means, but to my knowledge, there have certainly been many cases that could have been more successfully treated by other approaches.

In innumerable cases I have seen psychoanalysis serve the crippled individual as a crutch which, as long as the analysis was available, would not be thrown away and allow the patient to begin walking on his own two feet. It is a great comfort to the patient to be made to feel that his parents were responsible for his present difficulties, that his personality was malformed by one or both his parents or whoever else may be held responsible. All this may or may not be true; but in any event, this piece of information is very gratifying, and the thankful patient, having been relieved of the responsibility for himself, comes to regard the analyst with the feelings he should have had for his parents. This projection of such parental feelings on the person of the analyst is called the transference. It is at this stage that the patient becomes the analyst's "child."

The most perfervid and loyal supporters of psychoanalysis have been the analysands while in analysis. It may be good to have friends in court, but if the ends of justice are not thus best served, it is not good. The children of foster parents are not their best judges. Anyone who becomes emotionally involved in the issue is not likely to be the most balanced and dependable of critics. Love is blind. Nor have the patients who have not developed too deep an involvement in their analysis likely to prove any better critics. Too often they are more or less profoundly disturbed by their failure to benefit from the analysis, and about this they often tend to be bitter or emotionally critical.

Psychoanalysts themselves are highly unsatisfactory on the effectiveness of psychoanalysis as a therapeutic method. Much is written and said by them about its effectiveness, but evidence that would satisfy a genuinely critical intelligence is seldom offered. When evidence, in the form of a case history, is offered, it is sometimes very striking and convincing, and one wishes that psychoanalysts would publish the evidence that would make it possible for others to judge the success or failure of their therapeutic method. Instead, psychoanalysts usually consider themselves to be above this sort of thing, for they are singularly reticent about publishing résumés of their case histories in which the facts are plainly stated. Were such collected series of cases to be published, the census of cases would not, there is very good reason to believe, be favorable to psychoanalysis as a therapeutic method.

The fact that psychoanalysis serves to maintain the patient in his neurosis is gratifying to him, and having in this way convinced himself that he is at last dealing with it, coming to grips with it, he is confident that progress will be made. Sometimes progress is made. I have seen it. I have also seen other cases in which no progress was made, but in which during the term of the analysis the patient was convinced of a progress that was evident to no one else and eventually not even to himself.

The length of time an analysis takes, its high cost, and its dubious outcome make it a highly impractical form of therapy. I believe this is slowly coming to be realized in the United States. Psychoanalysis as a therapeutic method has had a long trial, and it has been found wanting. Undoubtedly many of the insights with which it has provided us can be adapted to more effective forms of therapy, but the long-term analysis, it would seem, has no future. What is needed are short-term therapies, therapies which will relieve the patient of his symptoms or else enable him to accept and live with them. In the hands of a competent therapist this can sometimes be accomplished in a matter of hours. One of the principal aims of the therapist should be to make the therapy as brief as possible so that the patient may return as quickly as feasible to a relatively more healthy life. Psychoanalysis, with its indefinite, interminable, and open-ended attitude toward time and the patient, has served to retard the development of short-term therapies. With more attention and research directed toward the development of a variety of short-term therapies, instead of the *vis a tergo* of psychoanalysis, there is every reason to expect that such endeavors would meet with success.

Sex and sex education

A RECENTLY CONVICTED PUBLISHER of a sex magazine is reported to have declared that sex is what life is all about. Judging from the preoccupation with sex in America, it is not surprising that within a year of issuing his quarterly magazine devoted to erotica, at an annual subscription rate of twenty-five dollars, he should have obtained 150,000 subscribers! Had the magazine not been put out of business by the government, it would undoubtedly have attracted many more subscribers. Americans do seem to be by sex obsessed, but although some may, most Americans clearly do not think that sex is what life is all about. They have many other sports. In any event, it is not Americans, but the male of the species who tends to be preoccupied with sex. The success of such magazines as *Playboy* and *Esquire* testifies to the overweening interest of many American males in sex. I do not, however, believe that American males are more preoccupied with sex than males tend to be elsewhere in the world. Sex is everywhere a male preoccupation and is by no means a peculiarity of the American male. If there is a difference in the expression of sexual interest in America compared with other lands, it is probably due to the fact that, as in so many other things, Americans make more noise about sex than other peoples, but I very much doubt that they are more obsessed with sex than other peoples.

The real difficulty, as I see it, is not that too much but that too little is made of sex. Christian, Puritan, Fundamentalist, and other influences have served to obscure and pervert the understanding and meaning of sex, not alone in America, but wherever these influences have made themselves felt. The result is, particularly in America, that sex is equated with sexual intercourse and all the titillations that lead to that climactic experience. Instead of the uniquely beautiful enchantment that sex should be, it has been degraded to the crass status of a male relief mechanism for the pressures of the sex drive. This is principally a male psychosis, and this male attitude toward sex is extremely hard on the female and is not a little responsible for the frequent unhappiness of the American wife.

No one having taught him anything of the meaning of sex, except what he has picked up adventitiously, the American male at about sixteen discovers yet another dimension of the process of growing up into which he must enter and which he must conquer. And since sexual conquests are considered to be the mark of a genuine he-man and are made in the context of a pseudoromantic glow, aided and abetted by TV, the movies, the press, and the like, in which love constitutes the theme and sex its realization, sex and love come to be identified as one.

The identification of sex with love is quite disastrous. Sexual attractiveness becomes the basis upon which marriage is contracted and maintained. With the cessation of the sexual attractiveness, there is in most cases a cessation of the electrical bond which held the marriage together, and what was formerly a positive force now becomes a negative polar force, and the two bodies involved tend to separate. In this manner many marriages come to an end. The breakup is largely, if not entirely, the doing of the male.

The divorce rate is sufficient testimony to the flimsiness of the grounds upon which most Americans marry. About one out of three marriages in the United States ends in divorce. The remarriage rate is also quite high, higher for men than for women. Hence, the institution of sequential polygamy or serial monogamy, in which instead of having parallel spouses at the same time, one enjoys them serially or sequentially. The obsolescent model is turned in for the new one. The consequences of these shallow confusions for the family, the children, and society are extremely disordering.

Proper sex education is not going to cure this situation, but it would undoubtedly greatly contribute to its cure and, indeed, will constitute an indispensable part of it. To learn to love, one must be loved. It is not possible to learn to love from books or lectures on the subject. Similarly, to be sexually healthily developed, practice and experience are necessary, guided by knowledge and healthy values.

It is scarcely believable that in the second half of the twentieth century sexual intercourse is prohibited by the mores for everyone except in marriage. Sexual intercourse during adolescence is considered especially heinous. Few ever ask why or what sense or purpose lies behind this prohibition.

The strength of the sexual drive is so great that every society has always had to control its expression. Every variety of such control is encountered in human societies, from permissive to repressive. On the whole, most nonliterate societies tend to be permissive with respect to premarital intercourse. In such societies complications are unlikely to arise. The reason for this is that marriage generally occurs when the girl achieves menarche (the first menstruation).

Before menarche (and for some time thereafter), a young girl is rarely capable of conception; hence, she may indulge in as much intercourse as she pleases without fear of pregnancy. In civilized societies in which the age of marriage has been postponed to her late teens and even later, a female is capable of conception and bearing a child, and this can be socially very disruptive. Unmarried mothers and illegitimate children constitute problems in all societies. Civilized societies have in general been unable to cope with this problem, except by branding premarital intercourse as immoral and to be met with severe social disapproval. However, with the invention of effective contraceptives the danger of conception has been reduced to the vanishing point so that the principal objection to premarital intercourse is no longer valid. This being so, the time has surely arrived when Americans would do well to reconsider their attitudes toward sex and especially toward premarital sex as a preparation for and the practical education in the appreciation of the art of sex.

Sex education in America has been one of the most slighted of subjects. The facts about the bees, the birds, and the beasts may be very interesting, as may those about human beings, but they are practically of no value in helping anyone learn the skills and techniques of sex, in the only way in which such techniques and skills can be learned. In Scandinavia, particularly in Sweden, this has long been recognized, and young people are encouraged to acquire the practical experience of sex in a gratifyingly healthy manner. Promiscuity is strongly discouraged, but sex between steady friends, who may take off together for the weekend or longer with the blessings of their parents, has long been customary, without either causing the collapse of these societies or having anything but the most beneficial effects on everyone concerned.

What misery, what disasters, what unhappiness, what trag-
edies would be avoided, were young people to arrive at
marriage without the fears, anxieties, lack of knowledge, lack
of understanding, and lack of skills which have so often
resulted in the most unhappy and often only too enduring
consequences. How much more healthy, promising, sensible,
and gratifying, when the partners to the marriage arrive with
all the experience, knowledge, art, sympathy, and understanding that the premarital sexual experience has given
them! And how much better that the premarital sexual
experience be engaged in a permissive and sympathetic environment than in a guilt-producing one in which premarital
sex has to be indulged in furtively and with little or no
understanding of it as anything other than a guilt-laden
pleasurable forbidden physical act!

In a nationwide survey conducted in 1965 by the Health
Guidance in Sex Education Committee of the American
School Health Association, a study designed to discover what
was being done about sex education in American schools, the
appalling number of forty out of the many thousands of
schools that were circularized replied to the questionnaire.
Of this small number, about 80 percent had some form of sex
education, but quite clearly in most cases it was of the most
inadequate kind. In California, that land of perpetual pubescence, only 26 percent of schools have courses in family living
or sex education in their curricula.

In 1965 the School Health Education Study sponsored by
the U. S. Public Health Service, the National Congress of
Parents and Teachers, the American Medical Association, the
U. S. Office of Education, and the National Education Association inquired into the subject of sex education in 1,101
elementary schools with an enrollment of more than 500,000,
and from 359 high schools with more than 300,000 students.

This study revealed that resistance on the part of parents and the community to the discussion of sex, venereal disease, and related matters constituted the main cause of the general ignorance among children of these important aspects of health. Other factors were ineffectual instruction methods, inadequate time devoted to health instruction, inadequate preparation of teachers, and indifference on the part of some teachers, as well as students, parents, health officers, administrators, and other members of the community. It was found that more than 70 percent of high school seniors entertained some rather serious misconceptions concerning sex and health. It is just this sort of ignorance that can be corrected in our schools. Sex education, however, should begin long before the child enters school. It should begin in the home and should be carried on through the elementary grades through high school and in college. In the schools the teaching of the facts about the psychology and physiology of sex, graduated to meet the developing maturation of each child, should occupy an important place in the school curriculum.

The venereal disease and pregnancy rates among adolescents have risen spectacularly. The only way to meet these problems is to solve them before they occur—namely, by education. As every investigation has amply demonstrated, the teaching we give our children in our schools lacks clear and constructive goals. Our educational ideals are confused; they are not geared to the world in which we live. To fit young people for wholesome productive relationships in the modern world, they must be taught what wholesome productive relationships are, and they must be taught what the modern world is and exactly what their place in it should be. In this connection the principal element lacking in the education we give the young is a sense of involvement and commitment to the whole human enterprise. We too often tend to leave our young people with the feeling that the world is indifferent to them and that they can therefore afford to be indifferent to it, that they are to be outsiders, onlookers, who will never be called on to contribute in any significant way to the making of their society and of the world and to the humanizing of human relationships.

There is a direct relationship between the disproportionately high incidence of venereal disease and unmarried mothers in metropolitan areas and the increasing population pressures of those areas, for the possibilities for individual development decrease as the square of the population increases. Not only do religious, educational, recreational, and other constructive cultural influences lag behind population growth in such areas, but the population pressures themselves also make for a breakdown in moral values. The stresses put on family living under crowded conditions and in socio-economically depressed environments tend to produce intensive individual and social disorganization.

Although the importance of adequate housing and recreational facilities in contributing to the alleviation of the problem cannot be overemphasized, adequate sex education is of paramount importance, and it is an innovation about which something can be done immediately. The blight that traditional attitudes toward sex have produced must be removed, and the subject of sex must be approached with dignity, understanding, sensitivity, and frankness. A good understanding of the basic facts of reproductive physiology, of the psychology of sex, and of whatever other facts may be considered necessary to provide the student with an understanding of the meaning of sex should be the goal of a sex education which forms an indispensable part of the school experience.

It is necessary to learn to read the music before one can

play a musical instrument, but no amount of music reading will ever enable one to play the instrument. That one can only learn by practice on the instrument itself. The reading, the theory, the harmony, and the interweaving of all these develop with practice. This is a matter of great delicacy and must be treated with all the sensitivity and understanding it demands.

It would, I am convinced, greatly contribute to the mental health and stability of our society were adolescents permitted the self-development and self-discipline of premarital sex— *not* the encouragement of licentiousness or promiscuity, but the encouragement in the growth and development of a mature and healthy personality, a growth and development in which the experience of sex as the beautiful and greatly humanizing event it can be plays its necessary and proper role.

One cannot help wondering how long it will take Americans to take seriously such views as I have expressed here. It may not be too long, for the younger generation has, to some extent, already taken the matter into its own hands. This generation will soon be adult and very much more understanding of the meaning of sex and what one does about it than its parents were.

Honorary degrees

UNIVERSITY AND COLLEGE degrees granted in course at the satisfactory completion of the requirements set by the examining bodies constitute an honorable evidence of one's having passed through a certain kind of learning experience. A bachelor's degree constitutes evidence of four years' academic work. A master's degree is evidence of at least two years' graduate work and the presentation of a satisfactory thesis. A doctor of philosophy's degree is evidence of the satisfactory completion of an additional several years of work and the submission of an acceptable piece of original work as a thesis. These degrees represent the fruits of application and labor and serve to qualify their holders for the skilled performance of certain tasks. And this applies to all other degrees. The higher degrees—that is, the doctorates—constitute evidence of high professional competence. As such, in general, they constitute all the evidence normally required to vouch for the technical competence of the holders of degrees —with few exceptions.

The practice of conferring honorary degrees, *honoris causa*, is an old one. Its original and largely continuing purpose was to recognize the merits of the person upon whom the honorary degree was confirmed. It was and is a well-meaning gesture. But the custom has been greatly abused, such degrees being conferred in large numbers upon utterly meritless persons and not altogether by utterly merit-less institutions. But let us not make invidious distinctions.

The honorary degrees usually conferred are Doctor of Laws (LL.D.), Doctor of Civil Laws (D.C.L.), Doctor of Humane Letters (D.H.L.), Doctor of Literature (D. Litt.), Doctor of Divinity (D.D.), Doctor of Theology (D. Theol.), Doctor of Education (D. Ed. or Ed. D.), and a few others. Those named are the most popular.

I believe it would be to everyone's advantage if the practice of conferring honorary degrees were to be altogether discontinued. There are many objections to honorary degrees. In the first place, they compromise the value of the earned degree and so serve to bring it into disrepute, and in the second place, they frequently confer on their recipients a status and a quality which are altogether unmerited. For the shocking and dismaying thing is that in America, unlike Europe, those who receive honorary degrees frequently thereafter adopt the honorific and call themselves and are called by others Doctor. This is bad taste, bad manners, and, in my opinion, downright chicanery. University and college degrees should not be abused in this way. Everyone has encountered either in print or in the flesh "Doctors" like Dr. Billy Hargis, who enjoys an honorary doctorate in theology from Bob Jones University in South Carolina, and there are innumerable presidents of so-called colleges who bask in the glory of an honorary doctorate conferred on them either by the college over which they preside or by some equally edifying educational institution. This is to make a mockery of what should be an honored and respected accolade, bestowed on its holder as a recognition of years of formal study and research satisfactorily completed.

An honorary degree should be accepted by no one of academic integrity. All holders of degrees should decline such empty flattery. I know a distinguished American academic who declines all offers of honorary degrees on the grounds that he worked very hard for the one doctorate he earned in the course of a regular university career, that he didn't see any point in accepting one for which he had not worked, and that, in any event, one doctor's degree was enough.

It is an example which I hope will be widely imitated. Failing a sufficient number of college presidencies to go around, one could always console the generals and admirals with such honorary degrees as were still being conferred. But the hope is that even generals and admirals would eventually come to understand how asinine such honorary degrees are— and come to hold them in the same contempt as they hold the Southern honorific, so freely bestowed, of Colonel.

Reference to the asinine recalls the historic event when a horse that had served a certain university nobly for some ten years was to be retired to oats. At the meeting of the trustees at which the decision was approved, one of the trustees said he would give the university a million dollars if it would confer an honorary degree on the horse. So at the next commencement the horse was led up onto the platform, the dean of the faculties pronounced an oration celebrating the merits of the horse, and the hood of Doctor of Humane Letters was hung over its neck, whereupon the president rose and, turning to the assembled audience, said, "Ladies and gentlemen, in my twenty years as president of this institution this is the first time I have had the pleasure of conferring an honorary degree upon an *entire* horse."

And that, I believe, puts honorary degrees exactly where they belong.

On the right to vote

THE RIGHT TO VOTE implies, or rather should imply, the realization of the right to be intelligent. To be intelligent is a moral obligation. Those who voluntarily choose to remain unintelligent or who deny others the right to be intelligent should not be permitted to participate in what is done about the government of the people by the people, for only those who have earned that right should be privileged to enjoy it.

A voter should be capable of arriving at reasoned conclusions concerning the issues on which he is to render his decision. If he is not able to, then he should not be asked to participate in a process for which he is unequipped. The unintelligent should under no circumstances ever be put in a position of voting the unintelligent into the ditch. In a democracy, in which issues are decided by a show of hands, it is *vitally* necessary to guard against such a contingency by making as reasonably certain as possible that the heads that go with those hands know what they are doing. The best way to do this is to start at the beginning by teaching the child how to use that delicate instrument with which it is endowed —its brain. To turn that brain into a mind which is capable of sound reasoning and feeling should be the fundamental task of education.

Quite clearly, to judge from the majority of candidates who run for and are elected to national office, something must be seriously amiss somewhere. The cause of the trouble is, I believe, in our so-called educational system. That so-called educational system constitutes a dense jungle of weeds overgrown by centuries of error and outmoded ideas. In that jungle wander teachers and children alike, seeking the light and warmth that escapes them, seemingly forever retracing their tracks in the dark disappointingness of it all. A few there are, pupils and teachers, who sometimes find their way out. But they have difficulty making themselves heard or understood by those who remain. Those within mostly listen to echoes and are not attuned to the vibrations of a new voice. But where the spirit is willing, there is hope. And if a sufficient number of people will express that willingness in the form of practical action, we may yet achieve a citizenry that is capable of voting—that is, of arriving at clear, sound judgments by the conscientious use of intelligence.

Before we permit anyone to practice medicine, law, engineering, pharmacy, or numerous other occupations, we see to it that they are properly trained and are licensed to practice only after they have been certified as proficient in the field in which they have qualified. But when it comes to the making of decisions that will affect the lives of large numbers of human beings, no qualifications whatever are required—simply a residence requirement, registration, and the ability to raise one's hand or make one's mark or pull a lever. It is a ghastly thought, and it happens to be a ghastly fact. We, who would not dream of entrusting the disposition of our property without resorting to the necessary legal assistance, do not hesitate to allow millions of individuals, without any qualifications whatever, to decide vastly more important issues affecting the lives of untold numbers of others, to cast their vote. It is madness. It is worse: it is calamitous.

The kind of people who vote for a Bilbo, Rankin, Strom Thurmond, Byrd, Joseph McCarthy, Lester Maddox, and their like, whose numbers everywhere run into the hundreds of thousands, are not fit to vote and should not be permitted to vote, even for the election of a local keeper of the dog pound. This is, of course, a most dangerous kind of statement to make, for were it to be irresponsibly acted on, it could lead to conditions even worse than the disorder we would want to cure. But, of course, we should want to see it responsibly carried out or not at all.

I suggest a national intelligence test for all ages beginning at eighteen. This test would be designed by a specially appointed board of experts, who would be independent of any form of government control. This test would be designed to ascertain the fitness of the individual to vote in local and national elections. Indeed, I would extend this test to the right to vote on anything whatever. Such a voter's test would soon become as established and as taken for granted as any test of intelligence or literacy or as the tests taken in school to measure competence in any subject. What the voter's test should measure in the person desiring to vote is his ability to think. It seems to me that the simplest and most dependable measure of the citizen's competence to vote would be such a test.

If the establishment of such a test meant that for many years a large number of individuals, even if this turned out to be a majority, would be disqualified as voters, and that the voting would for a time be done by a minority of qualified voters, it would be far better for everyone that a minority of intelligent and honest citizens should be considering the issues and voting upon them, rather than a minority of machine politicians in the legislatures, put there by an unintelligent majority. Health and illness are best overseen by qualified physicians. Similarly, social health and illness are best dealt with by those who are qualified to do so. The social health of the community is a complex condition to maintain, to diagnose when it begins to show early symptoms of a departure from health, and to prescribe whatever may be necessary for continued improvement.

Ignorance, emotion, prejudice, and complacency are simply not good enough. Human beings are worth more informed attention than that, and the uninformed and the ignorant, the prejudiced and the complacent, if they do not agree, should nonetheless not be permitted to compromise the future of the informed and the understanding.

I know all this has an authoritarian ring about it, and I don't like it. I can see very clearly how such ideas could be terribly abused. Perhaps the whole idea is silly, impracticable, unworkable. Perhaps there are more efficient, less dangerous ways of securing an intelligent electorate. I am sure there are. But until we apply those methods and develop such an electorate, the process might be accelerated by the kind of voter's test I have suggested. Perhaps, when such a test has been developed, the test itself could be tested on a sample community. It would be worth trying. H. G. Wells once remarked that civilization is a race between education and disaster. Until the time when through education we shall have achieved an intelligent electorate, it might well be worthwhile considering a voter's test. If we don't do something of the sort, it may be that disaster will catch up with us before education has an opportunity to.

Overpopulation and being human

OVERPOPULATION, MOST AMERICANS seem to think, is
something from which other peoples suffer, but not Americans. This is not so. Overpopulation for most people errone-
ously means that there are too many people for the land to
support, that there is not enough food to feed all the hungry
mouths. This is certainly so in many parts of the world, and it
is a very serious problem, threatening the continued existence of not only those countries, but the whole world. In
spite of the existence of more than 12,000,000 really poor
persons in America, America is able to feed its population
more than adequately. In the last fifty years, food production
in the United States has multiplied more than six times.
There is not only plenty of unsettled land in America, but
also plenty of food—enough, and more than enough, to feed a
much larger population than our present 200,000,000.
Hence, most Americans behave as if their own country were
not suffering from overpopulation. They couldn't be more
wrong.

They will admit, perhaps, that overpopulation is a problem in some crowded cities and that food is a problem for the
12,000,000 impoverished, but that these are very different
problems from those which face the overpopulated nations of
the world. Are they?

A country may well be supplied with land and food and yet be overpopulated. Land and food are by no means all that it takes to make a human being or to make a nation worthy of the name. The very name "human being" tells us what the most important quality of such a creature is. It is *being human*. It is the quality of humanity that is the mark of a human being, and whatever threatens, endangers, or abrogates that humanity to that extent obstructs and denies his birthright. That birthright is development, the fulfillment of the individual's potentialities for being a realized, creative, healthy human being. The greatest danger of overpopulation is not overcrowding or starvation of the physical conditions of life, but overcrowding and starvation of the spiritual conditions of life, the imperiling of the quality of humanity.

In a land in which quantity has been elevated to the status of a supreme value, in a land in which Americans feel that they have the most, the biggest, the largest, the longest, the tallest, the greatest, etc., it is likely to be overlooked that quantity is not exactly the same thing as quality and that, indeed, under certain conditions as quantity goes up, quality goes down. This is really the heart of the matter: the debasement of humanity to which overpopulation leads. Even in a land of great affluence, not only can cities be overcrowded, but families can be, too. It is in the overcrowded family that the greatest damage to humanity is done—both to the individual and to society—for not only do overpopulated families lead to overpopulated societies, but their worst and most damaging effect is the deprivation of development and the impoverishment of humanity to which such overcrowding leads.

By virtue of the fact that he is born a human being and that he is therefore dependent on other human beings for everything he comes to know as a human being, every human being's birthright is development—the creative development of his potentialities for being human. Such development takes a certain amount of unharried time. The conditions in which parenthood becomes a reality, uncomplicated by the consequences of irresponsible parentage, need to be relaxed.

It is apparently very necessary to distinguish between parenthood and parentage. Parenthood is an art; parentage is the consequence of a mere biological act. The biological ability to produce conception and to give birth to a child has nothing whatever to do with the ability to care for that child as it requires to be cared for. That ability, like every other, must be learned. It is highly desirable that parentage be not undertaken until the art of parenthood has been learned. Is this a counsel of perfection? As things stand now, perhaps it is, but it need not always be so. Parentage is often irresponsible. Parenthood is responsible. Parentage at best is irresponsibly responsible for the *birth* of a child. Parenthood is responsible for the *development* of a human being—not simply a child, but a human being. I do not think it is an overstatement to say that parenthood is the most important occupation in the world. There is no occupation for which the individual should be better prepared than this, for what can be more important to the individual, his family, his community, his society, his nation, and the world of humanity than the making of a good human being? And the making of a good human being is largely the work of good parents. And it *is* work—hard work—not to be irresponsibly undertaken or perfunctorily performed. Yet parenthood, perhaps like politics, is the only profession for which preparation is considered unnecessary.

Why do people have children? Not surprisingly it is a question seldom asked. It is usually taken for granted that following marriage, it is the normal thing to do. But how many who marry are really fit for marriage? How many who marry really understand what marriage means or what parenthood means? Very few. Added to this is the problem of the large increase in the number of children born out of wedlock.

Very few Americans are ever taught the art of parenthood—an art one learns best from the example of parents proficient in it, or failing that, one doesn't learn at all. The schools, in which these matters are tabooed, could do a great deal to remedy this and related deficiencies.

At this moment (1966) there are some 70,000,000 children in the United States under the age of eighteen, and of those 70,000,000 children, 12,000,000 live in the most abject poverty. Eighteen out of every 100 children living in the most affluent country with the highest standard of living in the world live under physical and moral and intellectual conditions which are nothing short of catastrophic. Most of these 12,000,000 children should never have been born, for the simple reason that there was no one to give them the care they deserved. They represent a disaster. No one cares for them. In 1964, 750,000 children were arrested in the United States. In New York City alone, in the same year, more than 40,000 children were arrested. This is, of course, only a proportion of the total number of children who committed indictable offenses. The increase in the calendar of serious crimes—murder, rape, assault, arson, larceny, theft—has been spectacular.

These tragic children are not simple statistics but reflect the alienation and indifference of a delinquent society. Every one of these children is a human being who has been failed in the most basic of his rights, the right to fulfillment. A society unable to satisfy the needs for development of more than a certain number of its citizens should see to it that more than that certain number is never exceeded. And when this has been said, that is the long and the short of the story.

Birth control has been discussed and debated for well over 100 years, and in some places the idea still meets with as much irrational opposition as it ever did. Although it is perfectly true that there is no adequate defense, except stupidity, against the impact of some ideas, the impact of the facts of overpopulation has been such in recent years as to cause a perceptible and hopeful rise of interest in the heading off of the disasters that overpopulation brings in its wake. In a State of the Union Message, President Johnson said, "I will seek new ways to use our knowledge to help deal with the explosion of world population and the growing scarcity of resources." Former President Eisenhower has put the issue very clearly: "The population explosion has become one of the critical world problems of our time. It threatens to smother the economic progress of many nations and endangers the free world struggle for peace and security. Greatly expanded public and private efforts must be undertaken to contain this human explosion." Progress is being made, but it must be accelerated. More and more persons practice birth control, increasingly greater numbers desire to, and many governments have recognized the pressing necessity of teaching their citizens to do so. Every government ought to have a department of population control. We have a Department of Agriculture, which controls the reproduction of plants and animals, but we do not have any governmental means of controlling the reproduction of people. Such a department exists in Japan, the only land which has really satisfactorily solved its population problem, to the extent that a labor shortage threatens there! Japan reduced its birthrate, by control and legalized abortion, from 34.2 per thousand in 1947 to 17.2 per thousand in 1957, to 7.0 per thousand in

1964. In other words, in ten years the birthrate was cut in half, and seven years later by more than half again.

Governments have many departments organized to defend the people against threats originating from without their borders. But scarcely any have a department designed to protect the people against the most dangerous of all threats from within their borders. I say "the most dangerous" because I believe, in common with many others, that the devaluation of the quality of humanity by the uncontrolled increase in its quantity constitutes a vastly more tragic loss than the reduction in its numbers by the evils of famine, disease, or war. Liberty, privacy, and freedom for human development decrease as the number of people increases, opportunities for growth and development are curtailed and frustrated, and self-realization assumes not even the semblance of a dream, and "like this insubstantial pageant faded," under conditions of overpopulation, most men are destined to "leave not a rack behind."

When the size of a population increases beyond the limits consonant with the requirements of individual development, individual development is necessarily slighted. The very pressures for survival produce the atomization of human relationships, disengagement, alienation, and indifference to the lot of others—a state in which everyone must sink or swim by his own efforts without expectation of support from others.

Increases in the size of human societies tend to increase the complexities with which such societies are confronted out of all proportion to the actual increase in quantity. And one of the first things that suffers under such conditions is the quality of human relationships. Consider, for example, the United States. It is a big country. It has grown at a rapid rate. Our rates of crime of every kind, lawlessness, disorder, disorganization, wastage, immorality, injustice, and vast num-

bers of other problems are among the highest in the world.
We have grown too large too quickly. And the result has
been that we have grown into the habit of paying more attention to things than to human beings. Human beings create
the need for things, and the business of dealing in things
yields greater cash returns—or, at least, so it is believed by
those who believe in consumerism—than enabling human
beings to fulfil themselves. If you can go into the business of
making money, like General Motors, by providing these
problems in search of a solution, with things that will tend to
make them feel that they are on the road to fulfillment, you
cannot, as General Motors has abundantly demonstrated,
possibly fail. Was it not a president of General Motors who
said, "What is good for General Motors is good for the
country"?

In our worship of quantity and things, we have forgotten
that the only genuine wealth of a people lies in the quality of
the people. What is the sense of having 27,500 students in a
university and often more than 600 students in a class?
Certainly it is possible to instruct such numbers, but it is
impossible to educate them, for in the process of education
one is concerned with a dialogue between student and
teacher. The student is recognized as a unique person, and
the exchange that should be unhurriedly proceeding between
teacher and student should serve to minister to the individual
needs of the student, so that he may grow and develop as a
human being, in the increase in his sensibilities, in the
broadening of his vision, in the deepening of his understanding, as well as in the enlargement of his mind and the increase of his knowledge. To do all this is difficult, if not
impossible, under crowded conditions. Under such conditions the precious gift that lies within the power of the
teacher to offer his students—his own personality—is aborted

and diminished, if not altogether lost. And what is worse, so is that of the student who is pressed into a mass conformity, instead of being helped toward the development of his own individuality and the service of his fellowman, by the pressure of the overcrowded institutions in which he finds himself and which reflect the consequences of the general overpopulation of the country.

What happens to a country when it becomes overpopulated is in macrocosm what can be observed occurring on a smaller scale in a city that becomes overpopulated. It matters not how materially prosperous the country is; the complexities produced by overpopulation constitute a human and social disaster for most of its inhabitants. Consider New York, Chicago, Los Angeles, Paris, London. What becomes of humanity in such cities? What will happen to human beings when populations double and treble in size? Altogether apart from the fact that we in the cities are already engulfed by automobiles and overcome by smog, the struggle for survival will become even more severe and there will be vanishingly less time and thought available for the development of the individual. The individual, indeed, will tend to get lost in the crush. Schools and teachers will be insufficient to take care of the swelling masses of unplanned children; schools and classes will be even more crowded than they are today, with a consequent lowering of standards. Parents will be able to pay even less attention to their children than they do today. Delinquency and crime and poverty will increase, and social disorganization rather than organization will spread.

At the end of this century it is estimated that there will be some 350,000,000 Americans. The number of automobiles will have increased from the present 80,000,000 to 170,000,-000. If anyone desires to see what the future America will look like, let him go to that disaster area California. In

California there are the largest, biggest, and most complex freeways in the world, where often to drive under seventy-five miles an hour is to court death. To drive on these freeways is an open invitation to death, anyway, so this last statement was rather redundant. Into California pour 1,600 people a day, 500,000 a year, and for every 1,000 increase in population, 240 acres of arable land are lost to asphalt or buildings. Before one's very eyes one can see 3,000,000 acres of open land disappearing before the inundation of people. It all looks like a tentative preface to extinction, especially of the human spirit, as recent political and social events in California serve only too gloomily to indicate.

With the continuing drift of the rural population toward the cities we are producing that urban sprawl which accounts for so much of the destruction of the land which we see acceleratingly proceeding apace. Anyone who travels in America has not far to go before he observes the human and natural devastation that is everywhere about us, the debasement of the human spirit, the disinheritance of the birthright of millions of human beings, the disengagement from humanity, the progression from cruelty to callousness to indifference to unawareness. If the human landscape has been devastated, what shall one say of the natural landscape, the congenial environment in which man once lived? Here there has been not only a destruction of the natural beauties of the land, but also an unspeakable uglification of it. The living creatures that once freely roamed over the land are threatened with extinction. Virtually everyday, numberless animals, birds and butterflies, beautiful and enhancing, cease to be before the onrushing masses of reduplicating human beings and the poisons they produce. The air, the land, rivers, lakes, and streams are unconscionably polluted, as the silent spring bears poignant testimony to the degradation of the human spirit. We are turning God's own country into God's own junkyard. Is this what we Americans want? It is certainly what Americans have in the past done nothing to prevent. But the signs are not unhopeful. Increasing numbers of Americans are beginning to realize what has happened to their country and are increasingly beginning to make themselves responsible for doing what is required: planning their own families, helping others to plan theirs, and supporting those organizations that are dedicated to the protection of the land and its inhabitants against further deterioration and to the improvement of its natural resources—the land and its people.

The new wasteland

THERE ARE MEN in America who on perceiving a green field or a meadow begin to slaver at the gills and, like Uriah Heep, start washing their hands with invisible soap at the contemplation of the thought, nay, the beatific vision, of a glorious development on the site or a nice four-lane concrete highway, with all the trees cut down, the ponds and streams filled in, and lovely gas stations, hot-dog stands, and billboards usefully replacing all the land that was going to waste. Land in its natural state is regarded as so much wasteland by such men, to be recovered for its proper use— that is, its destruction and uglification. Cut down the trees, bulldoze the earth, and cover the ravished land with asphalt and developments.

Oil-cracking plants, refineries, factories, railroads, sidings, junkyards, hoardings, dumps of every description—these are the true marks of material and spiritual progress.

When citizens of Chicago recently attempted to protect the trees that were to be destroyed to make way for a new highway, the mayor of that city deplored their backward behavior. "You can't stop progress," said he. Can't we? That kind of progress leads straight to hell. It is not for nothing, perhaps, that hell has been described as a pocket edition of Chicago. The mayor's kind of progress leads onward and upward, for when enough highways have been built in Chicago, and the traffic has come to a standstill, it will be necessary to build a second story over the town, and then a third, and a fourth, and so on, ad infinitum. The prospect may please the mayor of Chicago and the developers, and it may even please the majority of Americans; but in that kind of progress lies disaster.

The unmerciful destruction of trees has created the worst kind of erosion problems. The destruction of the beauties of the land, the bulldozing of orchards to make way for the slums of the future, the scarring of hillside and mountainside by carving them into terraces upon which houses are erected and roadways are built, all opening onto the most deadly freeways, the eateries, the shopping centers, the pollution of rivers, lakes, soil, and air, the slaughter of wildlife—all this is thought of as progress: the progress which leads straight into the ditch of inhumanity.

The callousness and brutishness that this rape of the land reflects are found among all levels of Americans. In Washington there are permanent real estate lobbies whose job it is to see to it that as much land is prevented from being nationalized as possible. These lobbies are powerful. They have fought every inch of the way against the nationalization of parklands and the preservation of many historic monuments. The outdoor advertising people have done the same. How little Americans care for their country, so beautiful, so various, so fair, is something to reflect on. Lovely country roads are used as garbage dumps by automobilized Americans, who will think nothing of strewing their garbage along the sides of the road. Beer cans, bottles, paper plates, napkins, newspapers, paper cups, and the rest are indifferently strewed wherever these good Americans choose to picnic. Even at picnic grounds, where receptacles are provided for refuse, the inconsideration of the delinquent American picnicker is evident.

Americans, who constantly protest how much they love their country, litter, despoil, and deface it unconscionably. To be a litterbug is for many Americans a privilege of freedom, *not* an abuse of it. Cities employ street and park cleaners whose task it is to remove the litter. Millions of dollars are spent annually to clean up the mess created by so many thoughtless Americans who are constantly engaged in soiling their own nests.

One of the more vile habits of gumchewing Americans is their practice of expectorating their chewd cuds onto any surface that presents itself. Hence, every sidewalk throughout the United States is disfigured by the flattened dark globs of chewing gum virtually incorporated into the surfaces upon which they have been dropped, pounded into the hardest surfaces by the thousands of feet that have passed over them. The same globs may be seen on subway and station platforms and on the tiled, paved and inlaid floors of innumerable public buildings. At great expense of time and money men are frequently employed, with an instrument specially devised for the purpose, to scrape these blobs from such surfaces. It is an extremely difficult job.

An interesting thing about lawbreaking, irresponsible, thoughtless Americans is that on occasion they are capable of the worthiest kind of respect for the law. It is remarkable. For example, on the New York public transportation system it is not permissible to smoke on any of its vehicles. In forty years of traveling on such vehicles I have never seen anyone smoking. If Americans were only encouraged to observe the law, not alone of man but of nature, we would succeed in banishing the junkyard appearance we have given to so much of the land. We would also be making a good beginning, by creating the proper attitudes of mind, toward preventing its further spoilation.

Competition and cooperation

AT CHAMBER OF COMMERCE lunches and on similar occasions one not infrequently hears the orator of the day asserting that "America owes its greatness to the spirit of competition." I would like to suggest that the evidence indicates that whatever greatness America has achieved, it has achieved in spite of competition, *not* because of it. But this is not the main point I wish to make here. My main desire is to clarify the ideas of competition and cooperation as they are actually found to work in an industrial society.

Competition means to strive *against* others to achieve the same or similar goals. Cooperation means to strive *with* others to achieve the same or similar goals. A principle of the American way of life is the idea of competition. This takes the simple form of going out and doing better than the other even if you have to do him and his family injury in the process. *That* can be none of your concern. After all, you have *your* family to think of. This kind of indifference to the consequences to others of one's competitiveness is inherent in the principle of competition. Our studies have shown us that this kind of competitiveness is extremely damaging to everyone and everything that comes within the orbit of its influence, to none more so than to the successful competitor, for the spoils, he finds in the end, do not belong to him; instead, he belongs to the spoils. This is the kind of competition that leads to high frequencies of ulcers and nervous breakdowns; to high delinquency rates, divorce and separation rates, and homicide rates; and to violent crime rates that are the highest in the world—as they are in America.

It has been said that no man is an island because every man is so much at sea. There is a modicum of truth in that statement. No man is an island because every man is involved, by his natural endowment, in every other man. Not only are other men parts of our environment, but they are also *necessary* parts. We are involved not only in other men, but in their welfare—or we should be. The competitive frame of reference is antithetical to such a way of life. It misplaces the emphasis on oneself rather than upon the other, and such value as it affords to one, it validates in terms of externals instead of in terms of internals. The principle of conspicuous consumption—in plain English, keeping up with the Joneses —is perhaps the clearest illustration of the misplaced emphasis. Driving up to your neighbor's house in the "right" car may spell prestige in a society of false values, but the proper value of a man lies, not in the quality of his car, but in the quality of self—the most precious of all his possessions.

In America we have often tended to place too much value on things and not enough on people. This is because we have desired to "arrive" in terms of things rather than in reference to people, a state to which competition inevitably leads.

On the other hand, cooperation, striving *with* others—*not* against them—is a far more efficient way of achieving any objective than competition is. Cooperation seeks to bring out the best in everyone. Competition, in spite of oft-reiterated statements to the contrary, in the long run has the effect of making it impossible for large numbers of individuals to exhibit what is in them. This is where competitive examinations so often fail and where in a cooperatively designed examination much greater justice would be done to the individual, with correspondingly greater benefits accruing to his society.

It is far more efficient to cooperate with one another to help bring out the best that is within us than it is to compete with one another in order to do so. As industry, as well as many another group, is slowly learning, cooperation pays higher dividends than competition does; this is not to say that all competition is bad. Cooperative competition, the kind toward which American industry has been developing, is perhaps better called competitive cooperation, in which different groups, formerly competitors, agree to join forces and cooperate.

The violent American

IF AMERICANS ARE NOT the most violent people on earth, they are certainly not far removed from that position. The violence of America began with its settlement, with its "defense" and "protection" against the Indians, "defense" and "protection" being the euphemisms for the deliberate and merciless murder of whole tribes, for the gloss of instituting the practice of scalping and then saddling the Indians with the crimes we taught them. That violence was licensed and intensified by the ever-widening encroachment of the settlers on the territories of the Indians and by the establishment of the frontier, with every white man a law unto himself by force of his firearms, is a matter of the historic record. The myth of the savage Indian, against whose allegedly murderous ways it was necessary to defend oneself, made it mandatory that every American should enjoy the right to bear arms. In the Declaration of Independence every American was informed, as was the rest of the world, that the king of Great Britain "has excited domestic insurrections amongst us, and has endeavoured to bring on the inhabitants of our frontiers, the merciless Indian Savages, whose known rule of warfare is an undistinguished destruction of all ages, sexes and conditions."

In this manner every settler engaged in opening up the country was made to consider it a patriotic duty and a moral obligation to shoot up as many "Indian Savages" as he could manage to dispose of.

> It is surprising how indifferent people become to the sight of violence and bloodshed in this country. Here we have almost daily rows, attended with loss of life, and we look upon these scenes with the greatest callousness of feeling, at the same time being well aware that in any of these rows one's own life is just as much in danger as another's. A man now fires his pistol on the slightest motive for quarrel, with the same readiness that in another country he would strike a blow with his fist.

Those words were written during the 1849–1852 gold rush in California by William Perkins, a Canadian.* Have conditions much altered?

The romanticized cult of the frontier and the "Indian Savages" is still with us, with its glorification of violence and unrestrained individualism. The Wild West and the Western represent the glorifications of a libertinism of violence. Billy the Kid is an American folklore hero, and every kid develops more than a sneaking sympathy for the two-gun fugitives whom Marshal Dillon and Wild Bill Hickok bring in, either dead or alive. Cowboys and Indians is a game played not only by American children, but also by children almost everywhere in the world. The example of America has not been parochial, but its effects have been greatest on location. Small boys at an early age are often attired in cowboy uniforms, complete with replicas of revolvers, holsters, and gun belts neatly filled with imitation bullets. With this armament they fire away in emulation of their adult models. The incitements to the use of firearms are everywhere. Comics, storybooks,

---

* William Perkins, *Three Years in California: Journal of Life at Sonora, 1849–1852*, with introduction and annotations by Dale L. Morgan and James R. Scobie (Berkeley, University of California Press, 1964).

movies, TV, magazines, tabloids, newspapers, F.B.I. reports, the murders, muggings, gang wars—adult and juvenile—the rapes, stranglings, police brutality, and much else combine to make violence an everyday part of the American scene. America has the highest rate of violent crime in the world. J. Edgar Hoover of the Federal Bureau of Investigation expresses himself forcibly on the subject several times a year, but no one seems to pay him much attention. In March, 1966, Mr. Hoover announced that preliminary figures for the calendar year 1965 disclosed a nationwide rise of 5 percent in the crime index over the preceding year and that for the country as a whole, all crime classifications were up in volume. Violent crimes recorded increases of 6 percent in murder, 7 percent in forcible rape, and 3 percent in aggravated assault. Aggravated assault by gun rose 12 percent, and armed robbery increased 6 percent. Since 1949 the violent crime rate was up by 40 percent.

Americans are violent in their sports and in their entertainments and are constantly in search of thrills. With their principal means of terrestrial mobility, the automobile, many Americans are engaged in an undeclared war against their fellow Americans, with a casualty rate of staggering proportions. The automobile accident rate reflects something of the violent attitudes that characterize so many individuals. This is particularly evident in certain teen-agers and young "adult" males. One teen-ager I encountered boasted that he has had seven serious automobile accidents. The comparatively light injuries he has sustained far from serving to deter him from driving dangerously, have had the effect of encouraging him to continue in his reckless driving. Why the parents or guardians of this menace have not taken the indicated action to prevent him from continuing to endanger the lives of others, as well as his own life, is a mystery. Nor can I understand why official action has not been taken to ground this irresponsible youth permanently. A car can be used as a lethal weapon, and those who reveal the slightest tendency to use it as such should not be permitted to do so.

This brings us to yet another aspect of violence in America. It is the disgraceful laxity of our courts. I do not refer to the police. The police are generally much more alive to and concerned with this than the average citizen or, apparently, our courts are. Judges and juries, on purely technical points of the law, are only too often persuaded that the offense, such as motoring down five innocent pedestrians and killing them, is only a minor one and no occasion for court action or is at most to be dealt with in a perfunctorily legalistic manner. Such behavior on the part of judges and juries makes a mockery of the law, a principal function of which, we had understood, was the protection of the individual, if necessary even from himself, and certainly of the society of which he is a part.

I refer to laxity in enforcing the laws governing the possession and use of lethal weapons, whatever form they may take, not from any belief that the proper enforcement of the law would solve the problem of violence, but from the belief that the lax enforcement of any law serves as a *de facto* encouragement to its violation. It is not an accident that America is the most lawless country in the world. Lawlessness is an American tradition, and lawlessness prospers in America because its expression has never been seriously or adequately controlled.

It is not alone what Americans do but also what they fail to do in the home that contributes so much to the violence of the American character. The great failure in the American home is the lack of a loving discipline—a discipline in which the child comes to understand that always within the warmth of his parents' love he can depend on them for what he has a right to expect from them, the spiritual, material, and social supports he requires for development. At the same time he must be taught that there are many things his parents have a right to expect from him so that they, and others, may be able to depend on him to do the right thing. A child who knows he is loved will soon learn that when his parents say "No" and mean it, their disapproval is as well intended for his benefit as is their approval. Love has a firmness and a discipline all its own, and the child thrives on it. The child takes delight in a firm hand at the helm, especially at such times as he himself may be rocking the boat. It gives him confidence, for he fails to enjoy the insecurities and dangers of being in a boat no one knows how to handle. He wants to hear the orders delivered in a firm voice, in a voice that inspires confidence, whatever the orders, because he knows they are the right orders. He does not want to be left to sink or swim on the ineptitudes of those who do not know what orders to give and so either give none or give confused ones.

Any order that is accompanied by corporal punishment is wrong. It is wrong for many reasons, the principal one being that it teaches violence, the infliction of pain on others, as a permissible form of behavior. By being violent to a child, we teach him to be violent to others. In this manner the child is taught to believe that violence is inseparable from the human condition, that violence is a fact of nature, something to be taken for granted. In such an atmosphere the child accumulates a considerable amount of repressed hostility, as a consequence of the punitive frustrations he has so often experienced.

Permissive violence in the home and the lack of discipline designed to build those inner controls which would inhibit every tendency to violence, together with the piling up of large stores of repressed hostility, constitute a formidable combination. There are millions of Americans with such a contagious family history, with their repressed hostilities ready to explode into violence at the slightest provocation.

These words were written before the horrifying events that took place on the campus of the University of Texas at Austin on August 1, 1966, when Charles J. Whitman shot and killed fourteen people and wounded thirty-one others, having previously killed his mother and wife. Whitman was brought up in a home in which guns were the playthings of a violent-tempered wife-beating father, who boasted that he "raised" his "boys to know how to handle guns." A photograph has been published of Whitman as a small child with a rifle in each hand.

The panel of thirty-two physicians and psychologists appointed by Governor Connally to inquire into the causes which led Whitman to his murderous rampage reported that it was deeply concerned that the Whitman incident and others similar to it indicated a growing tendency to violence in the United States. It recommended that a massive nation-wide study be made to find out if this was true and, if so, what should be done (*The New York Times,* September 9, 1966).

Such a study is long overdue. It is greatly to be hoped that it will be carried out and that its findings will be seriously acted upon.

The National Rifle Association's response to the unfavorable publicity resulting from Whitman's addiction to firearms was to buy newspaper space to advertise that "America needs more straight shooters." Apparently thoroughly in agreement, the United States Senate has bottled up the bill to curb interstate traffic in firearms in its Judiciary Committee.

Not only should all forms of violent behavior be discouraged in the home, but so should all instruments of violence, real or imitated. Guns are not playthings, and no child should ever be allowed to believe that they are. To regard a lethal weapon as a toy, even in toy form, is to train children in the belief that a gun is something with which to have fun. In a world torn by war, filled with superweapons and daily talk of armament and violence, with the hunting of animals a major sport, the gunplay of TV and the freedom, frequency, and fury with which guns are almost uniformly fatally employed in that medium, aided and abetted by the movies, make the taking for granted of guns and violence on the American scene a matter of course. Add to this the fact that our policemen, state troopers, and other uniformed law enforcement officers freely display upon their persons guns in holsters and belts arrayed with bullets, and we have legal sanction placed on the free and easy acceptance of the display of arms. What this open display of arms by the police teaches is that Americans are so violent that the police must be armed in order to protect themselves and in order to restrain, capture, or shoot the lawbreakers. In response, the lawbreakers arm themselves. In addition, the very knowledge that a policeman may shoot a lawbreaker gives others the feeling that they are free to do likewise under similar conditions. Mr. Ruby, for example, felt among other things, as every member of a vigilante mob has felt, that the law would be saved a great deal of trouble if he took it into his own hands and settled everything by pulling the trigger. It was simple. It was easy. Everyone had a gun. He had a gun, and what are guns for, if not for use? What better use could his gun be put to than to mete out punishment to a man who had already been judged guilty of murder by the mass media, the police, and the district attorney?

If it had been made difficult socially, psychologically, by public opinion, and legally for Oswald and Ruby to think of guns as most Americans do, there would have been no tragedy that fatal day in Dallas. Both Oswald and Whitman had been trained by the American Army as first-class marksmen.

The National Rifle Association, a powerful lobby against any regulation of the ownership of firearms, tells us that 30,000,000 Americans own and know how to use firearms. Article II of the Bill of Rights secures every American in the "right . . . to keep and bear Arms." But times have changed since the eighteenth century, when there were no police and firearms were a necessary precaution against marauders. The National Rifle Association says that these 30,000,000 gun owners constitute a bulwark against any threat of invasion by a foreign power. This suggestion is laughable. The National Rifle Association and 30,000,000 gun-using Americans resisting the nuclear weapons of a foreign power would be a spectacle to behold.

Since the year 1900 more than 750,000 persons have been shot to death in the United States, a number considerably exceeding the 530,000 who have been killed in all U.S. wars!

Every year in the United States, many men, women, and children are shot and killed because of the ubiquity of and easy access to guns. The number shot is well over 28,000, of which about 9,250 are murders. It is time that it was agreed that a gun is a lethal weapon and that it should be treated as such. This means that no child should ever be permitted to play with a toy or real gun and that no one should ever be issued a license to own a gun under any circumstances whatever, with the exception of a duly authorized and certified official. Anyone desiring to own a car must first obtain a license to drive one and must simultaneously register his ownership with the state. A car may be used as a lethal weapon, but its presumed primary purpose is transportation. The purpose of a gun is to wound or kill, yet there are only seven states in the Union that require a permit to carry a gun. In 1964 a Gallup Poll showed that 78 percent of

Americans are in favor of some kind of registration of guns. If guns are not registered, we can depend on it that crime by handguns will continue to rise. The unlicensed manufacture, sale, and possession of firearms should be made a criminal offense, and if this requires an amendment to the Constitution, then that is what should be done. This would mean that hunting would be outlawed. Where it would be necessary to control the numbers of animal populations, this could be effectively and safely left in the hands of officially appointed members of the conservation corps—a step which is, in any event, long overdue.

We Americans must grow up and stop playing with guns, whether it is as children or in the guise of an adult hunter. A gun gives a weak man or an intemperate one the kind of power that should never be placed in his hands. Law-abiding citizens must demand the right to be protected from the weaknesses of such individuals. They must use their own authentic strength to help the weak and protect them from themselves. The weak must have the help of the strong. If Oswald had received the necessary help from the strong when he most needed it, instead of being failed as he was, there would have been no tragedy in Dallas in November, 1963. We consistently fail the Oswalds because we will not, as individuals and as a nation, honestly and squarely face the fact that there are at work in America many socially disorganizing forces which cannot be abandoned to the private agencies so inadequately organized to deal with them. The relatively few good and intelligent individuals who make these agencies possible cannot provide more than the most inadequate palliatives. The problem of violence in America concerns the nation as a whole and every American without exception. These problems should be the concern of the government. Private agencies can help, but the federal, state, and local governments must assume the wise and beneficent use of their own powers and strengths in relation to the rest of the community's weaknesses.

In 1965 five serious crimes were committed for every minute of the twenty-four hour day. Every two minutes someone was killed, maimed, robbed, or beaten with a gun. There was a murder every hour; forcible rape every twenty-six minutes; aggravated assault—that is, assault with intent to kill or inflict grievous bodily harm—every three minutes; burglary every twenty-eight seconds; robbery every five minutes, and auto theft every minute, and each year these rates rise. Guns are only a symptom, not a cause, of this destructiveness. The removal of guns will not cure the disease, but certainly it will greatly help reduce the expression of the disease in one of its most dangerous forms. To discontinue the availability of firearms would be a first step in the desired direction. In 1963 in New York City, which requires the licensing of guns, 25 percent of murders were committed with guns. In the same year in Dallas, which does not require the licensing of guns, 72 percent of murders were committed with guns. Governor John Connally of Texas, who was himself seriously wounded by the assassin of President Kennedy, does not think that any new firearms control laws are needed (*The New York Times,* August 4, 1966).

The shots that rang out in Dallas in November, 1963, seem to have taught us nothing. All these years after the murder of President Kennedy, virtually nothing has been done to regulate the interstate traffic in firearms or to institute uniform regulations in each of the fifty states controlling the use of firearms. Among other things, it would be heartening to see the 750,000-member National Rifle Association die of inanition, instead of having our government, as it does, continue to supply it with millions of rounds of free ammunition.

The beauty of American women

HUNGARIAN WOMEN, it is said, are the most beautiful in the world. Possibly they are. Certainly those I have met or seen strikingly live up to their reputation. On the basis of my own sampling experience I would think it likely that Hungary has a high frequency of exceptionally beautiful women. Looking at American women, I can conclude only that a large number of Hungarian women—in addition to the Gabors—must have emigrated to America, for America has by far the largest number of beautiful women I have seen anywhere in the world. Since I have never visited Scandinavia, it is quite possible that, per centum of population, Scandinavia has a higher frequency of beautiful women, but surely not as great a variety.

When I arrived in America from England, a land in which women tend to be plain and forty years ago were the most dowdily dressed in the world (in addition, they knew virtually nothing concerning the use of artificial embellishments), the contrast presented by the American woman was almost overwhelming. Until I landed in the United States, I had no idea that there were so many beautiful women in the world. Even the nonbeautiful ones were somehow attractive; they had not given up on themselves, and this was admirable.

[119

How to account for this high frequency of beauty? It could not all be due to a Hungarian or even Scandinavian influence. A probable explanation is hybrid vigor, the kind of vigor that accrues to the offspring of admixed types. More people—about 40,000,000—have entered the United States from a greater variety of lands and ethnic groups than has even remotely been the experience of any other country in the history of mankind. With this enormous diversity of national and ethnic origins there was bound to be a greater variety of gene mixtures than had ever occurred before. And it is therefore not surprising that among the evidences of this should be an increase in the frequency of beauty—not alone feminine, but also masculine. In addition, sexual selection has played an increasingly important role—altogether a combination of factors sufficient to explain the frequency of beauty in the United States.

Several other factors contribute to the appearance of beauty in American women. These are clothes and artificial embellishments. American women are, I believe, the best dressed in the world, and certainly they use makeup with considerable sophistication. The result is that the beauties look even more beautiful, and women who would otherwise look quite ordinary become extremely attractive.

The antiprivacy conspiracy

PRIVACY IS A RESERVATION of civilized life which Americans do not cherish. Hence, high walls, green hedges, or fences do not separate them from their neighbors, and picture windows are an open invitation, if not to come in, certainly at least to look in. Mowing the lawn at all sorts of hours disturbing to one's neighbors—were those neighbors disturbable—is considered, if it is considered at all, a right of every homeowner, and that last infirmity of the surburban mind, the manicured lawn, the pride that only too often goes before the fall, is the occasion of all those pesticides and weed poisons, powders and potions which are thoughtlessly injected into the air for one's neighbors to take into their lungs, whether they desire to do so or not. The children run all over the place, shouting at the tops of their voices, and grow up to be so fond of noise that they come to identify it with gaiety. If foreigners find Americans objectionably noisy, it is because they fail to understand that Americans do not consider that they are really having a good time unless there is a certain amount of noise associated with it. To Americans, noise is neither irksome nor disagreeable, as it is in other countries, but a reassurance that while there is noise, there is life. Hence, the great popularity of the detonations that are a part

[121

of the essential structure of modern popular music. It is loud; it is rhythmical, gratifying, and vibrant evidence of the fact that one is both alive and kicking. *Yeh. Ye-eh-eh.*

Is it that Americans are so fundamentally insecure that they fear silence? That they identify silence, quietude, with death, nothingness? And that silence is equated with solitude? And being alone confused with loneliness? A room of one's own? Americans usually do not have one and, when they do, scarcely ever make use of it. The den is usually where the liquor is kept, along with the few books, which stand on their shelves unread, like so many tombstones in the graveyard of their keeper's good intentions. The American wife usually does not have a room of her own. American children are likely to share rooms and to run wild through the house, playing cowboys and Indians and generally whooping it up, so that noise becomes associated in their minds with fun. Hence, it is not surprising that being conditioned so early to noise, Americans should come to value it for itself and to find most of the noises that other people find intolerable, not only endurable, but even agreeable.

Homework is usually done to the accompaniment of the latest record, not to mention the other noises incident to daily life in the American home. Noise indeed comes to be, for the average American, an anodyne and an ameliorator of tension. Hence, quietude is the last thing one comes to associate with the American ethos. "The highest degree of earthly happiness," said Dr. Johnson, "is quiet." What an un-American idea! But then, Dr. Johnson was an Englishman and anyway lived in the eighteenth century. The fact, of course, is that earlier centuries, especially the eighteenth century were, not without their share of noise. It may be recalled that in that period Schopenhauer wrote an essay "On Noise," in which he bitterly complained of the brain-split-

ting cracking of the coachmen's whips and other objectionable contemporary eruptions of noise. Schopenhauer added
that "the amount of noise which anyone can bear undisturbed
stands in inverse proportion to his mental capacity, and may
therefore be regarded as a pretty fair measure of it." What
would Schopenhauer have thought of the noises perpetrated
by the modern automobile driver, the honking of horns, the
backfiring, screeching, groaning, swishing of automobiles,
trucks, and buses, the unthrottled infernal roaring and stac-
cato of motorcycles, the whining of jet aircraft, and the sonic
boom? It is far better he was spared the pain of having to
think about them at all.

This "stench in the ear," as Ambrose Bierce called it, these
damaging unwanted sounds, are appropriately coming to be
called noise pollution.

Yet Americans take all this din and discord for granted.
Scarcely anyone protests. Loud-voiced Americans are not
oppressed by loud noises. It is seldom that one hears a quiet-
voiced American. Conversations in public vehicles are usually conducted as if everyone else were an audience designed
to hear what one would have supposed was intended for the
private ear of one's companion. A loud voice—I think Socra-
tes said—generally betrays a shallow mind. America has no
monopoly on shallow minds, but it does seem to have a very
large proportion of loudmouths. Traveling, as I do, a great
deal in public vehicles, trains, buses, and planes, I find it is a
rare experience when I am not disturbed by some inconsiderate loudmouth. The loudmouths are by no means restricted
to the uneducated and the underprivileged—although these
are only too well represented among the noisy-mouthed—but
it seems to be a point among many who should know better
to make their presence felt by their raucous voices and
obtrusive disregard for the privacy of others, as if to make it

clear how much they think of themselves and how little they value others. That talk can be noise and an irritating invasion of privacy never seems to occur to them—these contributors to the little meannesses and diminishments of life.

The private poisoners of the atmosphere and disturbers of the peace make possible the public enemies of quietude. Among the chief offenders are the public-address systems which assault one's eardrums with their abominations, without as much as a by-your-leave. Up and down the streets mobile public-address units usually announcing the dubious virtues of a candidate for political office, are permitted to break in on one wherever one may be, one's home being no more sacrosanct than the open street. And not only from the streets but also from airborne vehicles the curse of Babel may descend on one so that there is no escape. And when it is not noise to which one is being subjected, these vehicles will either write their crapulous eructations in the skies or drag the lettered advertising behind them like some pennant announcing the edge of doom.

Some readers may recall that some years ago when a well-known railroad introduced a loudspeaker system on behalf of its advertising friends, the unconsulted captive travelers were not very upset. But some were, and among these was the late Harold Ross, editor of *The New Yorker*. He led a revolt against this unspeakable iniquity and succeeded in putting an end to an inexcusable invasion of the individual's privacy. This incident showed that "enough people" constitute a minority of one, a single individual who will take the trouble to protest and organize protest against such encroachments on one's liberties. I am not aware, however, that there has been an inclination to imitate Harold Ross' protest or that anything at all has been done elsewhere about restricting the liberty of advertisers and the like to trespass on the rights of others.

State and city authorities are no less guilty of contributing to the increase in the decibel count of noise. Such public agencies are among the most barbarous and inconsiderate of offenders. Their licensed noises are sanctioned iniquities. Are not the piercing shrieks of police sirens an offense unto the spirit of man? What is their purpose? I have always assumed that it was in most cases an act of consideration on the part of the police designed to apprise criminals of their impending arrival so that the criminals might be able to make a leisurely getaway. Other countries somehow contrive to manage these matters much more quietly and effectively. If a police car requires a right of way, surely there are superior means to announcing the official need for the right of way? Fire trucks, rescue squad cars, and ambulances—all are offenders. Surely a signaling system could be easily devised, with every car equipped with the necessary device which would enable official cars to announce their needs?

The barbarous custom that has developed in recent years of the continuous blasting of horns in automobile wedding processions should be altogether forbidden. Indeed, automobile horns should be used not as an expression of emotion of any kind, but exclusively for the purpose for which they were intended—as warning signals.

Speaking of automobiles reminds us of another recently developed fracturer of the sound barrier. This is the radio receiver with which many cabs are now equipped. It is seldom possible to take a ride in a cab without being exposed to the more or less continuous crackling of the dispatcher's voice—and whether male or female, usually a most gratingly unpleasant one. Surely a telephone would be a more thoughtful way of dealing with such communications.

American cabs are, of course, yet another example of the American's lack of interest in privacy. Whereas in other countries it is recognized that the passenger takes a cab as a means of getting from one place to another and that even under such circumstances he has a right to his privacy, as the driver has a right to his, this is anything but the case in America. The English taxi is equipped with a sliding partition which separates driver from passenger. Communication with the driver can be had simply by moving the partition. I hope we can start a movement to respect the cabdriver's privacy. He works hard at a frustrating job, and he needs as much protection from meddlesome passengers as he can secure. He should feel free to open and close his own windows, to smoke, sing, and drive his cab, without any unnecessary interference. He should be saved from the garrulous passenger, as he should be saved from the noxious fumes of his passengers' cigarettes and cigars. He should be free to listen to his radio as he drives, without comment or objection from a mere transient passenger who might seek to force his own taste on the driver. The sliding glass partition would take care of all this.

What a boon it would be to everyone if the English type of taxi were introduced into America! It might not solve many traffic problems, but it would certainly constitute a signal contribution to the amenities of civilized existence.

An especially loathsome intrusion on one's privacy is the telephone pirate who breaks into one's home with his mindless and inhuman speech. If every man's home is his castle, and the law protects the citizen against anyone who proposes to break into it, why cannot the law protect one against such telephonic housebreakers? They steal one's time and break into the quiet of one's home, which one has a right to believe is at least the one sanctuary which will not be despoiled by the hucksters of the outside world. TV and radio will provide more than enough of that kind of noise.

The advertising matter one receives through the mail may

be a minor invasion of one's privacy, but it is certainly a major waste of everyone's time except, of course, the advertisers and their clients. I have often wondered how many forests must be destroyed each year in order to keep this fallout of paper going. It must be a very large number. For my part I prefer the trees to the paper into which they have been transformed. I automatically throw all advertising mail into the wastepaper basket and burn it in the fireplace unopened. The two exceptions are the booksellers' and the publishers' catalogs. These I welcome. And, of course, there is the Sears Roebuck catalog, and I daresay others have their own particular indispensables; but most of us surely could do without the greater part of the advertising mail that descends on us. But until the government intervenes, I know that all of us will continue to be victims of the advertisers, for as a slogan in a mailing list catalog has it:

> We've got you on a list,
> We've got you on a list,
> And you NEVER WILL BE MISSED!

But do not be intimidated. All you need do is simply write on the container "Return to Sender," and even the post office may be persuaded it was time something was done about this junk mail.

Justice William O. Douglas has said, "The right to be let alone is indeed the beginning of all freedom." Americans, alas, have lost almost the whole of that kind of freedom. Anyone who chooses can break into your home by telephone, pry into every nook and cranny of your private life by employing private prying eyes. The government in this matter indeed sets the example, for the Federal Bureau of Investigation has millions of records on the lives and activities of citizens on file in Washington. The files of the Un-

American Committee, misnamed the Congressional Committee on Un-American Activities, are open to all right-wing individuals and organizations, for these are the only ones likely to be interested in them. Then there are the manpower lists, the biographical reference works, specialty lists, telephone books, black books, red books, yellow books, who-knows-what books, the scandal-mongering yellow press, private eyes, public eyes, F.B.I.'s, wiretapping, bugging devices, Dun & Bradstreet ratings, TV and radio brainwashing, "the hidden persuaders," subliminal conditioning, and so on.

So little do Americans think of privacy that they are strongly disinclined to protest its invasions. Noise, doorbell ringers, invaders by telephone, mailbox, and TV, far from being discouraged, are, if anything, cordially invited in. Were this not so, they would long ago have gone out of business. Instead, they flourish.

It seems, then, that most Americans are so accustomed to the abuse of their privacy that not only do they take it for granted, but they also fail to notice that it is even being abused. This is dangerous, dangerous because it reflects the decreasing sensitivity of the individual to his rights as a person and therefore an accompanying desensitization to the rights of others—and that way great abuses lie. How good is the man with others who cannot be alone with himself?

Government: a few modest proposals

THE AMERICAN FORM of government may not be the best that has ever been devised, but if it is not, it is certainly one of the best of all compromises that has ever been developed for the government of men.

A great scaffolding for a noble edifice was erected by the Founding Fathers of this country, a scaffolding which many enemies of the grand design they planned have ever since been busily engaged trying to tear down. If they have not altogether succeeded in their efforts, it is because there have been many Americans who have wholeheartedly identified themselves with Abraham Lincoln in the work of nobly saving rather than meanly losing this last, best hope of earth. Another reason is that the Constitution and the Congress have a way of eventually nullifying even the temporary successes of the wreckers. If the mechanics of government do not always work perfectly, it is, perhaps, because nothing human ever does. It has struck me, as it has undoubtedly struck many other Americans, that there are some ways in which the mechanics of government in America could be improved. Over the years I have made a list of them as they occurred to me, and here they are.

1. *Elections held every four years.* This means that neither the people nor the Congress can effectively express its dissatisfaction with the party in power and, whenever this seems desirable, call for a vote of confidence and a new election.

2. *The weight of decision on the President is too great.* As Harry S. Truman once remarked, "No one can really fill the Presidency. It is an executive job that is almost fantastic. No absolute monarch has ever had such decisions to make or the responsibilities that the President of the United States has." "This splendid misery," as Thomas Jefferson called it, is and for a long time has been the toughest job in the world. The Founding Fathers, in Article II of the Constitution, resolved that "The executive power shall be vested in a President of the United States." It is a power which can be regulated by the legislative and judicial branches of the government, but it ever-increasingly continues to constitute a crushing burden on its incumbent. The major departments, bureaus, sections, services, branches, offices, divisions, administrations, agencies, areas, boards, commands, commissions, corporations, groups, headquarters, authorities, and miscellaneous units of government over which the President is expected to watch and control run into the many hundreds, as do the documents he has to sign each week, not to mention the innumerable decisions he is called on to make which truly decide the fates of millions of human beings everywhere in the world. I do not think the power of the Presidency should in any way be curbed. I believe this would be both unnecessary and dangerous. The Twenty-second Amendment was a bad thing, limiting the Presidency to two terms. That amendment was aimed by a jealous party directly at the heart of a President who threatened to be elected by the will of the people every time he chose to stand. There is and was nothing wrong with that. What is wrong is that we attempt to kill our Presidents

while they are in office by the impossible burdens we demand that they bear. How precisely these may be reduced I don't know. I am not an authority on the subject. But there must be plenty of authorities who do know, and it would be good to hear from them.

3. *The immense difficulty of interpreting or changing the Constitution.* "The American Constitution," wrote Lord Bryce, "has been changed, is being changed, and will continue to be changed by interpretation and usage. It is not what it was even thirty years ago; who can tell what it will be thirty years hence?" This is perfectly true; nevertheless, it often takes decades before the Supreme Court hands down an interpretation of a particular article or amendment and before that interpretation assumes the force of law. Changes in the Constitution are notoriously more difficult to achieve than interpretations of it. Is this as it should be?

4. *Seniority basis of committee chairmanships.* This unfortunate practice often amounts to the disqualification of the qualified and to rule by senility, not to mention the obstruction of much-needed legislation of which the chairman happens to disapprove. To see such great power placed in the keeping of incompetent and senile hands greatly undermines the confidence of the people in its government. The ignoble and antidemocratic activities of committee chairmen who have often held their position for decades for no better reason than they have managed to get themselves continuously reelected in their constituencies are matters of unhappy history. The pestilential elder Lodge, the windy Senator Borah, the incredibly hopeless Pat McCarran, the unspeakable Joe McCarthy, to name but a small sample, all were chairmen of strategically, highly important committees. As a consequence of their chairmanships, they were able to do such mischief, so harmful to so many, that it may never be possible to repair

the damage they have done. The seniority rule should be abolished, and competence for the job, granting so much formal power, made the only criterion of *election* to committee chairmanships. Nothing in government should be automatic.

5. *Congress takes too long to get through its business.* The delays are endless. What Congress needs is a thoroughgoing restudy by a group of experts with a view to recommendations leading to the improvements in the efficiency of the conduct of the business of Congress which are so long overdue.

6. *Residence qualifications for Congressmen.* This is idiotic. The locality rule has the effect of debarring from election to Congress highly qualified people who almost by definition would do a far better job of representing their country than the resident candidates. The residence requirement ensures the election of a politician of the dominant party from a district in which he has secured the nomination against a limited field of competitors. The Congressman should be representing his country first, his state second, and his district last. Surely, it should make not the least difference where a representative of the people has lived or lives for him to be able to do all three jobs well. If Churchill had been dependent on a residency rule for election to Parliament, there would have been no Churchill. The residence rule denies the right of election of its representatives to the people and restricts it to a small number of ward heelers in a district. It is the sheerest folly and cries out loudly for correction.

7. *Patronage system of public appointments.* All nonelective public offices should be filled by people whose qualifications for the job have been tested by public civil service examination. Every nonelective public office should be in the civil service and *achieved* by examination by a civil service

examining body, having no connection with political parties whatever. Patronage is evil, wasteful, enormously costly, and inefficient, and it ensures the worst possible service to the people.

Imagine the consequences of appointing a man to be a surgeon by patronage! Yet this is the manner in which large numbers of operators upon the body politic are appointed by our legislators.

8. *Lobbying of vested interests.* There are hundreds of lobbies in Washington, the majority of which are opposed to the best interests of the people and its institutions. These lobbies are often enormously powerful and constitute an unelected second government of the United States. Their interest is usually entirely selfish. All lobbies, without exception, should be completely outlawed. It should be made a heavily punishable offense to attempt to influence any government official for the benefit of any individual, organization, or whatnot by offering any kind of gift, reward, blandishment, or whatever else it may be.

9. *Uncertainty whether Congress or the Supreme Court has the final word.* Surely the last word should be with the Supreme Court.

10. *Clumsy electoral procedures.* Who needs Republican and Democratic party conventions? The hotels and the convention hall owners? If the political parties want an occasional shindig, are there not better ways of having one? Who needs an Electoral College? This should go into the museum of political curiosities. Would it not be highly desirable to restudy all our electoral procedures, at every level, retaining what is desirable and changing what is not?

11. *Election of representatives every two years.* This hardly gives a man time to get into his job and causes him to spend much of his time away from Washington, attempting

to keep his memory green among his constituents. Four years is better than two.

12. *Unequal representation of rural or urban population.* At long last the Supreme Court has ruled on this, and proportionate representation will become the rule.

13. *Electoral apathy at the polls.* This can only be corrected by better education of Americans to their responsibilities as citizens. This should be done in the schools.

14. *Multiplicity of committee action in foreign affairs.* A great many committees go into action on matters affecting our foreign affairs which had far better be left to the experts than to the politicians.

15. *Interval between election of the new President and his taking office.* During the months which at present elapse, the outgoing administration can do a great deal of damage and put many spokes in the wheel of the next President's chariot. The newly elected President should take office immediately—ceremonies can be held later—and from the hour that the new President has been elected by the people, the old should cease to have any Presidential powers whatever.

17. *The filibuster.* This disgraceful and utterly immoral device should be completely abrogated.

The practice of medicine in the United States

ALMOST EVERYONE is aware that all is not well with the practice of medicine in the United States. From the practitioner of the noblest of arts, the image of the doctor has changed and tarnished to a money-hungry businessman to whom the practice of medicine has become a bonanza profession. Indeed, it is not alone the doctor whose image has become tarnished, but virtually every aspect of medicine; nurses, hospitals, the American Medical Association, the cost of drugs, the unwillingness of doctors to make house calls, the cost of medicine, and the overspecialization.

Before proceeding further, I should perhaps make it clear that I spent twenty years of my life teaching medical and dental students human anatomy in medical schools. I speak, therefore, not alone from a knowledge of the patient's point of view, but also from a knowledge of the preclinical and clinical training of the doctor and of what goes on in hospitals and in private practices. I have spent much time with doctors of every specialty, and I have to add that I yield to no one in my admiration and respect for the superlative technical competence of the American medical man. And I speak with gratitude and affection, for many reasons—above all, because neither I nor many members of my family would today be alive had it not been for the skill of certain doctors. It is also true that several members of my extended family have been more or less badly maimed for life as a result of the incompetence of some doctors and that I have been almost killed by the ineptness of a doctor and, on another occasion, almost sent on my way by the unknowingness of a hospital staff. I remember the magnificent doctors. I know what a good doctor can be. I know how he can be made. And I also know how he can be unmade. And I know how a promising medical student can be turned into an unpromising doctor.

Everyone takes the practice of medicine for granted, and scarcely anyone asks what the practice of medicine is for. The main purpose of the practice of medicine surely should be the maintenance of health, the health of the members of the community. Surely the most precious possession of the individual and of the community is good health. The principal interest, the exclusive interest one sometimes feels, of the medical profession is not in health, but in disease. The periodic checkup, a much to be encouraged development of recent years—however, too often perfunctorily performed— constitutes an advance in the right direction, with the emphasis on preventive medical care and the maintenance of health rather than on giving the patient some attention only when he is ill. Prevention *is* better than cure, for everyone concerned, but even though this is so, the medical profession has not done anything like the necessary job in the furtherance of the idea of preventive medicine. An adequately developed and applied program of preventive medicine would reduce immeasurably the incidence of disease and disorder and would make so great a contribution to individual and social welfare that the whole quality of life would be changed.

The principal complaint against the medical profession is the high costs of its services. The high costs of hospital services are understandable, but the high charges of medical men are not (any more, for that matter, than the high costs of lawyers' services). The charges of doctors are simply not related to the distribution of incomes. The general principle which doctors seem to follow is to charge as much as the traffic will bear. It is only because patients have on occasion refused to pay the charges and the matter has gone to court that we know what elevations these charges can sometimes reach. Some years ago a surgeon sued a patient, upon whom he had performed an appendectomy, for the payment of his bill for some $2,000. The patient declined to pay this amount on the ground that it was excessive. The surgeon claimed that his fees were scaled, that he treated some patients who were poor without charge, and that those who could afford it should bear the cost of his services to those who were unable to pay for them. The court took a dim view of this doctrine, and the surgeon had to be content with a reasonable fee for his services. But the practice of "as much as the traffic will bear" goes on. But the traffic will not and cannot bear as much as some doctors think, and the day of reckoning is therefore rapidly approaching.

It is rather belatedly coming to be realized in America that as its most precious possession, the health of the individual must be a principal concern of the community, for it is the health of the community itself that is involved. The health of the community is far too important a matter to leave to a private monopoly devoted to what might not be altogether unjustly interpreted as its own self-interest. Nor is the focus on disease rather than on health a desirable approach to the welfare of either the individual or of the community. The simple and unfortunate fact is that most medical men are not concerned with human beings, but merely with their illnesses and the remuneration their treatment can provide. This appears to be only too evident to most patients, and they dislike the transaction. What, indeed, they most dislike is the businesslike detachment of the doctor. This is the most frequently heard complaint. In the doctor-patient relation, the patient is hoping for someone who is sympathetic and understanding, as well as competent.

It is the pooled experience of doctors that more than 80 percent of the patients who visit them really have nothing more seriously wrong than the need to talk to someone who will listen sympathetically. Most doctors assert that there isn't the time and that they cannot get emotionally involved in every patient they see. Such involvement, they claim, would interfere with their ability to do the job that must be done. This is, of course, no answer at all. It is a rationalization. No one expects the doctor to become so emotionally involved with the patient that he cannot get his work done. What the patient does have a right to expect from any human being is that he shall be treated as a human being, not as a bundle of symptoms or a name or a number or a bill or a chart or a bulge on a billfold, being surveyed by a computer having the semblance of a human being. What needs to be done is to take the money out of medicine and put the humanity back into it.

The doctor needs to learn that the care of the patient begins with caring for the patient, that this is an essential part of the treatment, and that the practice of medicine should never be treated as a business, because human beings are human beings and not businesses. The attitude of the doctor should closely resemble that of the minister to his parishioners. In an age of psychosomatic medicine there ought to be little difficulty in understanding that the care of the psyche and the care of the soma go together and cannot be dissociated.

As a member of his society, the doctor is as subject to its pressures as much as other people. The cult of success is no less a part of his religion than that of other people—perhaps more. But this is not what serves to dehumanize the doctor. What serves to dehumanize him is the training he receives in medical school and hospital. There are many grounds upon which the organization of medical school teaching can be criticized. I shall restrict myself here to those aspects of medical school training which make the doctor the poor example he too often is of the art of human relations.

It requires to be pointed out that the average doctor's general education ceases when he leaves high school or its equivalent. He enters a college or university and takes the premedical course. This concentrates on biology, mathematics and physics, and chemistry. He then enters medical school, prepared to pursue the special subjects that will turn him into a technically competent practitioner of medicine. When the average student enters medical school, he is frequently characterized by some originality of mind and usually an earnest interest in human beings. At the admissions interviews of prospective students, one of the most frequent answers to the question, "What led you to choose medicine as a profession?" is, "I read the story of a great doctor, *Arrowsmith,* by Sinclair Lewis, and that made me want to be a doctor."

The noble doctor, Martin Arrowsmith, is the model on which they want to form themselves. I have known a fair number of such students, and I have seen what happened to most of them as they progressed through their courses and examinations in medical school. As a result of this training in normative standards, in techniques and skills, in syndromes and symptoms without sympathy, in the focus on cases rather than on human beings, the student tends to lose any originality and creativity with which he may have entered medical school and to have most of his interest in human beings completely flattened by the steamrollering requirements of his teachers to depend on the rote-remembered facts which must be regurgitated at examinations if the M.D. degree is ever to be acquired. Once the degree is obtained, the worst is yet to come—the year of internship which must be completed in a hospital before the license to practice may be granted. As an intern, the young doctor is finally deprived of any remnants of humanity that may have remained. This, of course, does not occur in every case, but the pressures are very strong. In the first place, the intern is treated as a slave. He is scandalously underpaid, a mere pittance in fact, and exploited, all in the name of continued training for which *he* should really be paying—according to his exploiters. The intern's average rate of pay is four cents an hour! It is not an accident that as a consequence of the intern experience, the young doctor should develop an exploitative attitude toward his patients. As an intern, he receives the final indoctrination in how to relate to human beings in the impersonal, antiseptic, dehumanized, marketing manner so characteristic of too many of our hospitals.

The many years spent in preparing for the practice of medicine puts the doctor into the labor market at a rather advanced age. In this manner he comes to feel that he must make up for lost time, and so he drives himself into an early grave—the age at death of the average doctor being fifty-nine years. The average for men in general is sixty-nine years. The loss is great to everyone, and everyone would be better off if doctors were more human and did not have to drive themselves as they do but had the time to lead a more balanced life, instead of one wholly devoted to their profession.

The average medical man is ill educated and politically conservative and is a member of a profession which is the most reactionary in the land, headed by a trade union, the American Medical Association, which is among the most hidebound in the land. The association has fought every measure designed to bring government aid to the health of the people, has taxed its members in order to do so, and has employed advertising agencies, at a cost of millions, not to mention other dubious procedures, to defeat such measures. It has been and continues to be a sorry spectacle, and it constitutes one of the major reasons for the tarnished image the doctor has developed in the public eye. Like most people, the medical profession in the United States declines to learn from history.

The truth is that the medical profession everywhere in the world has fought the attempt by government to protect the health of the people. The most recent case in point is England. In spite of the opposition of the medical profession and the Conservative party, Socialized medicine was established in England in 1946. Although it has effectively reduced the income of the average doctor and caused some doctors to emigrate to other lands, the medical profession is today quite reconciled to the benefits of Socialized medicine, and indeed, its staunchest defenders are the doctors. Socialized medicine is in England to stay. No government would dream of abolishing it, and were this remote possibility ever to be contemplated, there would be a rebellion on the part of the people. In spite of the fact that there are still too few hospitals, that many of those that do exist are antiquated and unsuited to the requirements of the contemporary period, that there are long waiting lists for surgical treatment, everyone agrees that the system works extremely well and constitutes a great advance on the medical facilities that were available in former days.

Throughout Europe and most recently in Saskatchewan, Canada, every medical care bill proposed by a government has been fought tooth and nail by the medical profession. In Saskatchewan and in Belgium the doctors even went on strike. Yet the story has everywhere been the same: once the government reform has been introduced, the doctors have finally become its most perfervid supporters. It will be the same story with Medicare, which the American Medical Association fought so relentlessly, and it will be the same with public, national, or Socialized medicine, or whatever name it is called by. Socialized medicine has had the dreadful bogey of Socialism attached to it, and as everyone knows, "Socialism is the back door to Communism." This kind of stupidity would hardly be worth noticing were it not for the fact that those who believe in stupidities are capable of great inhumanity. The Scandinavian countries have for many years had Socialized medicine, as well as many other Socialized services, yet these welfare states are as far from being Communistic as one could imagine. Indeed, they are a great deal more democratic, as is England, than is the United States, in which the word "democracy" is perhaps the most frequently heard of any word in the vocabulary. In the United States we have a Socialized post office, a Socialized Public Health Service, Socialized National Institutes of Health, Socialized armed forces, and a good many other Socialized agencies, and although Mr. Barry Goldwater and Mr. Richard Nixon, John Birchers, Ku Klux Klanners, and their like pretend to find in such agencies the open door to Communism, and there are apparently millions of Americans who do likewise, such views are belied by the facts. There are some who hold that such agencies should be in private hands, that they would do a better job. But that is just the point: we know from experience that they would not and do not. And that is the principal reason why medicine will become Socialized—because it will do a better job than is at present being done by medicine as a private monopoly.

Courtesy

COURTESY IS NOT A QUALITY Europeans associate with Americans. Americans of lower-class or recent lower-class origin—no matter what class they have risen into—are not so much discourteous as noncourteous, for they are altogether wanting in courtesy. It is a dimension of existence of which they seem to be utterly ignorant. If it is maintained that the situation is not very different in other lands, the answer is that it is simply not true. For sheer barbarity of manners it would be difficult to beat the average lower-class American male *or* female. Comparisons are odious, and I shall desist from making them—or as one of my three-year-old friends says, "No, please."

It is Americans of lower-class origin, the common men, who have given America as a whole a bad name abroad. It was Abraham Lincoln who remarked that God must have loved the common man since he made so many of him. A corollary of that would then be that God must have much misliked the uncommon man since he made so few of him. But they do exist. Alas, abroad the civilized, well-bred, cultivated, and uncommon American goes unremarked. Yet for perfect manners, for genuine courtesy, I know of no country that can offer more perfect examples than are to be found in many Americans.

Is there anywhere in the civilized world a more perfectly mannered human being than a cultivated New Englander? Such poise, charm, and what I can only call a balanced relatedness to others, such thoughtfulness and grace, as I have observed in certain New Englanders, I have rarely observed elsewhere in the world. The so-called good manners of the "Southern gentleman" are too ostentatiously obtrusive and too self-conscious—though pleasant enough in themselves—to make even an approach to the quality of the New Englander's gentility. Indeed, I do believe that perhaps the most civilized, most humane beings in the world are found within a short radius of Boston—I do not refer to the corrupt Irish Catholics who have done their utmost to ruin the state of Massachusetts. I suppose the ancestors of the New Englanders I have in mind were largely English. Transported to the New World, the Puritan ethos and the fierce devotion to the principles of liberty and justice that they brought with them, under the challenge of the new environmental pressures, combined to form this remarkable New England character. In passing, it is of interest to note that by far the best English, not only in the United States but in the whole English-speaking world, is spoken by New Englanders. It is, of course, not surprising that the first blow against the tyranny of Old England was struck by the colonists of New England, for it was New Englanders who from the earliest times were the most active and zealous defenders of liberty and who have continued to be so down to the present time.

It is the devotion to the cause of humanity which, doubtless, contributes to the quality of the New Englander's courtesy, for its outstanding characteristic is the deep and devoted interest in the welfare of the other, a sensitivity to the qualities of others, and a respect for the other's uniquenesses and privacies. It is this kind of courtesy which, alas, so many Americans lack altogether.

Manners

I STILL RECALL the astonishment of a New York patrolman who, when I asked him whether he could *please* tell me where a certain street was. It was clear that it had been so long since he had heard the word "please" and so long ago that anyone had used the word in asking him for directions that it threw him off base. Shortly afterward I had a similar experience with the man in the change booth in the subway. Forty years later, on entering a taxi in New York and asking the driver to *please* take me to my destination, he was so overcome by the "please" that he delivered himself of an address on the subject so charged with emotion that he had obviously been suffering for years from the privation of this simple courtesy. He was hungry for a gentle word, and when at last he heard it, he was overcome. He was a tough man, but not yet so hardened to the ways of New Yorkers that he had lost all capacity for responding to the right word. But, alas, he practically never heard it, and he suffered, as everyone does, from the lack of ordinary good manners.

New Yorkers are notorious for their bad manners. Perhaps the reputation is deserved. I don't find American manners much better elsewhere in America.

It is something of a paradox that Americans who are so

energetic should be so lazy about their manners. Americans are the most generous, and certainly among the most hospitable, people in the world, and withal among the most lacking in that politeness and courtesy which constitute the signature of the civilized.

In a land in which the tough guy is admired, politeness is widely considered to be effeminate. And in this male-dominated world the male still believes that women, females, are his inferiors. Hence, any suggestion that males could do with more of the gentleness with which women are generally endowed is greeted with active hostility and rejection.

The tough guy is widely admired not only by men in America, but also by females. Mothers frequently encourage their sons to become the kind of "man" they think they ought to be and there is a widespread fear that a well-behaved boy is either turning into a "queer" or, if he is not rescued from his goody-goodiness, that he may become one. A boy has "got to be a football hero to make a hit with the beautiful girls"; we have it on the authority of a popular song of several decades ago. And mothers, as well as fathers, see to it that their sons are men, and no mistake about it! If their manners are a little rough, well, so much the better. It proves that they are men. And in this way rough, bad manners come to be not only tolerated, but even encouraged in the American male.

Beating the rap, American style

As EVERYONE, especially the criminal, now knows, the law is on the side of the criminal. Virtually any criminal, no matter what crimes he has committed, with a "good" lawyer to represent him, may escape the penalties prescribed by law on the basis of some technicality or other. Murderers, gangsters, the Mafia, rapists, mobsters, and the whole company of criminals are so little concerned with the legal consequences of their conduct that they scarcely give them a thought, secure in the knowledge that, with the aid of the law, in one way or another, they can "beat the rap." The result is an enormous increase in virtually every kind of crime, disrespect and contempt for the law, the complete demoralization of the law-enforcing agencies, and the dismay of the citizen. The letter has completely replaced the spirit of the law.

If law and order are to be preserved in any society, then respect for law and order must be maintained. But the law, the judges, and the lawyers themselves make the law ridiculous and bring it into contempt, in the very name of the law and order they are employed to maintain.

Murderers, mobsters, rapists, and every other kind of criminal can secure bail and freedom to pursue their criminal activities often indefinitely—by the delaying tactics of

their lawyers—and can then on some technicality be completely freed to continue to prey on their innocent victims.
Again and again one reads reports of criminals with innumerable arrests who were freed on some technicality and who
have for years pursued their criminal activities in the secure
knowledge that however often they might get caught, there
was always a lawyer and an obliging judge somewhere who
could get them off in a matter of hours.

I have discussed this matter with many lawyers, and the
stock argument with which I have been met is that it is better
that a hundred guilty men should go free than that one
innocent man should be found guilty. This seems to me a
wholly irrelevant argument, and in any event it is not a
matter of a hundred men but nearer a hundred thousand. I
do not believe that punishment is the proper way in which to
handle criminals. The bankruptcy of that approach should
by this time be clear to everyone, but until the time when we
have reached the level of social development which will
enable us to deal with criminals more humanely as sick and
wronged individuals in need of treatment as such, the law
ought to do what it was designed to do: making it impres-
sively clear that just as privileges entail obligations, so the
commission of crimes will entail penalties and that these will
be strictly enforced.

The law no longer has any relation to justice—discipline
transmitted through the alembic of love—but has become a
technical formalistic device for administering the judgments
of the court. These judgments are mostly based on the
language of the applicable laws. Interpretation of that language may vary, the judge may have made prejudicial comments, or he may not have said what he ought to have said, and
on a hundred and one other grounds, a case may be dismissed
on some such technicalities and the purposes of justice en-

tirely defeated—for it is not justice that is involved, but a technical point of law.

It is, indeed, naïve to think that lawyers are in the least interested in justice. Nor are judges concerned with justice: what they are concerned with is the interpretation of the law—quite another thing. As for the practicing lawyer, his point and purpose are to represent his client as well as he is able and to serve the interest of his client. The lawyer for the opposite side does *his* best to represent his client. As Carlyle put it, a lawyer is like a loaded blunderbuss: if you hire him, he will blow your opponent's brains out. If your opponent hires him, he will blow your brains out. The lawyer represents his client, and what "represent" in practice, in fact, means is that each side is bent on blowing out the brains of the other—on winning the case for his own client. This, it seems to me, is powerfully wrong. I don't think that any lawyer should work to win against the other side, but rather to see that justice is done. This, no doubt, is a great over-simplification of a difficult problem, but no doubt it is not. It seems to me that the law has become diseased with technicalities, hypertrophied with growths of extraneous matter, that defeat the very purposes for which the rule of law was created.

In the interests of justice the law is now the chief instrument for the defeat of the ends of justice. Morality, law, order, and freedom are increasingly threatened by the diseases to which the law has succumbed, and the increase in every kind of crime rate indicates that unless the courts have wise men appointed to the bench who, recognizing human frailty, are nevertheless firm in the enforcement of the law and genuinely understand the meaning of the relationship between law, society, and justice, we shall continue to observe the growing paradox of the law's continuing to serve the purposes of the lawbreakers.

American speech

AMERICANS ARE BRILLIANTLY inventive of colorful, original, and amusing ways of saying things—so much so that virtually the entire English-speaking world has adopted most of them. And yet the average American is a very slovenly speaker of his native tongue. Some of the ugliest forms of English to be found anywhere in the world are spoken in America. I don't know which is ugliest, Bronx or Brooklynese, certain Texan or some other Southern accents or Philadelphianese or some Middle Western awfulnesses. Bronx and Brooklynese speakers, in spite of the ghastliness of their speech, have been among the most creative contributors to the language. Most of these contributions to the language have the stamp of their Jewish origin on them: "Drop dead," "Be my guest," "Kibbitzer," "Schmalz," "Schlemiehl," "Nudnick," and numerous others.

The English spoken in the South has been largely influenced by the Negro. Southern Negro speech is pleasanter to the ear than Southern white speech. Southern Negro speech ripples with cheer. Southern white speech drawls with ennui, frustration, and repressed hostility. The tensions of life in the South make most Southern women nonstop chatterers.

Why Middle Westerners are so much addicted to talking through their noses, and why women frequently possess such

[151

high cracked voices, and why *o* is turned into *u,* as in "bux"
for "box," I don't know, but they grate on the ear most
unpleasantly. East New Yorkese is very ugly, but "erl" for
"oil," while constituting a fascinating linguistic phenomenon, isn't half as offensive, to my ear at least, as "bux" for
"box."

The best and purest English spoken anywhere in the world
is to be heard in cultivated Boston and Cambridge families
and in neighboring localities. The speech of the lower classes
in this region is, however, contaminated by the Irish influence, the flat *a* making an English speaker from this area
immediately recognizable.

The worst English is certainly not spoken in America, but
in England, the homeland of the tongue itself. For bloody
awfulness nothing can quite equal Cockney. And certainly,
from this judgment, "Orstryliyun" (*pace* Australian) should
not be exempted. Cockney is a genuine dialect, spoken exclusively by the lower classes of London south of the Thames,
and here, too, it is of interest to note that Cockneys have been
among the most colorful contributors to the language.

In vocabulary, grammar, and pronunciation, Americans on
the whole do at least as well as other English-speaking peoples. Where they fall short is in the carelessness, the sloppi-
ness, the slovenliness, and unconcern with the manner of
their speech. Far from making an effort to speak well, most
Americans appear to be wholly unconcerned with the manner of their speech. They slur their words, telescope them,
mispronounce them, misstress them, and if cigarettes are as
damaging *like* cigarettes are, it is perfectly "orright" with
them.

This slovenliness of speech is no more than a bad habit
within the power of every individual to correct for himself, if
only he were convinced of the advantages of good speech—the

pleasure, the sheer esthetic quality of good speech, the delight in the efficiency of communicating with elegance, clarity, and precision, and, finally, the sheer pleasure taken in the use of words, the delight in doing well something one does so often.

Here, again, the schools can do a great deal toward changing things in the desired direction. Careless, slovenly speech, like a careless, slovenly performance of any kind, should be strongly discouraged, and creative, esthetically pleasing speech strongly encouraged. In short, it is time that more of us were made aware of the fact that speech is a skill whose function serves to put man in touch with his fellowman and that as such, it is a skill that one must work at, at least as hard as one works at accomplishing any other skill.

American architecture

AMERICANS, IT HAS BEEN SAID, suffer from an edifice complex. The style of architecture in office and other buildings has been described as hemorrhoidal—that is, one huge pile. Neither criticism seems to me altogether just. Nineteenth-century domestic and public architecture was quite appalling. On the whole, there has been a great improvement in all forms of architecture, even though frightful architectural atrocities are still being committed in great numbers all over the country. It is a free country, and the freedom is freely abused; but it is also often constructively and sometimes even beautifully utilized. The new office buildings on Park and Third avenues in New York, for example, are on the whole really quite beautiful both outside and inside. How efficient or comfortable these glass houses are to work in I do not know.

The architecture of some of our recently built airports is magnificent. The Eero Saarinen T.W.A. Building at Kennedy Airport in New York is an outstanding example of such airport architecture. The history of airport architecture reminds one of the fact that foresight is the last of the gifts granted by the gods to man, for none of the airlines was able to foresee the tremendous growth in air travel and hence built one inadequate airport after another—and they are still doing it. Even now, some of the most recently built airports are proving unequal to the task of handling the volume of traffic with which they are daily confronted. The idea of each airline's having its own building and facilities is a good one where the traffic is as great as it is at New York, Chicago, Los Angeles, and San Francisco. But the idea is not altogether a success because of the long distances one has to walk in the buildings to and from the gates. Airports, I believe, are still in their primitive stages of development. In the course of time, I suspect, most large airlines will be forced to have their own airports in different outlying localities on the periphery of the town they serve.

Domestic architecture has not, I believe, kept apace of industrial architecture. Bathrooms have been greatly improved, and the old-fashioned homey kitchen has been replaced by something that looks like a highly antiseptic hospital laboratory. Laborsaving devices in the overapplianced house, which includes the washing machine, the electric dishwasher, the disposal, the walled-in chest-high oven and grill, etc., have set the pattern for the whole house, which must be spick-and-span and absolutely gleaming. Although the design of the interior of the house is usually quite unimaginative, the exterior exhibits even less of that estimable quality. At best it is more often than not dull and uninteresting.

The decline in the style and quality of domestic architecture is not peculiar to America. It is perhaps seen at its worst in England, where the decline set in immediately after World War I, when an enormous burst of building of "houses fit for heroes to live in," for the heroes who had escaped the slaughter of the western and other fronts, produced the largest number of jerry-built houses ever foisted on an innocent people. Semidetached, with a bay window apparently made of sticks, with a thin veneer of stucco for walls, they were built in endless rows, looking like so many reduplicated sets of identical twins produced on the assembly line of a manufacturer of toys. They all looked as if they had been stuck together with spit and sticks and paper, and it was generally predicted that they would fall apart in a short time. The astonishing thing is that they didn't and, most regrettably, haven't. They still stand like some accusing digit, offering mute testimony to the degeneration of taste, the breakdown in values, and the cupidity of man.

The same human cupidity seems to have been responsible everywhere for the decline in taste in domestic architecture. The developer and his developments are essentially the products of mass production, and it is easier and cheaper for the developer to achieve his kingdoms of earthly bliss through a single blueprint and the use of quantities of the same materials for all his houses than it is for him to see each one through the eye of a needle as a single unit, unique and individual in its own right. And this is precisely where the trouble lies. In earlier times each man built his own house, and whether good or bad, it was of his own design and making. Whether the house was built with one's own hands or by the hands of others skilled in such crafts, it was built as a living organism in adaptation to the needs and tastes of those who were going to live in it. The house was built by human beings for human beings, and every part of it was overseen and selected and approved by those who were to live in it. Today this sort of thing is a luxury possible for only a limited few. Most people are forced to live in houses that have been blueprinted for them by others. The individual no longer designs the house in which he shall live; it has been produced according to a master plan on a blueprint. Just as no great work of art has ever been produced by a group of experts, so in a creative work as personal as a house no developer has ever produced a beautiful house. It is individuals, with their own unique tastes, who do so.

It would seem to me that the limits of the beautiful attainable in domestic architecture were achieved in the Georgian period, about two centuries ago. Practically nothing built since has been as beautiful. The picture window is the most original and bathetic contribution to housebuilding since the Georgian era, and that should be commentary enough.

America's "great" architect Frank Lloyd Wright was in my opinion no architect at all, but a showman. His houses were hopelessly unlivable, dark, dreary, dull, and disappointing. His penchant for overhanging eaves was an atavistic throwback to the rock ledge of our prehistoric ancestors, shutting out the light and boxing in the gloom and dreariness of his interiors. Frank Lloyd Wright's arrogance was exceeded only by his bad manners in pretending to be an architect.

Most college architecture perpetuated during the last two decades is a disgrace. This is especially true of state colleges, where the blueprints are prepared in a central office, usually the comptroller's, and where buildings are then foisted on the institution without the slightest regard to their suitability. Esthetically they are an offense, a rape of the environment, and utterly defeat the purposes which college buildings should serve. But of this, more later.

As one travels about the country, the ugliness that has been forced on it is everywhere apparent—and appalling. The appallingness is especially striking in the newest towns. In a lovely natural valley, surrounded by mountains, a Tucson is perpetrated. The dreariest and most depressing buildings are erected without the least evidences of a modicum of taste

anywhere. The longest road leading into the heart of Albu-
querque is lined on each side with one building after another
vying with one another in ugliness and, at night, in garish-
ness. This is the worst kind of violation of the natural
beauties of the land imaginable, and it is not very different
anywhere else one chooses to alight in America. The exceptions happen to be the towns that are the oldest and have
been, as in some parts of New England, left relatively undisturbed.

Clearly, there is a strong case here for federal intervention,
before the whole of America the Beautiful is transmogrified
into the ugliest land on this once green earth.

No one should be permitted to erect any structure anywhere unless it has first been approved by a committee on
esthetics. No element of politics should ever be allowed to
enter into the choice or the activities of such a committee,
which should be made up of men and women who by
profession and achievement have demonstrated their ability
to distinguish what is beautiful from what is not. It must
come to this, and the sooner, the better, before America, one
of the most naturally beautiful lands in the world, is turned
into one of the ugliest lands in the world.

College Architecture

The banality and mediocrity of the buildings that have
been perpetrated on American college campuses in recent
years constitute a most saddening experience. Often it is
impossible to distinguish such buildings from the warehouses
which are not infrequently adjacent to them or from factories. Indeed, one receives the impression that it is not the
builders alone who conceive of a college building as a factory
for the production of college graduates. More often than not

it transpires, when I bring up the subject of the environment as part of the process of education, that it is a matter to which no one has ever given any thought. What those responsible for the erection of such atrocities evidently have never understood is the meaning of education. Had they even glimpsed the meaning and significance of education, they could not have brought themselves to commit such desecrations of the college campuses of America. What very few seem to understand is that the environment in which the educative process proceeds constitutes a highly influential part of that process.

A college campus defaced by excrescences which are indistinguishable from factories and office buildings and which are often even uglier inside than they are outside is likely to produce or reinforce one of the most damaging psychoses that one can ever visit upon a student—a coarsening of his sensibilities and an insensitivity to his environment.

Just as the greatest gift a teacher bestows on his students is his personality, so will the environment in which the individual has spent his student years leave its permanent impress on him. It is important that that imprint be of the right quality. Those ivy-covered walls possess more than a merely decorative value, for they should provide the setting for a unique sort of spiritual experience, and the setting is an essential part of the experience. Builders of religious edifices understood this fully in earlier times, although with the increasing secularization and materialization of human values, the architects of religious buildings in our own time appear to be insensible to the spiritual requirements that should be satisfied in the creation of such buildings.

The early colleges of Oxford and Cambridge were built by men who were profoundly influenced by the religious architecture of their tradition. The resulting buildings and grounds have a quality and an atmosphere which, during every moment of the student's life among them, remind him of the strange necessity of beauty and provide him with an ambience in which the pursuit of learning is beyond all else an education in the dignity and quality of *humanitas*.

There is a character and a quality about English college buildings of this period which is largely lacking in their more recent counterparts and, except at such places as Princeton and Yale, which are frankly imitative of the older English style, is almost wholly lacking in America. The quality of his college environment enters no less into the making of the student's character than the nonphysical aspects of his college experience, and if we are as genuinely concerned with the quality of education in America as we assert we are, it is high time that we devoted some of that concern to the quality of our educational buildings.

Something of the feeling the student experiences in the physical environment of such places as Cambridge and Oxford is something akin to that feeling we have upon entering a beautiful chapel or cathedral. It is an ennobling, a purifying experience, a replenishing of our nobler, better selves. It is this feeling, presumably, which causes us to seek out such buildings and burn the incense of our admiration at their shrines.

The singularity, the character, and the beauty of Cambridge and Oxford colleges have in no small part contributed to the making of English character at its best. Those who are exposed to an environment of beauty in their formative years will know what it is and will not, by default, allow beauty to be supplanted by ugliness.

Frank Lloyd Wright

THE LIFE of Frank Lloyd Wright as an architect could well serve as the point of departure for a discussion of what is both right and what is wrong with Americans. I do not say "with American judgment" or "American critical taste," for much more is involved than that. Wright, like the land of which he was a product, was full of promises, potential talents which by their very prodigality endangered their possessor. Talents require discipline, and the greater the talents, the greater the discipline required. What is talent? It is involvement. But involvement is not enough. What is necessary for substantive achievement is disciplined involvement, the devotion to the critical and systematic, the skillful organization of one's potentialities. Essentially this means the sharpening of one's wits on the whetstone of all the best that has been said, written, and done in the field of one's major interest. Genuis can afford to take shortcuts. Frank Lloyd Wright not only considered himself to be a genius, but also imperiously demanded of others that they be in fealty bound to his own valuation of himself—a valuation to which most Americans readily acceded. Americans like their geniuses to be flamboyant, especially when they are homespun, as Frank Lloyd Wright was, the "Prairie Genius," a gross national product, if ever there was one.

But Frank Lloyd Wright was no genius. What was he then?

He was a huckster who had somehow blundered into architecture, a vainglorious man of overweening arrogance, effrontery, hardness, and insensitivity; a snake-oil salesman who talked convincingly of organic architecture but who, when it came to putting the talk into practice, committed the most atrocious blunders. I suppose the supreme early example of Wright's idea of organic form is the Tree House in a Chicago suburb. Here Wright built the house around the tree. I forget whether the tree stands in the hall or in the living room—it doesn't matter which. What does matter is that the house is a monument of ugliness and at the same time a monument to the gullibility of mankind and the impracticability of a plausible theory.

Nevertheless, Americans went on taking Wright at his own valuation for more than two generations. Was not Wright a genius, the greatest of American architects? Was he not always unconscionably late, and with never so much as an apology? Were not his houses the most talked about in America?

One of the most endearing qualities of Americans is their willingness to try almost everything. Those who could afford the luxury were willing to try the conjurations of Wright and pay for the experiment he called a house. The houses were not entirely wanting in magical qualities, but they were for the most part unlivable. The overhanging eaves shut out the light, making the bleak interiors even more dingy than they already were, a dinginess which was further emphasized by Wright's penchant for the darkest woods, with which the rooms were frequently paneled. As Henry Hope Reed, Jr., recently wrote, "Many of his houses, even in sunny Pasadena, are so dark that you need a miner's lamp to find your way about them. And, alas, the houses designed for 'the prairie' are always to be found in second-class suburbs where 'the far-reaching vistas' consist of views of the neighbors."

Wright built houses for cave dwellers, troglodytes, it would almost seem as a practical joke practiced by the High Priest of Ugliness and Contempt for Humanity.

Being a short man, Wright designed his rooms with very low ceilings. This barbarity was made to appear as a very great innovation. It was Wright "lowering the room on the American household." What in fact "the Isadora Duncan of American architecture" was actually doing was to play an egomaniacal joke on the American public. He would show them what organic architecture was, and if he were unable to add a cubit to his own stature, he would bring them down to his own dimensions. And so he produced elaborate versions of the cave and perpetrated what can be described only as the abysmal errors. "Organic architecture," forsooth!

The last of Wright's organic follies is among the worst of all his uglinesses, the Guggenheim Museum in New York. This has been appropriately dubbed a huge spiral of contempt for its contents. As anyone who has visited the museum knows, it is scarcely possible to hang a picture properly on its leaning walls, and what is worse, it is hardly possible to view a picture comfortably. It was Wright's final testament to his contempt for humanity.

The tragedy of Wright was that he was denied the discipline his fellow Americans might have given him through their criticism of his work, a criticism which might have prevented the development of that corrosive arrogance and self-blindness which made Frank Lloyd Wright the colossal failure he was.

Clothes and behavior

CLOTHES ARE behavior. As such, clothes reflect the behaving person and, of course, the culture, the society, of which he is a part. It was Anatole France who remarked that if he were to seek the best source of information about the world, say, a hundred years after his death, he would choose a fashion journal, in preference to books on philosophy, *belles lettres,* or science. With his customary acuity Anatole France saw through to the heart of the problem and came up with the correct answer, for the vagaries of fashion well reflect the basic values of a culture. Clothes reflect the interior values of people, and clothes constitute a vastly more important form of behavior than most people are aware of or have been willing to grant.

Anyone who has lived through two generations of rapid social change cannot have failed to observe how often the first evidences of beginning fundamental revolutionary changes in human behavior were heralded by the changes in clothing styles. When during World War I women raised their skirts, it was the first intimation of the fact that the boom was being lowered on the empire of men. It was also the first intimation of the fact that a revolutionary change in the status of women was occurring, and it was the first intimation of the fact, concomitantly with the others, that a revolution in sexual mores was in process.

The contemporary change in men's fashions to a brighter, gayer apparel reflects the breakaway from the arch-conservatism and drabness of the nineteenth century's inflexible arbitrariness with respect to the conduct of men, the pillars of society, whose affidavit of respectability was the dreary, dull, disappointing drabness of their attire. Perhaps "habiliments" rather than "attire" more accurately describes their clothing; it has the proper mortuary tone. Shakespeare, in a famous passage in *Hamlet,* makes Polonius say:

> Take each man's censure, but reserve thy judgment.
> Costly thy habit as thy purse can buy,
> But not express'd in fancy; rich, not gaudy;
> For the apparel oft proclaims the man.

The Age of Shakespeare was an age of gaudy, fancy dressers, in which the men outdid the women in fanciness and color. It was only with the French Revolution that the fanciness and gaudiness were banished from men's clothes and even from those of children, although women were permitted greater, if restricted, freedoms. The latter increased during the Victorian period, and insofar as men are concerned, it was only after World War II that American men began to break out in fancy clothes, in the one area in which a certain amount of freedom was always possible—namely, in summer sportswear. From this beachhead a foray was made into the peninsula of ties, then hats, socks, colored dinner jackets, and the emancipation from winged collars to sensible dinner shirts. Now men are beginning to experiment with the clothes they wear daily. It may even be that we shall soon reach that stage in the evolution of men's clothes when it will be proper to speak of them, not as clothes but as raiment. However that may be, men and women are at last emancipated from the restrictive straitjacket of the sumptuary laws which regulated what men and women could wear in earlier centuries. It is not commonly known that such laws existed in many parts of Europe as early as the fourteenth century. For example, the Council of Zurich about 1375 ordered that no woman, whether married, widowed, or ecclesiastic, should put embroidery on any cloth, veil, silk, linen, or other material but should leave it as it was originally woven. This was designed to counteract the tendency to overornamentation. The ordinance went on to prescribe in great detail how clothes were to be made for women, men, and children, a subject with which John Martin Vincent in his book *Costume and Conduct in the laws of Basel, Bern, and Zurich, 1370–1800* (Baltimore, The Johns Hopkins Press, 1935) has dealt most interestingly. The purpose of these sumptuary laws regulating the quality and manner of dress was not only to prevent the lower classes from spending too much money on unnecessary clothes, but also to maintain distinctions between the classes in their dress, to prevent immodesty in dress, to regulate morals, and to arbitrate taste. These regulations and ordinances proceeded right into the twentieth century, not only in Europe, but also in America, as is witnessed by the arrest of women on beaches for indecent exposure when they put on what were so charmingly called bathing costumes. This was long before the bikini which, far from being a twentieth-century invention, was worn by Roman women as long ago as 400 B.C.

Fortunately, fashion is a rebel which, as Robert Lowie has said, has never known law, and no ordinance or regulation has ever succeeded in bridling it. It is clearly one of the most immediate means of self-expression, and on that precious quality no restraints should be put, except for those which come from self-discipline.

Clothing or dress is one of the languages of the imagination, and as such, it can be and often is a very beautiful thing
to observe and to experience. In the beauty of their clothes,
women by far outdo men. This is especially true in the
United States, where women are among the best dressed, if
not the best dressed, in the world, and men, however expensively, among the worst dressed.

The clothes of the American male reflect something of his
inner stresses and atomization. Nowhere in the world are his
clothes better made; they fit as if they had been poured out on
him in plastic form. The material could be better, but in a society characterized by conspicuous consumption, that material
must become obsolete as soon as possible and the old clothes
jettisoned for the new. However that may be, his clothes
are well made, even though the material from which they are
made is not. His suits are genuine works of craftsmanship and
of art. They are really admirable. But this work of art is then
associated with a garish tie, which puts the lights of Broadway
vulgarly in the shade, a tie which has no relation to the suit
and is in violent and disharmonic contrast with it. The shirt,
which is usually white, in no way blends with the suit in a
harmonic counterpoint but is usually in conflict with it, and
the hat is more often than not also out of harmony with what
should be an integrated color scheme, not a flamboyant
mélange of clashing incongruities.

What I have said about men's daily wear applies a thou-
sandfold more forcibly to men's summer wear. It is utterly
and completely without taste, offensive to the eye and depressing to the human spirit. Its one redeeming feature lies
perhaps in the evidences it gives of a breakaway from the
general ingloriousness of men's apparel. If this is indeed so,
then perhaps it will have been worth suffering the present

incoherently wild tastelessness and offensiveness of men's summer wear.

The art of being well dressed is surely to be so well dressed as to be unnoticed, precisely as good health, when it is enjoyed, is unnoticed by the enjoyer but is relished when it is reflected on. So the art of being well dressed is to be unobtrusively elegant, to make the best of oneself, without a blast of trumpets announcing the fact to all and sundry.

Garish dress is an intrusion on the right of others to remain unmolested by the disharmonic violence of the tasteless. It is to make the worst of oneself and to communicate that fact immediately to others, for clothes are a very direct form of communication and, like all art, a means of addressing humanity.

"Clothes make the man" is a very old saying, and it has a profound meaning. A resplendent uniform has turned many a pygmy into a giant. And I think it will always remain profoundly true, as Herbert Spencer put it, that the consciousness of being perfectly well dressed may bestow a peace such as religion cannot give. And what is this feeling of peace, if not the feeling of well-being which comes from the knowledge that things are as they ought to be, in the serenity that what has been done has been well done, in harmony and beautifully?

The American magazine

WHAT A LOOKING GLASS to the history and development of this country is the American magazine! Is there any country that has ever had a more interesting and bedazzling variety of magazines than this? I strongly doubt it. For vigor and variety, I think it would be difficult to equal the performance of the American magazine. One has only to glance through the four-volume work of Frank Luther Mott, *A History of American Magazines* (Cambridge, Harvard University Press, 1957) to appreciate this fact. When that magnificent work is read, it becomes clear that a free and vigorous society is likely to express itself more freely and frankly through the pages of its periodicals than through newspapers or any other public record it creates. Written for the day and the fray, the topics with which the magazine deals are likely to be those which most exercise the minds and the imaginations of the most forward-looking thinkers of the time.

Nothing is more contemporary than the magazine, and hence, its pages constitute a living repository of events and issues. In the pages of the magazine we see the community, as it were, in vital motion. Its values and conflicts, its causes and alarums, its tastes and dislikes, its political and social struggles, its fads and crazes, the poor and the good judgment, the true and the false estimates, the concern and the curiosity, the fashions and the frenzies, and the state of culture, science, theology, and the law—indeed, the whole social scene—pass before our eyes like a film in many dimensions. If one wants a social history of America, one can do no better than to look for it in the magazines. Together those magazines constitute a cultural history of the United States of immense scope and variety.

The first American monthly magazine, *The American Magazine,* made its appearance at Philadelphia on February 13, 1741. Franklin's magazine saw the light three days later. He called it the *General Magazine,* and it was published by that title to the year 1850. Since 1741 a huge variety of magazines, literally hundreds, have come and gone. Most of them deserved to live a great deal longer than they managed to do, and one cannot help regretting that so much labor and devotion should so often have come to naught, but then, as Noah Webster remarked in his *American Magazine* in 1788, "The expectation of failure is connected with the very name of a Magazine." The chief difficulties faced by magazines in earlier times seem to have been the indifference of readers and of writers, lack of adequate means of distribution, losses in the collection of subscription accounts, and manufacturing embarrassments. These difficulties have continued to plague American magazines throughout their history, and pretty much the same difficulties face most magazines today. The little magazine is a particularly poignant example of the vulnerability of a valuable public organ which to this day regularly succumbs, mainly to the indifference of readers. This subject has been ably dealt with by Hoffman, Allen, and Ulrich in their charming book *The Little Magazine* (Princeton, Princeton University Press, 1946), a book which was itself remaindered because there were not enough people interested in one of the most important media of cultural progress. Doubtless the little magazine will always continue to exist and cater to small and select groups.

At the present time America has a large number of magazines of high quality: *Partisan Review, Commentary, Kenyon Review, Poetry, Sewanee Review, Hudson Review, Texas Quarterly, American Scholar, New York Review of Books,* and others, as well as a host of little magazines. They do much better here than in England, if a comparison may be forgiven. In England such magazines have always eked out a precarious existence, and in recent years one after the other, literary magazines have fallen by the way, whereas in America they manage somehow to exist. Can it be that general cultural interests are greater in America than in England, or is there some other explanation? Since the evidence suggests that there has always been a more widespread, if not a more profound, interest in culture in America than in England, it is perhaps not surprising that there should have been so great an efflorescence of magazines in this country, compared with England, and that this factor, in spite of all appearances to the contrary, should still constitute an important influence today. It is a melancholy experience to go over Walter Graham's excellent book of a generation ago, *English Literary Periodicals* (New York, Thomas Nelson & Son, 1930), and to discover how many admirable English periodicals have become extinct during the last hundred years. It is unlikely that in America we shall ever decline to England's present low estate of half a dozen first-rate magazines, to make the comparison with England's present status on a proportionate population basis. America's intellectual vigor happily grows greater rather than less, and we may expect this to be paralleled by an increase, rather than a decrease, in the number and quality of its magazines.

Newspapers

AMERICA WHICH certainly has the finest newspaper in the world, *The New York Times,* as well as some other excellent newspapers, also has some of the ghastliest—and not only the ghastliest, but the largest number—of such abominations. The good newspapers are very good, but the bad ones are horrid. That so many millions of Americans voluntarily support the kinds of newspapers they do is in itself commentary enough, not so much on the newspapers as on the masses of Americans. Not that Americans are in any way unique for the bad newspapers they support—every country seems to have them—for it would appear that the masses everywhere must have their quota of blood, murder, rape, violence, circuses, and cheesecake. And that is what so many of the most successful newspapers, like England's *News of the World,* gives them.

It is of interest that almost all these ghastly newspapers are reactionary in their politics, obstructionist in their attitudes toward social reform, and utterly lacking in taste. The kinds of creatures employed as columnists by these antinomian sheets are often so unspeakably monstrous that were it not for their actual being, it would be difficult to believe that they really exist outside straitjackets. But happily their day seems to be passing. The few that remain make their egregious presence only too obtrusive, for like a powerful bad odor, their stench is as penetrating as that of the animal they in this respect so closely resemble, the skunk. But this is unfair to the skunk who uses his scent glands for defensive purposes. The calumniasts, as these public conveniences of the yellow press may appropriately be called, have no such excuse. They produce their noxious effluvia for profit, for the entertainment of millions of readers who luxuriate in the bad smells they emit. One of the most notorious of these calumniasts earned the sobriquet of "Poison Pen," which aptly described him; another was described as having the kind of attraction for the reader that a fatal accident has for most people. Crude, illiterate, tough, utterly wanting in sense or sensibility, these creatures often attain immense power, achieve coast-to-coast influence over TV, radio, and the movies, battening all the while on their calumnies. Insured against lawsuits by their employers and by libel laws which protect the libeler, they get away with almost anything. Like pimps in the service of a whore, they are rewarded for the juicy morsels they supply.

As I have said, things are getting better, and most columnists today are not anywhere nearly as objectionable as most columnists used to be. Some of the finest political and social criticism comes from newspaper columnists. On the whole, they are to be applauded.

Some years ago *The New York Times* undertook to publish a Western edition for the benefit of Californians. But Californians didn't want to be benefited. They preferred their, on the whole, parochial sheets, whose quality has to be seen to be believed. The truth is that the daily *New York Times,* even though it is the world's best newspaper, has a relatively small circulation, a total of about 600,000, whereas the *National Enquirer,* a lurid newspaper published in New York, specializing in such banner headlines on its front page as DAD BURNS HIS THREE BABIES ALIVE FOR INSURANCE and MAN EATS DOGS, has a circulation of about 1,200,000.

While a free press is a vital necessity for every free society, the abuse of freedom is not. In America the press often tries a case even before it is heard in a court of law, and many a newspaper has set itself up as court, judge, and jury. The Roman holiday a newspaper can have with a good case—a good case being defined as one which lends itself to being made the most of—can send the sale of newspapers rocketing. So trial by newspaper has become a profitable industry in America. Certainly when others fail in their duty, the press serves a useful function when it forces the law to take action against offenders who would otherwise escape the consequences of their conduct. But apart from that and the unprejudiced reporting of arrest, charges, and trial, no pretrial discussion of any case should be permitted in any of the mass media reporting the news. In England the law has for long been explicit on the subject, and any newspaper that chooses to break the law is subject to the severest penalties. Fair comment is allowed; but the English judge rules on that, and any journalist or newspaper overstepping the bounds, publishing anything considered prejudicial to a fair trial, may be imprisoned or heavily fined. This is not the case in America where, at most, a judge can lock up the jurors, prohibit them from discussing the case outside the court and jury room, selling stories on the case, and posing for pictures; if all else fails, he may grant a change of venue—that is, he may order the transfer of the trial to another area. None of this is good enough. Judges seldom order a change of venue, and the appellate courts seldom reverse a judge of a lower court for refusing to grant a change of venue.

A free press should not be incompatible with a fair trial, and a decent press aware of its responsibilities would police itself so that it would never embarrass in any way the chances of a fair trial. Every individual, whether a citizen or not, has a right to due process and a fair trial. The Sixth Amendment guarantees everyone the right of trial by an impartial jury. It is an abuse of the First Amendment, which guarantees the freedom of the press, in any way to interfere with the fair working of a judge and jury in the trial of a case. It is proper and desirable for the press to be free to criticize judges, the courts, and the administration of the law, but it is neither proper nor desirable for the press to conduct the trial of a defendant in its columns either before the case has come to trial or during its progress.

The good taste and objectivity of the public news media have on more than one occasion been questioned by the higher courts, but it was not until June, 1965, that the Supreme Court found the conviction of Billie Sol Estes unconstitutional, simply because TV cameras were allowed in the courtroom. This is a beginning in the right direction, and it is to be hoped that it will not be long before the press and all other news media will be forced to conduct themselves in a manner which does not prejudice the due process of law and the fair trial of all defendants.

Broadway and the theater

BROADWAY IS PROBABLY the greatest impediment to the development of the theater of any institution in America. Broadway's measure of the worth of a play is the box office, and the box office is the supreme dictator. This means that, with rare exceptions, new ideas, originality, and the encouragement of creativity are most unlikely to receive a helping hand from Broadway.

It is the off-Broadway theater that has done the most for the theater in America. At any one time the plays most successful on Broadway are likely to be trivial and, although box-office successes, of ephemeral value. Off-Broadway can do a play at a fraction of the cost that Broadway requires for its production, and has successfully staged the first plays of playwrights who wouldn't have stood a chance on Broadway. Among these are Tennessee Williams, Bertolt Brecht, Samuel Beckett, and Jack Gelber.

The classics of the theater have been mainly produced off-Broadway and there have had their longest runs. The newly discovered Haydn, *A Voyage to the Moon*, which I would gladly have gone round the world five times to see, was produced in Greenwich Village. I have not heard of it since 1948 when I first saw it, but I would never have heard of it or seen it if Broadway had been the only available means for staging this long-lost and hitherto unknown opera of Haydn's. This is equally true for the magnificent dramatization of *Ulysses* with Zero Mostel in the lead and so many other delightful plays of permanent value, whose permanence, alas, depends on the noncommercial theater, for these plays will never be seen on Broadway.

The off-Broadway theater deserves all the success it has enjoyed, and all lovers of the theater are deeply in its debt. It deserves every encouragement, and long may it flourish in all the cities of our land. But what is needed is a national theater. Early in 1954 the English instituted the National Theatre, and its success has exceeded the fondest hopes of everyone connected with it. Every production has thus far been sold out—in fact, well over 100 percent—and the critical reception has been superlative. The National Theatre is wholly government-supported, and because the National Theatre is independent of what happens at the box office, it is able to produce any play it desires. It is in its early development, and there is a sizable annual deficit which the government makes up. But there is the expectation that although it may never become wholly self-supporting, the deficit will ultimately be reduced.

In German-speaking countries the state theater has long been established, and with great success—each state vying with the other to produce the best theater. Our own state organization lends itself admirably to the institution of a state theater in each of the fifty states and dependencies.

A national theater must be the work of the Congress, that work being restricted to the passage of the necessary bill establishing such a theater and supplying the annual funds with which to support it. Each state should contribute to that support a certain adequately proportional amount, and that is where the state's involvement should end. The state should have absolutely no word in what plays shall be produced or in what manner. The production of plays should be left to a board elected for a period of a few years, and the board should consist of people experienced in the theater. In this way we may yet see a theater in America that is worthy of the name. Repertory companies, resident theaters, and community theaters are good things, but they are no substitute for the national and state theaters.

American jazz

ONLY AMERICANS can play jazz. One has but to hear an English band attempting to play it to know the reason why. Essentially jazz is a free-swinging natural expression of feeling, of emotion. That is why it lends itself so well to improvisation. Americans are very good at that. The English are not. Louis Armstrong once put it in a hemisemidemiquaver. Asked to define jazz, he replied, "If you have to ask what it is, you'll never know."

Jazz, as the whole world knows, is an exclusively American invention and one of America's more considerable contributions to the jollity of nations.

Pop music is an expression of America's cultural diversity, unified. Rock 'n' roll in its contemporary form may be new, but it is so only in the sense that it represents an evolutionary form of a quite old style of music and dance. Pop music is music in evolution. It goes all the way back to the music of our pioneer ancestors. One can still hear the bagpipes, the fiddle, the Irish jig, the Elizabethan melodic elements, and the melancholy of the Jewish folk song in much of the popular music of our day.

Deep in the roots of this multiple American tradition the great river of American popular music has flowed into musically replenishing and refreshing waters. The Scotch-Irish tradition of the Ozarks and Appalachians, with the fiddle, banjo, and mandolin playing in bluegrass or country style; the Negro spirituals and Negro church music entering into the gospel and blues feeling of so much of jazz; and the folk music of southeastern European Jews—all have contributed to the popular music and especially to the development of jazz.

No one knows quite where or when, but it is generally agreed that jazz originated around the turn of the century, maybe in New Orleans and maybe in New York and maybe in the coming together of the early jazz makers somewhere along the road between—the product originally of American Negroes and subsequently of American Jews, by no means exclusively, but certainly in a major way. The Negroes and the Jews brought something of the African and Jewish feeling and style for musical expression to bear on the already uniquely styled American music and proceeded to make it swing. W. C. Handy and Irving Berlin, the one a Negro and the other a Jew, were among the earliest creators of jazz, whoever may finally claim to be its actual parents. Following them by far the larger contributors to the making of jazz in America were Negroes and Jews: Jelly Roll Morton, Fats Waller, Louis Armstrong, Art Tatum, Duke Ellington, George Gershwin, Jerome Kern, Benny Goodman.

All the many non-Negro, non-Jewish jazz composers, instrumentalists, and singers of distinction were influenced by the style of the creators of jazz and helped establish it as the thoroughly American medium it is.

Perhaps there somewhere exists a non-American band that can play jazz. It is possible. Experience, however, tells me that if such a band does exist, then it must rank among the rarest things on this earth. Foreign bands seldom manage the rhythm or the beat, and almost invariably they are lacking in that quality which Louis Armstrong undoubtedly had in mind when he said, "If you have to ask what it is, you'll never know." That quality is oomph. You either is or you ain't, and that's the long and the short of it.

Some people believe that English plumbing is to be reckoned among the four wonders of the world. They are wrong. Let them listen to what an English band imagines it is doing when it attempts to play jazz. Such a caterwauling was never heard anywhere else on this earth. The poor things haven't the slightest notion of what the music is supposed to do, and so they are unable to get with it. This difference in the ability to produce and play jazz is anthropologically very interesting. It is not that the English lack the necessary musical genes that so disable them, but rather, we may suspect, it is their cultural conditioning. The English have not enjoyed an environment, such as Americans have, with a polycultural population of immigrants drawn from almost every country in the world. Nor have the English until the last dozen years or so enjoyed a sizable Negro population. The Jewish population has always been relatively small. The relative homogeneity of English cultural pressures has constituted the chief impediment to the development of any original musical contribution in England—with one exception that we shall soon note. The cultural crosscurrents that would spark the kind of creativity that produced jazz in America were virtually entirely wanting in England.

A widespread current myth is that Negroes are born more musical than whites. If that were really so, then given the opportunities for musical development, Negroes raised in any musical environment should exhibit superior musical abilities to whites. Anyone who has observed Negroes' musical performances in England, especially in English nightclubs where the best Negro talent is to be found, will know that Negroes raised in England are as unable to sing and play jazz, let alone compose it, as are the English. It is something to experience. Neither Negroes, nor Jews, nor Englishmen in England produce jazz for the simple reason that the necessary chemical alchemy it takes to synthesize jazz is incapable of occurring in the uncongenial climate of England.

It is, of course, possible to claim that Negroes, like Jews, possess the genes for musical ability but that the English environment simply fails to afford opportunities for their development. This is evidently the case, but it throws no light on the question of the superior musical abilities that Negroes and Jews are supposed to possess. The English in Elizabethan times were the most musical people in Europe. Whatever happened to the "superior" musical genes of the English in the centuries following? Did they suffer a molecular or a cultural eclipse? The answer is surely clear. Whatever the causes, England has for the last three centuries failed to provide a favorable climate for the development of musical talent. America during the last hundred years and more very clearly has. The combination of Negro, Jewish, and other ethnically derived talents gave us jazz and its developing offshoots. The interaction of these with other American influences produced the American musical.

Jazz and the American musical have reached their highest development in America as a result of the unique interaction of so many ethnic elements, a unique intermingling of many musical traditions.

American pop music has now spread all over the world, and the appearance of such phenomena as the Beatles in England is largely due to that influence and possibly to the influx of a large number of Negroes. The Beatles' principal contribution seems to have been long hair—a fashion which has now spread all over the heads of young men over a large part of the globe. But who can really rationalize the charm and appeal of the Beatles?

Luck and the stock market

COULD AN APE play the stock market? Of course, he could—with as much success as most Americans play it. Playing the stock market constitutes the most abject form of gambling, because most people who play it can play any card game better by about a measure of a hundred times. There is one infallible rule about the stock market: the way to make a small fortune in the stock market is to begin with a large one. The stock market exists in what the Greeks used to call the aleatory element, the element of luck, that is, for most people. Otherwise, it is a full-time job, requiring the closest attention, experience, and intelligence. Anyone lacking in just one of these desiderata should enter the stock market only if he is ready to lose most of what he invests and to lose it with grace and good humor and the awareness of the fact that he is a damn fool anyway, whether he wins or loses. About 25 percent of Americans are actively engaged in playing the stock market.

People who spend a good part of their time straightening nails, saving string and wrapping paper, taking subways instead of cabs, and eating hamburgers instead of *filet mignon,* who save pennies all the days of their lives, and to whom a hundred dollars is a lot of money will think nothing of investing large sums of money in the uranium stock on which they have received a tip or in whatever else it may be that some crony has told them to put their shirt on. It doesn't even have to be a crony: anyone with a hot tip will do, for the stock market operates largely in the area of magic. It is for most people a secular equivalent of magic. It is the world of fantasy, the dreamland in which one's wishes come true, in which one can grow rich quickly and achieve one's heart's desires. It is like the one-armed bandit. You put in your money, pull down the lever, and out rolls the money—not maybe the first time, but if you go on long enough, you're sure to hit the jackpot. Anyway, whether one wins or loses it is exciting. And as every gambler knows, part of the pleasure of gambling is not so much the contemplation of future riches as the excitement of the game itself—no matter whether one wins or loses. This keeps a lot of gamblers in the stock market.

There are so many chance elements involved in gambling on the stock market that in order to do so anywhere nearly successfully, one must devote as much time to it as one would have to do if one were going to be successful at any other discipline. Not even then is there any promise of success, for many more chance elements enter into the practice of the stock market than enter into the practice of any other discipline one might choose to follow.

The medicine men of the stock market, the brokers, know very little more about the stock market than do their customers. But the very little more they do know amounts to this: they know that they, the brokers, will grow rich on the follies committed by their customers, for customers will buy, and they will sell, and every time their customers do the one and the other, they, the brokers, will grow richer.

Play the stock market, and with one lucky break I will

become a millionaire. It has happened to many people. Why not to me? So the sorcerer's magic goes. One pronounces the spell, one does something, and the supernaturals, whether they like it or not, are compelled to do one's bidding. The aleatory element is at one's command. Fortunately, it is not so. The element of chance remains, and no amount of either black or white magic will in any way influence it. Yet most people continue to behave in relation to the stock market as if they were living in the world of magic. Let a perfect stranger approach you and say, "Buy American Utensils," and then as rapidly disappear, as likely as not you will begin thinking about it and will finally decide to take a chance on the mysterious stranger's tip. After all, there may be something in it. The chances are, of course, that the mysterious stranger knows even less than the average broker, who knows everything about the mechanics of the stock market but nothing whatever about the direction in which any one stock may take it into its head to suddenly start moving. The broker, unlike his customer, does not believe in magic. He tends to be a hardheaded realist, who knows that stocks, like the stock market, go up and go down and that no one can predict their movement. The broker's advantage lies not in his ability to divine which way a stock is headed—he has no such ability—but in the fact that whether his customers gain or lose, he will always win, for the commissions are always there.

In the stock market, as in life in general, one tends to regret the things one did not do rather more than those one did do. And the thing one tends to regret most is that one did not stay out of the stock market altogether and put one's money in the bank or under the mattress. But this is a counsel for the timid. Most gamblers, that is to say, a fair proportion of Americans—will continue to align themselves

with the brave Earl of Montrose, who lost his head in 1650 at
the age of thirty-eight and who wrote these immortal lines:

> He either fears his fate too much,
>   Or his deserts are small,
> That dares not put it to the touch,
>   To gain or lose it all.

The Boy Scouts and big business

THE BOY SCOUT MOVEMENT in America is big busi-
ness, and so far as I can make out, it is little more than that.
An immense business is done in uniforms, accessories, and
the various publications issued from headquarters at New
Brunswick, New Jersey. In England, where scouting originated, the movement constitutes a powerful influence in the
formation of character, in addition to the many skills boys are
taught to acquire. In America, it seems to me, scouting
consists largely of being required to purchase additions to
uniforms, paying dues, attending disorganized sessions of play
and drill, during which the boys are put through dull and
unhelpful routines which eventually lead to a badge, which,
of course, must be purchased. Once a year there is the
ceremony of awarding prizes and the announcement of pro-
motions. Seldom on these occasions is anything said worth
remembering, and seldom is there in evidence any sense of
the dignity of the occasion. The ceremonies are usually
wholly unimpressive. The outings on which the boys go are
too frequently a fizzle, essential pieces of equipment usually
being left at home because no one had issued the proper
instructions.

Of course, there are exceptions—fine leaders, fine troops,

and great benefits derived—but these appear to be the exceptions rather than the rule. I don't think that Americans really get the point about scouting. When Baden-Powell created the Boy Scout movement, he had in mind essentially the training of character, as well as the training of skills. Training in character seems foreign to American ideas of what a boy's club should really be doing. Indeed, training of character does not seem to enter into the purposes which educators in America envisage for what should be going on in the schools. Why then should one worry about character training in such an organization as the Boy Scouts? It is a question.

Being a Boy Scout should be made to mean more to children than it presently does. As in England and in other countries, scouting could constitute an auxiliary educational experience, completing, applying, and enlarging the experiences of the home, school, and outside world.

Baden-Powell, as a result of his experiences as a soldier in the Boer War, perceived that the qualities most desirable in any individual comprised a combination of practical preparedness, theoretical know-how, physical fitness, character, and consideration for others. In Europe the scouting experience often makes the difference between success and failure in later life for many individuals. There is no real reason why scouting could not be made to be an equally significant experience for boys and girls in America. It would, of course, take leaders and scoutmasters who really understand the meaning of scouting. I don't think the organization known as the Boy Scouts of America understands that meaning.

California: decline and fall

THE STRIKING THING about California is not so much
its sunny skies as its parochialism. It is the land of perpetual
pubescence, where cultural lag is mistaken for renaissance.
The continuous sun is merely a bore. Continuous sunlight is
no substitute for a good climate. But the sun worshipers of
California do not seem to be aware of this. The climate one
prefers is, of course, a matter of taste. There are those who
prefer the stimulation and variety of the changing seasons to
the monotony of continuously cloudless blue skies, with the
sun turning everything to yellowish brown.

There is, I suspect, a highly significant correlation between
California climate and the character of its population. The
very fact that the sun shines continuously, that the air is
warm, comfortable, and only occasionally cold, attracts individuals who are interested primarily in creature comforts. A
high positive correlation is likely to exist between a devotion
to physical comforts and a lack of interest in the spiritual, the
essential, qualities of humanity. The more one values creature comforts and physical things, the less likely is one to
value those qualities of humanity without which human beings are in danger of losing themselves, of losing what is
essentially best and most important for themselves. More so

[190

than anywhere else in the land, Californians strike me as so many lost souls, living in a land which looks like a tentative preface to extinction, frenetically searching for a solution. Perhaps that is why California is the haven and the home of so many cults and religions. There is a famous line in *Charley's Aunt:* "You know, Brazil, where the nuts come from." There is no doubt where they go to, with possibly more of them in and about Los Angeles than anywhere else in the world.

A correlation is an association between variables, and associated variables are not necessarily causally related. An interest in creature comforts is not alone the cause of a lack of interest in humanity, in what it is to be essentially human. There is nothing in the least wrong with being interested in creature comforts. What is wrong is making them the major focus of one's interest in life. And what makes the interest in creature comforts a major focus of interest is not the interest in creature comforts, but surely something else—although the interest in creature comforts may become so consuming that it may crowd out interest in most other things.

The concentration of interest on creature comforts is a characteristic of the materialist, the individual interested in things rather than in humanity. It is the individual whose values are already dehumanized or seriously depleted in humanity to whom the bright sun and creature comforts make an irresistible appeal. Children raised in such a dehumanized creature-comfort sunny environment stand the best chance in the world of becoming the physically healthiest dehumanized brutes.

Lotus-eaters as concentrated on the fleshpots of existence as are Californians are likely to become increasingly more concentrated on the externals of their own limited world—a world hardly extending beyond the narrow boundaries of

California. Hence, the parochialism. The Western edition of *The New York Times* was too urbane for Californians. They preferred such apologies for a newspaper as the Los Angeles *Times,* a reactionary sheet of the dreariest small-town kind. A survey of almost any Californian newspaper would hardly lead one to suspect that the world extends beyond the boundaries of California. One gains much the same impression from conversation with Californians. There is a kind of disengagement from the rest of the world and an unconcern. There are, of course, exceptions. I am speaking here of the average Californian, *not* of all Californians.

This lack of involvement in anything but themselves is a characteristic seen most markedly in the young. The Californian teen-ager is a phenomenon in himself. Every physical comfort has been lavished on him so that his preoccupation with things and creature comforts appears to be the main driving force of his life. In summer he swarms to the beaches like one of a horde of lemmings, girls and surfing being his principal devotions. His ambition in life is to have lots of money, a beautiful house with a swimming pool, and a properly proportioned girl for a wife. Such aspirations are the result of his conditioning, and if as a youth, he is a blond beast, as a man, he is a great deal worse. It is no accident that the state he inhabits is the homeland of the antihuman Birchers, the fair housing referendum rejectors, the rejectors of Rockefeller and the endorsers of Goldwater, the electors of a song-and-dance man to the Senate of the United States, and if all goes their way, the electors of a former movie actor, Ronald Reagan, to the governorship of California. Some people think that Lassie ought to be a candidate. The state that could elect Max Rafferty Commissioner of Education and remove books containing favorable references to the United Nations from school libraries at the behest of self-appointed vigilantes—all this in a state in which the higher educational system can compare with the best anywhere in the world—has somewhere something askew.

But when one has said that, one has not said much, for the kinds of educational systems we have anywhere in the Western world, not alone in America, don't really do much for the humanization of the student. This is especially the case in California, where the classes are likely to be large and the schools overcrowded, particularly at the college level. Under such conditions it is quite impossible to establish anything resembling a humanizing relationship between teacher and student. On the other hand, the educational system of California serves largely to confirm the young Californian in the frenetic pursuit of material ends, instead of helping him understand the folly of such pursuits.

Extracurricular activities play a large role in the life of Californian youth, and his car, which is his shepherd and for which his parents see to it that he shall not want, leadeth him into ever greener pastures. In other parts of the world, youth lasts a reasonable period of time; in California it lasts a lifetime. Here it is the young who set the standards for the old, and there is a consequent blurring and confusion of roles. Youth seems to enjoy virtually complete autonomy, in which the parents willy-nilly concur. The result of this is a telescoping of development from childhood to technical adulthood without the intervening benefits of a gradual adolescent development, an adolescent development in which one gradually matures into adulthood. The consequence of this is a state of arrested adolescence, which persists into old age—hence, the Peter Pan quality of so many Californians who never seem to grow up. It is not altogether an attractive quality. There are great advantages to being one's age. Californians, on the whole, tend to be handsome, but there is a striking shallowness to their handsomeness. Tanned and tough Californian youth is possibly the physically best developed in the world. The same, unfortunately, cannot be said for his intellectual development. The too abundant pleasures of material life are almost antipathetic to a concern with the things of the mind. Several years ago, when I asked a distinguished professor on a certain university campus how many students there were on campus, he replied, "I should say about one in a hundred."

As for the California public school system, Dr. Max Rafferty is Commissioner of Education—the majority of voters elected him in preference to a good man—and no more need be said about that than that. As for the University of California, it has some of the finest research men and teachers on its campuses—but it is a factory, an assembly-line organization, instructing, rather than educating, students on a mass production basis. Six hundred or double that number of students in a class is a quantity that some teachers flatter themselves on, as if quantity were in any way related to the quality of the teacher. Such a relationship may very well exist in some cases, but classes running into the hundreds constitute an educational monstrosity. No one can educate anyone with so many students in a class; one can only instruct them. Obviously a close association between teacher and student becomes an impossibility under such conditions, and there exists a distance between teacher and students which is the very antithesis of the relationship that should exist between teacher and student. Not only do most of the branches of the University of California operate as if they were factories, but they also look like factories. Architecturally, inside as well as outside, they no more resemble what a university should look like than the miscalled *Encyclopaedia Britannica* resembles what an encyclopedia should be. An instruction factory is not a university or even a place of learning. It is far better than nothing at all. Alas, the so-called educational institutions of California reflect the ethos, the cultural values, of the people in being so devoted to things that even students are treated as if they were things—mere units, if that, in an undifferentiated mass, for quantity here is a value, as it is everywhere else in the United States.

California has, however, made what is in the opinion of many the greatest contribution to education anywhere in the world. This is the junior college. In 1966 there were more than eighty junior colleges in California, and more were in process of building. What California originated and developed is today being widely imitated throughout America. It is a great contribution. Investigation shows that junior college students entering a four-year college as juniors on the whole do better than the juniors who are already there. This is the general California experience, and it speaks very well for the teaching in the junior colleges and the motivation of the students. These colleges have, to my knowledge, been the means of saving many a youth for a happier and more useful existence than would otherwise have been possible for him. Without the junior college these young people would in many cases have been lost. In the junior college something is provided for everyone—machine work, police work, medical technician—in addition to the usual academic subjects.

But what an environment Californians have made for themselves! They have taken a beautiful land and destroyed it. Raymond Dasmann, a native Californian, has movingly described *The Destruction of California* (New York, Macmillan, 1965), in his book of that title, for those who have never seen California, as well as for those who have. It is a tragic story of wantonness and irresponsibility. The word that most fittingly describes physical California was used by a young Eastern woman whose husband was a graduate student on one of the University of California campuses. "Junky" was her description of "Sunny California." It is exactly my impression. I have visited California for many years several times a year, and each time it strikes me as having grown considerably junkier.

The whole state is junky, untidy, haphazard, and messy. Its towns with few exceptions, are ugly, slummy, and entirely wanting in taste or beauty. San Francisco is an attractive big town, but its suburbs are usually quite unattractive. The Monterey Peninsula is lovely, and Carmel is a pretty town in a mannered sort of way. The Hollywood Hills are fetching, but when this has been said, it can, I think, be truly said that California has been transformed into one of the most unattractive regions in the world. The bulldozing of innumerable orchards and groves in order to turn them into the slums of the future yields high profits to the developers, and the scarring of the hills by digging into them to make the terraces on which further developments will be built proceeds everywhere apace, for the 1,600 or so people who enter California to settle there every day of the year must be accommodated somewhere.

Everywhere there are tremendous freeways, on which millions of automobiles travel at speeds of seldom under seventy miles an hour, extending an open invitation to annihilation to everyone who uses them. The towns are engulfed by automobiles spewing out their poisonous gases, and the smog grows thicker by the hour. In October, 1965, the smog level had become so high in Los Angeles that the authorities issued an appeal to industry and automobile owners to reduce their contribution to the pollution of the atmosphere. It was a vain appeal.

If present trends continue, there can be little doubt that

California will become as reactionary politically as the South is today. It will be an extreme rightist form of reaction, and it will be a reaction which will do neither California nor the United States any more good than the South has achieved for itself and the land of which it is a part.

The American woman

IT IS TRUE that "Age cannot wither her, nor custom stale her infinite variety." Nevertheless, the American woman is under attack. We are told that she is a monster who devours her mate; that she makes a domestic animal of her husband, designing him to her requirements while he lives and driving him to an early grave, wearing himself out in the attempt to maintain her in a manner to which no woman should be accustomed; that she emasculates the male, thus bringing about the peculiarly American phenomenon of the he-woman and the she-man.

America, we are told, is a matriarchy in which women rule and momism is a way of life. The greater part of the wealth of the country is in the hands of women. Women run not only the home but also every member of the family, and although it is the function of the American wife to maintain her husband in the illusion that he is master of the household, he is in fact, as everyone knows, nothing more than chairman of the entertainment committee. It is true that American women are physically the most attractive in the world, that they make the best of themselves, but this only goes to show that they are too preoccupied with sex without being sufficiently sexual. American women, we are further informed, suffer from the Puritan blight. They are cold, calculating, and demanding. Women of other countries make better wives.

Of course, a great deal else has been said about American women, but the above represents, I believe, a fair digest of the most frequent criticisms. What about these criticisms? Well, there is just enough truth in most of them to constitute an inducement to further inquiry. Were the accusations that are today increasingly being hurled against the American woman not so seriously a misunderstanding of the true situation, they could be appropriately dismissed as strictly for the birds.

It may be suggested that what the American woman stands most in need of is not blame, but understanding, and this applies, also, to the American male—who is not entirely free of the responsibility for the confusion.

Women are no longer clear on what it is or should be to be a woman, and although men tend to have pretty definite ideas on that subject, they are not altogether clear on what their own role is or ought to be.

In seeking to escape from the oppressive mythology of inequality with which men and the millennia had saddled them, women were forced into the position of having to prove—to themselves, as well as to men—that they were as good as men. This meant, for many women, that they must prove that they are equal to men, that they must compete with men on their own ground and emerge from the competition at least as well. For many women this meant identification with men and envy of masculine roles. For others it meant attempting to achieve what was formerly regarded as male status by playing male occupational roles, while at the same time attempting to hang onto their own femininity. For still others the inability to play masculine roles, an "impediment" brought about in most cases by marriage and a family, has resulted in a certain amount of chafing at the bit.

The sad thing about all this is that a good many women have paradoxically sought to validate themselves (as persons) not as women, but as men. This is a typical minority group reaction. Anything associated with the higher caste is considered desirable and is, by any means, worth attaining.

This is a perfectly understandable human response, and so is the confusion of values that produces it; but it is nonetheless a most misguided, unsound, and adaptively inefficient one. Considering, however, the conditions under which such responses are made, any other is hardly to be expected.

The male of the species, far from being a help in bringing about a more reasonable adjustment, helped produce the very response in the female which, with the logic characteristic of the "masters" in such situations, they now find so little to their liking. For if men maintained that women were not the equals of men and were therefore not entitled to equal rights, women understandably but misguidedly felt that in order to attain equal rights they must demonstrate that they are the equals of men, so they proceeded to make themselves as much like men as possible. Bloomers were developed to replace skirts, masculine attire was imitated, masculine habits, such as smoking and drinking, were adopted, and such strenuous sports as were formerly the preserve of the male were indulged in.

That political and social equality rests on an ethical principle, not on a biological one or even achievement, seems to have escaped both men and women in the struggle for women's independence, just as it escaped most of those who were involved in arguing for and against the racist position. Whether a person is entitled to all the rights and privileges of development and as a citizen of the community depends not on his biological background, but rests solely on the consideration that as a member of the human species, he is entitled, without discrimination, to all the rights and privileges of his birthright, which is development.

And yet who knows? By bringing out any inequalities that may exist, we may find ourselves unexpectedly enriched. To attribute artificially created inequalities to natural causes is one of the most vulgar errors. In rebelling against the consequences of this particular epidemic error, women fell into the opposite one of proving that with the removal of the artificially created handicaps they could assume virtually every one of the roles traditionally played by the male. The greater the obstacles that men placed in their paths, the more determined they were to overcome them. In short, women responded to the challenge which men threw down and to the conditions set by the men. These conditions were, in effect, that if women could do as well in any of the roles in which men traditionally excelled, men would, to say the least, be surprised. It was with something more like consternation that men viewed the response that women made to their implicit challenge.

Women are today engaged in every occupation in which men are employed and are emerging as significant figures in the arts and sciences. There are few who any longer doubt that women are a great deal brighter and more capable than they were at one time thought to be. That is all to the good. But among the changes that have come about are some that are not so good. Among these changes is the psychic masculinization which has affected many women, the tendency to identify themselves with males, to think and act like males, and to aspire to masculine roles—with resulting turmoil and confusion. As women have become more masculinized, men have become more disoriented, so that the male is about as confused concerning his own role in the world as the female is befogged about hers. Both sexes feel that something is out of joint somewhere.

American women, in great numbers, go to their psycho-therapists and complain that their husbands are not as they would have them be, he-men. American men visit their therapists and complain that their wives are not as they would have them be, she-women. The women would like to be more like women themselves, and the men would like to be more like men; but by the time they get to the therapists, the difficulties seem to be insurmountable. And, indeed, the problem is a difficult one. For male and female roles in all cultures are largely a matter of conditioning. This condition-ing is thoroughly completed in our civilization by the time the sexes are ready for marriage or, let us say, by the end of adolescence. It is never an easy matter to take asunder the elements that have gone into the making of a personality and reconstruct them to the heart's desire.

The manner in which we may most helpfully regard the present relationships between the sexes is that they are in a transitional phase of development, that in the passage from the "abolition" phase of "emancipation" a certain number of predictable errors were committed.

The logic of the situation actually led to the most grievous of the errors committed. This was the argument that insofar as political and social rights were concerned, women should be judged as persons, not as members of a biological or any other kind of group. As far as it goes, this argument is sound enough, but what seems to have been forgotten in the ex-citement is that women, in addition to being persons, also belong to a sex and that with the differences in sex are associ-ated important differences in function and behavior. Equal-ity of rights does not imply identity of function, yet this is what it was taken to mean by many women and men. And so women began—and in many cases continue—to compete with men as if they were themselves men, instead of realizing and establishing themselves in their own right as persons. Women have so much more to contribute to the world as women than they could ever have as spurious men. And it is the clarification and recognition of what it means to be a woman, of the nature of the potentialities and capacities with which women are biologically endowed, which should make it possible for women to become happily reconciled to themselves and gratefully accept themselves as women.

Women have great gifts to bring to the world of men: the qualities of love, compassion, and humanity. It is the function of women to humanize, since women are the natural mothers of humanity. Women are by nature endowed with the most important of all adaptive traits—the capacity to love—and this it is their principal function to teach men. There can be no more important function. It could be wished that both men and women understood this. Once women know this, they will realize that no man can ever play as important a role in the life of humanity as a mentally healthy woman. By mental health, I mean the ability to love and the ability to work. Being a good wife, a good mother, in short, a good homemaker, is the most important of all the occupations in the world. It surely cannot be too often pointed out that the making of human beings is a far more important vocation than the making of anything else and that in the formative years of a child's life the mother is best equipped to provide those firm foundations upon which one can subsequently build.

When the male acquires a true understanding of the importance of the mother in the life of the child, especially during its first years, he will realize that he has a principal function as a husband and father to enable his wife to perform her maternal role as happily as possible. As the child grows older, the role of the father becomes increasingly more important, and that is to serve not merely as an appanage of the female, as a useful household gadget and a good provider, but by his example to help all the members of the family to develop their potentialities and to teach them the meaning of freedom, discipline, courage, and independence. A psychiatrist has sagely remarked that fathers are parents, too!

Whether the American woman carries her need to compete into the family in order to prove herself and achieve her ends, I am not sure, but certainly she frequently gives that appearance. For example, a common method of discipline used by American mothers with their children is the method of "conditional love." Mother, in effect, says to her children, "Mother won't love you unless you behave and do as she requires." Love is the one thing in the world that should be unconditional, and the American mother makes it conditional, a commodity for which one bargains. The training in conditional love thus received by boys and girls has the effect of teaching the female that she can use conditional love as a device for obtaining concessions from the male, and the male learns that love is something that one gets from women only if one "behaves." The American male has learned that love (which becomes identified with sex) is something you purchase by agreeing to the conditions set by the female. This puts the male in a weak and frustrating position in relation to the female, engenders hostilities in him toward her in the marital relationship, and further serves to flatten and debase his conception of love. It is not to be wondered at that the vendors of cheap substitutes are so numerous among us; that sequential polygamy has become a sanctioned form of plural marriage for those who can afford it; that husband and wife only too often find each other inadequate; that women come to be regarded as cool and calculating monsters who devour their husbands, and their husbands come to be regarded as emasculated weaklings.

Observing the marked asymmetry of the roles played by his father and mother in the home, the great power wielded by the mother and the comparative weakness of the role of the father, the male in America grows up to know where his "proper place" is—namely, anywhere but in the home. The "boss" is mother, and if father has been properly brought up, he is perfectly willing to grant that, and often jocularly—with the jocularity of the jest spoken in truth—refers to his mate as "The Boss." It is not for nothing that the comic strip that has enjoyed perhaps the longest continuous popularity is entitled "Bringing Up Father."

The view of the "proper" relations of the sexes is further reinforced by the manner in which boys are indoctrinated with the idea that females have a right to expect them to be chivalrous, kind, thoughtful, and gentlemanly and that even in the face of abuse from a woman, a male must never respond in kind. In effect, this means that women enjoy special privileges denied to the male, and it further has the effect of often rendering the male helpless, as an adult, in holding his own against the designs of an aggressive woman.

A further shrinkage in the American male's ego is brought about by his wife's having more time than he does for reading and the enjoyment of various other cultural activities, and so the American woman generally succeeds in becoming a more cultivated and knowledgeable person than her spouse. This is a fact commented on by most foreign visitors to America. I have often heard it said by such observers that the only people worth talking to in America are the women, the men, on the whole, being described as bores. However this may be, the truth is that most men are willing to admit that their wives read more "and keep up with things more" than they do. Such an admission further serves to demote the male in his own self-esteem.

We perceive, then, that women unwittingly serve to increase, rather than to diminish, the disequilibrium that at present exists between the sexes and that men by taking the complacent position they do—"for the sake of peace," as they so often say—are aiding and abetting the process.

One of the principal areas in which men combine with women to confuse the roles of the sexes is education. It is through the agency of education, particularly college education, that women have been especially trained in a confused perception of their roles. The chief error has been to educate women as if they were men. In most of our schools and colleges there is scarcely any recognition given to the fact that such a difference as male and female exists. In most of our women's colleges, women are educated in precisely the same manner as men are in men's colleges. The effect of such misguided education is that women are encouraged to develop aspirations which were designed exclusively to meet the needs of men.

With but a few superb exceptions, our schools and colleges encourage women to go into the world to compete with men as if they were men. They are not told what it means to be a woman or what a woman's role should be in the home and in the community. But they have been led to believe that a woman can be an engineer, a doctor, a writer, a career woman, or anything she desires to be.

Of course, she can! But she can, and ought to be, a great deal more. And so the better educated a woman is, the more likely she is to be confused about her role as a person. She feels frustrated as a homemaker; she has been educated for "better" things. There she is with her B.A. and, as it were, nowhere to go with it. She has been expensively prepared to play a role she is prevented from performing by the frustrating and dulling duties which cut her off from that other world of affairs in which she had hoped to play a significant part.

Such women are confused and unhappy. Those who get out of the home and realize their "otherworldly" aspirations are only too frequently equally confused and unhappy, however successful they may be in their "careers." Of course, there are a good many women who are both good homemakers and happily employed outside the home on full-time jobs, but these are the women who have no children in the home or whose children are of adolescent age. I put it down as an axiom that no woman with a husband and small children can hold a full-time job and be a good homemaker at one and the same time. The early years of family life constitute a full-time job, and while a homemaker needs rest, change, and diversion in sufficient frequency to maintain her freshness of interest and enthusiasm for her job, there can be no doubt about the totality of the demand that homemaking in the early years of family life makes on the homemaker. Hence, any feelings of frustration, of inadequate fulfillment, of dissatisfaction with one's lot, owing to the confused understanding of what her lot should be, creates a state of unhappiness. Such a state exhibits itself in the common response to frustration—namely, in aggressive behavior of various kinds. Such aggressive behavior on the part of the married woman may take any number of forms, such as inadequacy as a homemaker, sexual inadequacy, nagging, and the like. The wife may begin to compete with her husband at home, by assuming various dominant roles, which in a hundred and one ways subtly undermine the power of the male. Most women are quite unconscious of the fact that they are engaging in such competition with their husbands and are hurt and bewildered when they are accused of doing so. And this is the tragic element in the situation, for American women mean to be as good wives as women are anywhere.

Comparisons are notoriously odious, but it is true that on the whole European women make better wives than American women. Such a statement is no discredit to the American woman. The American woman has had to pass through much more turmoil and change than her European counterpart to attain her present freedoms, while the historical necessities of her development in this country have been quite different from anything that occurred in Europe. I am referring, in particular, to the pioneering spirit which the American woman was called on to exhibit in common with her husband in the settlement of America and the consequences of this for both sexes. From the first, women played a more dominant role in the family in America than they did in Europe. However this may be, in Europe women can accept the fact that they are women and be glad of it. The European woman is not bedeviled by doubts about her role; for her, it is precisely defined, and she suffers from no confusion of goals. Her life is focused principally on the happiness of her husband and children, and this is likely to be satisfying to everyone concerned. European women, it has been said, seem to behave as if they loved their husbands. In comparison, American women appear to behave toward their husbands as if they merely liked them. This is, no doubt, somewhat off the mark, but there is perhaps just enough truth in the comment to make it worth considering.

What the American woman needs is sympathetic understanding and help. She could be given a great deal more of both than she is now receiving, especially from that quarter to which she must look most for help—an adequate American male.

The American way of birth

In America almost 100 percent of women have their babies in hospitals. Ninety-six percent do not breastfeed their babies. Just as few doctors who would be willing to make a house call can be found, so there are practically no obstetricians who would be willing to deliver a baby at home. Yet that is, in my view, where babies should be born, in the home, in the bosom of the family, where they belong, not in a hospital. A hospital is a good place to enter, if one must, and leave as soon as possible. Disorder and disease may be alleviated in a hospital, but mother and baby are neither a disease nor a disorder, although they have been frequently treated as such by some obstetricians. This is absurd, atrociously absurd. The birth of a child is not a disease, a disorder, or an abnormality, although in a very real sense the medical profession manages on occasion to produce such conditions in what would in a home delivery have resulted in a perfectly healthy mother and infant.

Outside a sewer, a hospital is probably the unhealthiest place for a human being to be in. More people carrying a greater variety of bugs and parasites of all sorts congregate in a hospital than they do in any other place. Hence, the possibilities of cross infection are not inconsiderable, and cross infections in the nurseries in which newborn babies are kept constitute a problem in all hospitals.

The very fact that an institution is associated with disease and accident, with suffering and danger, would, one would have thought, have constituted a barrier against its ever having been considered as a place in which to have a baby. But the doctors did not consider it so. On the other hand, beginning in the sixties of the last century, they found it much more convenient to have all their "patients" about to have a baby in one place so that they were no longer obliged to travel all over the map to the homes of the impending mothers.

Whatever the rationalizations offered since, this was and continues to be the reason for the hospitalization of the "patient" suffering from the "disease" of pregnancy: the convenience of the doctors. But surely it is not so much the convenience of the doctor that should be considered when the birth of a baby is involved as the convenience of the mother and the baby, and let us not omit considering the convenience of the family.

The birth of a baby, the welcoming of a new member into the family, should be an event in which the whole family is involved—a family event, a family celebration. It is an event which is demeaned when it is treated as if it were a problem to be processed by an I.B.M. machine, yet that is very much the manner in which it is and has for many years been dealt with in the United States. In America there is a strong tendency to believe that if anything can be taken out of human hands, especially out of the human heart, and put through a machine, progress has been made. That is one of the reasons why Americans prefer factory-made goods to homemade goods. They would also seem to prefer factory-made to homemade babies.

The typical history of the birth of a baby in the United States is as follows: When labor begins, usually in the early hours of the morning, the husband telephones the obstetrician, who after a few inquiries either says, "Wait awhile longer," or says, "Take her to the hospital." At the hospital, where she may never have before been, the mother, now regularly experiencing labor pains, is taken into an office, while her husband waits outside, and she is there asked to give her biography and other details, all these irrelevancies at a time when more than at any other she is in need, not of an interrogation, but of a comfortable bed, the sound of a comforting voice, and the touch of a hand that is warm and reassuring. After the frequently agonizing experience of admission into this strange antiseptic environment, the abandoned mother is taken up to the delivery room, where she undresses, is put into a gown, and is emptied on to the delivery table, where, as she lies on her back, her legs are elevated and strapped into stirrups. In this undignified position she may be left alone for a considerable time, with an occasional nurse or intern popping in to inquire whether all is going well. It is not, but the poor abandoned woman rarely has the courage to say so.

The obstetrician may or may not arrive in time for the delivery of the baby. This is usually just as well, for most babies get themselves born without any assistance from anyone. With the arrival of the baby the cord is clamped or cut and tied, the cheeselike substance (*Vernix caseosa*) covering the body of the baby is washed away, and the two human beings who have been so long together are now, when they most need each other, put asunder. The mother is taken to her room, and the baby is carried away to the nursery, so called, of course, because no nursing is done in it. Here, the baby having been weighed, measured, recorded, and footprinted, a name and number are hung round the neck or wrist of the new arrival, who is then placed in a crib to howl away to his heart's discontent. And this is the way the American child is started off in life! On a wholly erroneous theory he will not be fed for at least twenty-four hours, and when he is fed, it will be with cow's milk, not the colostrum so important to him at this period, while his mother will be deprived of the benefits which his suckling will confer on her (constriction of uterine blood vessels, arrest of bleeding, detachment and ejection of the placenta, and beginning of the return of the uterus to normal size—which in the absence of a suckling baby it will never attain).

Meanwhile, the father has been kept anxiously waiting in a corridor, as abandoned by his wife and child as he has involuntarily abandoned them, when, of course, he should be participating in the birth of his child by his wife's side. That this is not permitted, except in a few hospitals, and that all the inhumanities that occur in connection with the birth of a baby should be as taken for granted as they are constitute an abject commentary on the average American's understanding of the needs and nature of human beings—infants, children, and adults.

Obstetricians consider any mother desirous of having her baby at home eccentric and strongly to be discouraged by making it quite clear that they will not be party to any such folly. Since they, the obstetricians, have rendered the midwife virtually as obsolete as the dodo, there is hardly an American woman under middle age alive who knows what a midwife is. What obstetricians are interested in is in delivering babies and charging the proper fee. This is one way to run a railroad, but it is no way to bring human beings into the world. I would like to see midwives restored to their proper place in American society. I would like to see them trained, examined, licensed, and encouraged to practice one of the most important professions possible for any human being. There isn't a thing the obstetrician can do that a well-trained midwife could not do at least as well. A woman, especially one who has had children, has a fellow feeling and understanding of the needs of a woman who is about to have a baby that no male obstetrician could possibly ever have. Another thing: there are not a sufficient number of obstetricians to take care of pregnant women either in the antenatal or the perinatal periods. Midwives could take a great deal of the pressure off obstetricians, could help them humanize the practice of obstetrics, and could leave the obstetrician to minister to the needs of mother and developing fetus much more effectively during the pregnancy period. The delivery of the baby can be safely left to the midwife. The whole business of birth—and it has become big business—has been so surrounded with mystery and anxiety and the fear that something may go wrong that most women have been led to believe that the presence of a highly qualified obstetrician is absolutely necessary at the birth of the baby, that his presence will ensure the maximum chance of everything's going well, that emergencies will be obviated.

The truth is, as I have already remarked, that most babies will get themselves born without assistance from anyone, that birth is not a hazardous process, but that it is rendered so by the fear and mystery and awe and danger with which it has been surrounded, and that "emergencies" at a generous estimate occur in 1 out of 200 cases. If a woman is the two-hundredth case, then surely she should have the benefit of the presence of someone who knows exactly what to do, and there is no reason why the midwife cannot act in this role. For emergencies of a serious nature, there is no reason why the humane community cannot have automotive units equipped with everything necessary which, upon the announcement of the impending birth of a child, can be waiting outside the home, with obstetrical intern and nurse who can be putting the time waiting to good use by studying the current literature or even playing a game of chess, for their services will rarely be required.

It is an interesting fact that not only are the mortality rates lower for the mother and infant delivered at home, compared with those delivered in a hospital, but even premature babies also do better in the home than they do in a hospital!

The little adults

AMERICANS PROBABLY have the shortest period of adolescence of any people in the world—not physiological adolescence so much as psychological adolescence. The situation is paradoxical. While there is a preternaturally high premium placed on youth, no one but the old really wants to be young, and in America one is old at thirty-five. The young want to be adult not as soon as possible, but sooner than possible. And adults cooperate with the young to help them achieve a spurious version of maturity. As soon as possible, the little "man" is put into long pants, and the little "woman" into high heels. In high school or even before, girls adopt high heels, lipstick, mascara, adult hairdos, and other badges of mature womanhood.

The only thing wrong with all this is that these little adults are masquerading under false colors. Lipstick is not an evidence of maturity, any more than long pants are. These external marks are a validation of nothing more than a counterfeit, a profound confusion of roles, statuses, and age grades. Too many parents actively contribute to this confusion, to such an extent, indeed, that it is often difficult to distinguish the parents from the children.

Children, it cannot be too often said, want their parents to be parents, not *pals*. They expect and want discipline. They want as firm a "Nay" as a "Yea." They want guidance, not a debating society in which everyone is equal. Children want parents to whom they can look up, not on whom they can look down. They want parents whose judgments they can respect and whose examples they can follow. Some years ago a visitor to these shores remarked how impressed he was by the American family. What impressed him most, he said, was the manner in which American parents obeyed their children! Too many parents are really afraid of their children. They are so afraid of doing the wrong thing that they do what is most pleasing, in their view, to the child. What is most pleasing to the child may be extremely undesirable for his healthy development as a human being.

One of the most undesirable weaknesses on the part of parents is to encourage or allow their children to assume roles which are the prerogatives of older age grades and for which they are in no way fitted. Development is a gradual process, proceeding step by step in an orderly progression. It takes years of gradually acquired experience in order to be able to leave one stage of growth before one is able to develop into the other. Growth is increase in dimension, in depth, in size. Development is increase in complexity, in understanding.

Adolescence, in particular, is the period during which one gradually grows out of childhood and prepares to develop into adulthood. It is a critically important period of development, which has to be taken slowly, gradually. Telescoping the whole period of adolescence into a short traverse, for the most part improvised, between childhood and technical adulthood is damaging and is to miss the whole meaning of development.

Someone once remarked that America may yet turn out to

be the only example in history of a society which has passed from barbarism to decadence without the intervening benefits of civilization. That observation may yet be reified. If it is, it may prove to be not unrelated to the fact that so many Americans have passed from childhood to technical adulthood without the intervening benefits of development from adolescence to maturity.

Because of this contraction of what should be a long-extended period of development, a great many Americans remain in a state of arrested adolescence all their lives. Older men and women call each other boys and girls and only too often behave as such. No doubt the cult of youth has something to do with this condition of arrested adolescence. Not being mature enough to appreciate the disadvantages of an arrested adolescence, they strive to perpetuate the state. Since they have never really ceased to be children, they deceive themselves in the belief that if they try hard enough, they need never cease being young.

It is, indeed, highly desirable to die young—late, maturely young, but not immaturely young. The immaturity of so many technically adult Americans is responsible for so much that is half-baked in American culture. Premature adults, like premature babies, are underdeveloped, and underdeveloped adults, no matter what their ages, are unfit for adult roles requiring maturity of judgment.

The sad fact is that there are millions of arrested adolescents masquerading as technical adults. They look like adults, their years would suggest that they are adults, and they play adult roles; but they are not in fact adults. They are adults only by law, but measured by the laws of maturity, they are children. The sooner we recognize this fact and its causes, the sooner we shall be in a position to do what must be done to help everyone mature at the rate at which they ought.

The cult of youthfulness

To be over forty in the United States is a sin against both the flesh and the spirit. It represents a fall from grace. There is no profit in it; the profits are all to the industries that cater to the young or would-be young. To be young, to be beautiful, to be handsome—what else matters? If a woman is young and beautiful, nothing else matters, and if she is neither young nor beautiful, nothing else matters either. Like a young beautiful woman, a handsome man can go a long way. In a man's world the premium placed on youth is far greater for women than for men; hence, women never tell their age, unless they are young enough to find it no handicap. Since men are a scarcity commodity—there are 3,500,000 more women in the United States than men—women are forced to make themselves as desirable as possible and to remain as desirable as long as possible to men—hence, the great preoccupation of women with youth and beauty and the high valuation placed on them by males. It is very hard on women and consumes an enormous amount of their time and energy. Young women have to catch husbands, and married women feel that in order to hold theirs, they must continue to look young—doesn't Clairol tell them so?

What is so iniquitous about the cult of youthfulness is that it places an unduly high value on a phase of development which is transitory and must in time pass for everyone. The trouble with youth, Bernard Shaw once remarked, is that it is wasted on youth, and he might have added that when it is gone, the no longer youthful try to make up for it. The emphasis on youthfulness is an evidence of insecurity, a fear of aging, of not being in the swing, of becoming superfluous, and ultimately an unwillingness to face the fact of human mortality. These are immature attitudes and reflect the failure of a culture to prepare its members to be their age and to define for them, and enable them to play, the roles appropriate to their age.

In a culture in which men place so high a premium on youthfulness in women and in which the workaday world of that culture places an equally high premium on youthfulness, youthfulness will understandably come to be regarded as a quality of the highest value. Hence, if the cult of youthfulness is ever to be relegated to the museum of false values, its damaging consequences will first have to be recognized, and healthier attitudes toward the various age phases will have to be cultivated. Since the whole of America is geared to youth—education, industry, advertising, the movies, the theater, TV, the magazines, the novel all are oriented toward the support and aggrandizement of youth—an implicit disrespect for and undervaluation of the older age grades become endemic. This is, of course, reflected in the manner in which Americans brush the problems of the aging, its so-called senior citizens, under the rug. For all practical purposes the aging do not exist, and if they do, then they do not matter. The disregard for the aging is one of the worst of the damaging effects of the cult of youthfulness. It is dehumanizing, and that is another of the detrimental effects of this cult. But most of all, it is damaging to the individuals who suffer from it, for what it does in effect is to focus their energies on remaining young so that they neglect attending to the process of growing old. Hence, when age finally catches up with them, they often experience it as a trauma, instead of what it could have been—an enriching and rewarding enlargement of one's life and horizons and, in many ways, a much happier period than that of the *Sturm und Drang* of youth.

The teen-age culture

TEEN-AGERS ARE PROBLEMS in search of a solution. Most of the problems they are seeking to solve were created for them by adults. It is, therefore, not a little amusing to hear adults complaining and criticizing teen-agers, whom, they declare, they cannot understand. The failure to understand is understandable and constitutes yet another testimony to the fact that human beings quickly forget what it was like to be a child, especially a teen-ager. They also forget or seldom seem to realize that teen-agers belong to another generation, with all the changes and problems which have accumulated with the passage of the years. It is not only old problems but also new ones, of which their parents are frequently unaware, that teen-agers are called on to solve, problems which have developed beyond anything with which they were challenged during their own teen-age.

It is not a new problem. It is as old as urbanism—which is about 10,000 years old—for age and youth to live in different worlds, with different interests and different aspirations. Shakespeare expressed it beautifully when he wrote:

> Crabbed age and youth cannot live together:
> Youth is full of pleasance, age is full of care;
> Youth like summer morn, age like winter weather;

> Youth like summer brave, age like winter bare.
> Youth is full of sport, age's breath is short,
> Youth is nimble, age is lame;
> Youth is hot and bold, age is weak and cold;
> Youth is wild, and age is tame.

Contemporary teen-agers are, however, something new in a new world. They have become an autonomous group, recognizing itself as such and more or less sequestrating itself from the adult group. What has appeared, probably for the first time in the Western world, is a teen-age culture, a way of life with which teen-agers, as individuals, identify themselves and which they find meaningful. The songs, the lyrics, the records, the dances, the clothes, and the like constitute the external evidences of a clear dissociation from the adult world.

Teen-agers have virtually declared their independence of the adult world. And in all this they are encouraged by a catering agent of the adult world, the world of business. The teen-ager is very big business. Since there are today more teen-agers than ever before, the encouragements each receives from the business world are considerable. The market being what it is, there is seemingly no end to the way in which it can be exploited. Even the hotel business has gotten into the act, and not only do teen-agers swarm to such places as Fort Lauderdale, where the boys are, but at their junior college recesses they also descend like locusts on such green isles as Bermuda, where the take is enormous.

Such phenomena as James Dean, the Beatles and their innumerable imitators, Joan Baez, and Bob Dylan would be impossible without the support of teen-agers. The magazines that cater to the needs of teen-agers constitute a very profitable industry, and a large number of TV programs are designed for the same market. So while the adult world of parents criticizes teen-agers on the one hand, the business world, on the other, gives them all the support and encouragement they need to go on doing all that the world of parental figures disapproves.

The truth is that teen-agers are the scapegoats of adults. Adults expect teen-agers to be problems, and so they specify the conditions and the behavior they expect them to exhibit, in a self-fulfilling prophecy, and that is exactly what they get.

It is not enough to say that teen-agers have weathered adults before and that they will do so again. Of course, they will, but it would be a great deal happier for everyone if the passage from adolescence to adulthood were made a little less stormy. Fortunately, there are at work today large numbers of students of the problem, whose findings, when taken seriously, hold out some promise for the future.

Times change—do people?

"TIMES CHANGE." It is an interesting expression. What it means, of course, is that in different periods, ideas, customs, and practices change. Time itself does not change, but conditions and events in the course of time do. Rates of social change vary. Whereas some social changes take place at a rate which renders it easy to adjust to them, others occur at a rate which not only makes adjustment difficult, but can also be very disequilibrating. During the last fifty years social changes have occurred at such an acceleratingly rapid rate that many of us have been hard put to it to keep up with some of them.

Two great world wars have transformed many of our institutions and have shaken others to their foundations. Among these, the character of the family and the roles of the sexes have been markedly affected. Not only have men and women changed in relation to one another, but they have also changed as parents in relation to children. Of course, children have changed, too. The interesting thing about this is that, without its scarcely having been noticed, children have for the first time in the history of Western civilization become agents, independent of their parents, of challenging social change.

[224

Within the family there has been a remarkable change in the roles played by parents. Whereas in former times father was the undisputed head of the family, today he remains so only in a titular sense. The situation resembles that of a constitutional monarchy, where the reigning sovereign retains his title, but the actual head of the government is the prime minister. The prime minister to her husband and children is the American mother.

The automobile has made it possible for father to work a considerable commuting time away from home so that he often rises before the children do and sees them only for a brief period on his return from work and during the weekends. The principal parental figure, therefore, is the mother. In earlier times father worked nearer home, was often home for lunch, and in the evenings saw a good deal of his children. He was a presence; today he is more nearly an "absence." The presence is mother; it is she whom the children see most of and whom they hear most from. It is she who is principally responsible for bringing up the children, and she is their chief discipliner. Nowhere in the Western world is there a father who less resembles a figure of authority than the American father. The American father has become a friend, a pal, to his children. It is he who often attempts to soften mother's disciplinary action and to intercede with her in behalf of the children on other occasions. The children will frequently call father by his first name, and father will often behave toward them as if they were members of his own age grade. Sometimes mother, in order to maintain a certain consistency in the relationship with the children, following the example set by father, will also permit her children to call her by her first name. But even where parents are called Mom and Dad, where the relationship is that of friends, rather than that of parents to the children, especially on the part of the father, children are seriously deprived of the example of a mature adult on whom to model their behavior.

The confusion of roles is further compounded for the children when they observe the generality of male adults to whom they are exposed behaving in the immature manner in which they usually do. There are in the United States vast numbers of technically adult males who have scarcely ever uttered a serious word in their lives. Their role in life seems to be to play the fool, to behave like a kid, a form of behavior which appropriately enough is called kidding. Of course, there are many men who do not behave this way. I am speaking only of the very large number that do.

Then there are the women who have been forced into the position of feeling that they must look and behave like girls. Times have changed since the days when a married woman was required to look and act like a mature one. Today she is required to look and act whatever age she chooses to arrest herself at. It is scarcely to be wondered that many such mothers fail to command the respect of their daughters. Mothers and fathers who cannot be their age cannot expect their children to be *their* age. The children, having no clearly defined age grades to fill, strive to become premature adults. They want to be grown-up as soon as possible, and so little boys are put into long trousers at an early age and are treated as little men, and as older children, they are dressed and encouraged to behave like adults. They drive cars as soon as, and often sooner than, the legal age permits, and in their early teens they date girls. Parents take pride in putting them into tuxedos and buying for them the corsage to present to the girl. The girl gets into high heels and silk stockings as quickly as she can, rouges her lips, paints her fingernails, and altogether makes it as difficult to distinguish her from her mother as she can. It is not that she wishes to be identified with her mother, but with her mother's age grade. She becomes a premature woman while she is still an immature girl.

The result of all this is that both boys and girls in America tend to miss out on a fundamentally important period of development, the period of adolescence. The average American tends to leap from childhood to adulthood without the intervening benefits of a normal period of maturation, maturation from childhood to adulthood. Adolescence is telescoped into a very short period and hurried through so rapidly that not only is there no time to prepare to be an adult, but there is also no time in which to leave childhood behind. This seems to me the principal, if not the exclusive, reason for the juvenile character of so many technically adult Americans.

Development is a steplike process in which every step must follow the preceding one in orderly succession. Omission of any step leads to incomplete development. Omission of a large number of steps leads to a massive failure of development. It is for this reason that so many Americans remain arrested at some stage of adolescence. It is an interesting fact, easily verified, that when one asks American adults what age, altogether apart from actual age, they think of themselves as being, they generally give an age considerably younger than they are, quite often in the teens. Altogether apart from the emphasis and high valuation placed on youthfulness, I believe, this identification of one's feeling tone about one's age with a developmental age much younger than one's chronological age constitutes an implicit recognition and evidence of the fact that in certain fundamental respects the individual has not developed beyond the age at which he thinks of himself.

It is no new observation that in America a great premium

is placed on youth. Men and women are often congratulated on their youthfulness when they should be commiserated with for their immaturity. Immaturity and youthfulness are very different things and should not be confused with each other.

Just as children expect and want their parents to be parents, not pals, so parents should help their children to be their age and assist them to pass from one indispensable stage of development to another as gracefully as possible. A certain amount of trauma, frustration, and turmoil is incident to and is a necessary condition of the process of growth. The adolescent is leaving the world of childhood behind him, seeking independence, while he is taking his first tentative steps in the direction of becoming an adult. And it *is* a becoming. When we interfere with this becoming and truncate it, as we so often do, the adolescent never succeeds in fully becoming an adult. The physical metamorphosis from child to adult is completed because there is not much that we can do to arrest that, but the psychological, the maturational, metamorphosis is never completed.

The consequences for any society of a large number of its members' remaining immature in a world requiring maturity of judgment and conduct can be serious, if not lethal. These are matters to which, I think, Americans ought to devote a good deal more attention than they have thus far done.

Arising out of the many social changes that have occurred during the last fifty years has been another unique development. This is the increased autonomy of children, especially of adolescents, their increasing independence of the control and discipline of their parents and other adults. This, in my view, is a very serious symptom of social breakdown, for children are not able to go it alone. Children, especially adolescents, need the help, support, and guidance of their elders. Because children have been set such poor examples by their elders and because of the weak self-discipline of so many parents in inadequate discipline and control of children, the latter tend to drift away from parents and other adult authority figures, who are promptly identified with weakness, into an undisciplined and disillusioned search for their own values. Almost all those who become beatniks are of this kind. The phenomenon is worldwide and represents a breakdown not so much in the discipline of children as in the discipline of those who become parents.

Premature imitation adults feel that they must marry as early as possible, and girls now do so in their later teens and boys in their early twenties. In this way they think to acquire the status of instant adulthood. In their mutual relations and in the raising of a family, the immaturities of such premature adults will inevitably be visited on each other and on their children. In this way their own immaturities will be perpetuated in their children. On a grand scale this is going on before our eyes, and most of us do not seem to understand what is happening. The most important and the most responsible job in the world, parentage, is being increasingly undertaken by individuals who are unprepared for it. Nowadays we often hear the trend to early marriage attributed to the consciousness of the young that they are living in a apocalyptic age, that there is not much time left, that they want to live while there is yet time, and that, therefore, they want to get as much as they can of life into as short a time as possible. These may well be contributing factors in many cases, but in a large number it is evident that the immaturity factor plays a highly significant role.

Just as the economic dependency of the young has been extended into adulthood, so the great change that has occurred in men and women is the increased extension of their immaturity. If I seem to belabor this point, I do so because I do not think that it has received the attention it deserves. The roles of men and women as parents have undergone revolutionary change, and on the whole this change has been for the worse—for the worse because the net result has been the weakening of parental discipline, the confusion and asymmetric sharing of parental responsibilities, and the devastating effects that these changes have exercised on children and the adults they in turn become.

Happily, human beings are the most highly educable of all creatures. The errors we have learned we can unlearn. The errors we have committed we can learn to correct. We can best begin, I believe, by asking ourselves the question of questions, no less than : what is human life for? Is the success of a human life to be measured by the material possessions and physical comforts with which one has been able to surround oneself, or is it to be measured by the quality of a life—a life that is lived in the endeavor to realize and fulfill its humanity, in the service of that larger humanity of which we all are an indissoluble part? The healthy functioning and the very survival of humanity have today become a joint enterprise in which everyone must participate. To participate in that larger humanity, we must first fulfill the promise of the humanity that is in all of us, and to that end all of us must be helped by those who are able to do so.

We often refer to ours as a child-centered culture, by which we mean not only that our attention is focused on children, but also that we believe that if we do the right thing by children, they will grow up to be the kinds of persons we would like them to be. The trouble with this viewpoint is that if those who are engaged in bringing up children are inadequate to the task, they will produce inadequate children and, therefore, inadequate adults. Quite clearly what is necessary at the present time is not so much a child-centered culture as an adult-centered culture. We need to focus more attention on ourselves as adults who stand very much in need of an overhauling, a self-examination, a self-maturing, and a self-disciplining, so that we become more responsible selves to the other selves we are engaged in creating.

A child needs to know that maturation is part of his development, and he has to have examples on which to base his own growth and development as a mature human being. These the parents should provide.

What parents can do to become more self-disciplined, more mature, and therefore more effective is to come to an understanding with themselves and with their spouse that parentage is a serious responsibility, no less than the making or unmaking of a life, and to realize that since it is from them that the children will learn most of the techniques of being human, it is up to them to assume that responsibility. To be responsible to others, one must be responsible to oneself for the government of one's own personality and affairs. The best model a parent can provide a child is a disciplined self-governing personality. It is never too late to begin. Without becoming too solemn about it and always retaining that interior perspective which is a sense of humor, one can begin the necessary changes in oneself by concentrating on the task of daily improvements in behavior by being loving *and* firm, by not being any more overpermissive with oneself than with one's children, by resisting all impulsive behavior, by thinking twice or even thrice before acting, by treating seriously and not frivolously all problems, by taking an active interest in social and political affairs, by being responsible to one's society, as well as to one's home, by ceasing to compete with others, and by exhibiting more cooperative behavior.

Respect for oneself must be accompanied by respect for one's children. One begins here by treating one's children as children, not as small adults.

Husband and wife can greatly help each other to achieve self-discipline and greater maturity by agreeing with each other to do so. Parentage is a cooperative enterprise, in which the roles of mother and father are complementary. Traits of character, responsibility, enterprise, resolution, courage, and dependability must be inculcated in children. In this the father plays a dominant role. He should attend to these traits in himself, for the old adage that children learn more from example than they do from precept has not been abrogated. Love, sweet reasonableness, orderliness, gentleness, altruism, idealism, habits of work, self-discipline, and the like are traits in whose development both parents must participate. Parenthood is itself a discipline that has to be worked at, and like all work that is to be well done, it must be taken seriously; taken so, it should be the most rewarding and pleasurable of labors.

The American father

IN RECENT YEARS we have heard a great deal about the serious effects of maternal deprivation on the development of children. Comparatively little has been heard concerning the equally seriously deteriorating effects of paternal deprivation. Yet a great deal of work has been done on this subject both in this country and abroad. The results are everywhere in agreement: father is not only necessary, but when he behaves as if he were not, the whole family, especially the children, suffer.

It is not surprising to learn from these researches that inadequate fathers are remote from their children in what has become an increasingly acceptable social way. Superficially the family appears adequately socially and emotionally organized, the husband seeming to exercise the usual controls. That is to say, he *seems* to be the head of the family, to play the dominant role, to be aware of his obligations, and so on. In fact, the husband's role as father is ill defined and weak. The breadwinner in such families does not participate in the making of family decisions or in discipline of the children. The mother in these families has taken over these obligations. Remaining on the outskirts of the family, such men were found to be neither happy nor unhappy with this arrangement. Social participation in the lives of their children was either negative or minimal. There was no involvement, such fathers pursuing a recreational and social life separate from or at most tangential to that of their children. Investigation of such men indicated that they had themselves not experienced satisfactory relationships with their fathers.

Research has shown that quite frequently such unsatisfactory father-child relationships are consciously or unconsciously fostered by the mother. Such women are usually unconsciously, but quite transparently, hostile toward men, unsure of themselves, and tend to be troubled by a feeling of personal unworthiness and incompleteness. Their relationships as children with their own father and brothers appear to have been unsatisfactory and frustrating. Such women tend to arrange things so that the father is excluded or isolated from intimate participation in the family. Father in this manner confined to the periphery of the family circle, mother makes herself the focus of attention, and the child tends to identify with her rather than with the blurred image of the father, with resulting serious confusions and disorders in the child. Some of the symptoms shown by boys in such families are underachievement in school; nervousness, overprotection, infantilization, and fearfulness; depression, crying spells, and moodiness; low self-esteem, easily hurt, few friends, shyness, and few outside activities; excessive daydreaming; overt anger; and effeminate behavior. Obesity, headaches, ulcerative colitis, recurrent vomiting, tics, bedwetting, and fecal incontinence are frequent associated symptoms.

The unfulfilled and unfulfilling father in such families, achieving none of the gratifications which come from involvement as a parent with his children, is naturally dissatisfied with the diminished position in which he finds himself in the home. Under such conditions he tends to seek release

from this attenuated status and to find expression for himself in the diversion of his available free energy into channels in which he can feel more adequate. The result of this usually is a worsening of his inadequacies as a father by overinvestment in gratifications obtained from activities away from the home.

The boy suffering from paternal deprivation lacks the opportunity for identifying himself with the male sex, while the girl is deprived of the opportunity for developing her own role in relation to men. Research has shown that this situation affects the development of the child's concept of himself and his ability to get along with others, and he grows up uncertain of his relation to others.

It used to be thought that the young child had a need only or principally of his mother. There is evidence he needs male adults as well. Young children, in America, are almost exclusively in the care of women during their early years—at home, in nursery school, in kindergarten, and in the early grades. This imbalance, however, can be corrected by the love and support a father can give a child at home. When this love and guidance are not present, children are often confused and upset. The child is going to live in a world of two sexes. Simply on the face of it, it would seem desirable that the child should enjoy the benefits of socialization by both males and females.

The art of parenthood is one that both males and females must learn. The young depend primarily on the example set by their parents. Girls have a head start generally on boys because a great part of their maturation is directed toward motherhood. The biological processes involved in the development of motherhood are somewhat more complexly developed in the female than in the male. Important as the father is, a mother, of course, is of necessity closer to and more deeply involved in her child, from the outset, than a father is.

To become a biological father is not difficult. To be an adequate father is quite another matter. It is an art—most proficiently learned from one's own father and from an awareness of what being a good father means.

What then is the role of the father, the good father?

From the outset the father's task should consist in assisting his wife in the care of the dependent infant insofar as he is able. This is not to say that the father is cast in the role of a mere appendage to his wife. But it is to say that there is a difference in the roles of mother and father. Where the mother is naturally prepared to minister to the infant's needs, the father must grow into the ability to do so. But in order to do so, he must *feel* involved. Being a good parent is a talent, and it is a talent which is essentially best expressed by the word "involvement."

The father's role complements that of the mother at every stage of the child's development. Within the first three years he will do whatever he can to lighten his wife's tasks and give the child as much attention as possible. From the fourth year on, while the mother's role will continue to be to attend to the needs of the child within the home, to ground him, as it were, in the domestic and humane virtues, the father's role will begin in the training of his child in the more character-building and urbane virtues. Maternal and paternal roles cannot and should not be dissociated from each other. Those roles will intergrade, overlap, complement, and support each other. It is, however, a help to know what the other parent's role should be. One of the difficulties with many contemporary families is that the parents have only the sketchiest and most confused ideas of their roles as parents. For such people, being a parent becomes very much a hit-or-miss affair, in which the child gets both hit and missed. In the contemporary family the mother has been forced to take over a considerable part of the role which should be that of the father.

It is true that children have been raised successfully without benefit of a father about the house. But in many such cases the exclusively feminine upbringing has resulted in more or less obvious failures of personality development. In the case of males there is often produced a feminization of personality in which masculine traits are more or less defectively, if at all, developed. Such persons can be and often are fine human beings, but they cannot be and in fact are not adequately developed males. In the case of females the result of an exclusively feminine upbringing tends to be excessive feminization, with the focus of interest directed toward other females and a concomitant inability to relate to males. In the absence of a male or males to relate to, they have simply failed to learn how to relate to males. An unsatisfactory father can produce exactly the same effect. His daughters reject him and, with him, all males and identify themselves with the father image of their own creation. Precisely the same mechanism is operative in boys in relation to their fathers.

The pattern of this type of rejection of the father may take other forms: in girls it may take the form of a contemptuous attitude toward males; in males it may, and, alas, only too often does, result in an equally contemptuous attitude toward females. When two such persons come together in marriage, the consequences for them, their children, and the community are not happy ones.

The patriarchal family of an earlier generation, in which the government of the family was conducted by the father, has in our own time given way to the matriarchal family, in which the governing force is the mother. Her rule is pervasive, if not absolute. The fiction that father is the head of the family and that he is master of the household is maintained, for purely bureaucratic purposes, but he is in fact seldom more than the titular head, a figurehead. Fatherhood has indeed fallen into low esteem, father having been the architect of his own fallen fortunes. A full day's work away from home, the distractions and burdens of his employment, his fatigue, and other preoccupations—all have contributed to his virtual abdication of his role as a parent, a father. Once a year, on Father's Day, that lucrative invention of the business world, he may be reminded of his putative role as a father, but his heart isn't in it.

So little do many men understand their role as a father and so little do they take that role seriously that many a father has experienced some difficulty in thinking of himself as such, except in the narrow technical sense. Instead, with the best of intentions, such fathers often think of their children as pals, buddies, friends. Good intentions are no substitute for the work that almost anything worth doing requires. It cannot be too often repeated that the father who treats his children as if they were his pals and encourages them to call him by his first name serves his children ill. Children are not the equals of adults, still less of their parents, and should not be treated as such. Children are growing and developing human beings, who need all the guidance they can receive from people whom they can trust, respect, and follow. Children don't want to be treated as equals, still less as pals. What they want is a firm hand at the helm, which will serve to pilot them into the safe harbor of their own growth and developmental abilities, upon which they may safely make their landfall. If they don't receive the help of father, they will have a hard time dropping anchor anywhere.

In the development of every human being the presence of

a mother *and* a father are essential and vital experiences. From the earliest days of his being, the infant grows to recognize that deeply involved in his welfare are two sorts of human beings, a mother and father, a woman and a man, who vary from each other in quality, appearance, touch, texture, voice, and smell. It is from these early experiences that the child learns to distinguish the maternal and paternal, the feminine and masculine roles, and to identify himself with the appropriate one, while incorporating elements of the other's qualities in himself.

A weak or inadequate father will produce an imbalance in both his male and his female children in response to the inadequacies of the experiences they undergo in relation to the father, and the absence of a father may leave a serious lacuna in the feelings of such children which they may experience great difficulty in developing later.

Children learn through the imitation and repetition of acts modeled on and conditioned by their parents. These are the images upon which the clay that is the child is molded. "And no man," as Plutarch said, "ever wetted clay and then left it, as if there would be bricks by chance and fortune." The clay and other ingredients out of which the bricks are made which go to build a human being have to be shaped by the parents. To the extent that parents fail in this task, to that extent, is the resulting edifice likely to be insubstantial and defective. The father's role as an architect of his children's growth and development is fundamental.

Fathers especially must face the fact that we generally expect our children to be better than we are ourselves, and we often expect more of them than we are ourselves willing to take the trouble to achieve. It is wisest to face one's own faults and inadequacies and to do something about them. Children learn quite as much from their parents' faults and deficiencies as they do from their virtues, and even more from those evidences, however small, of their parents' attempts to deal with their own problems.

We come now to the answer to the question we originally asked: what then is the role of the father, the good father?

The role of the father should be to behave toward the members of his family in such a manner that he confers survival benefits upon them in a creatively enlarging manner —in brief, to be loving toward them; to love with the firmness and the fairness which enables one to say "No" when that should be said and equally to say "Yes" when that is indicated; to build up a sense of justice, responsibility, courage, resoluteness, integrity, resourcefulness, honesty, sincerity, kindness, thoughtfulness, gentleness, and compassion—all traits that are within the power of a loving father to communicate and to make part of his children. It is unrealistic even to suggest that if a father will be all these things to his children, then this is what his children will always be. They may or may not. But certainly they stand a much better chance of being characterized by such traits than if they had not been conditioned in them. The whole history of the human species is there to tell us that if the father is the man he is to the child, the child will be the father to the man he becomes largely because his own father was the man he was.

Ultimately, when everything has been said and done, more will have been said than done, but whatever is done, right or wrong, let it be done with love. For love has a firmness and discipline all of its own.

One of the lessons the father, especially, has to teach his children is humanity—that the humane approach is always to be preferred to any other in the resolution of any human problem, that violence should not even be considered as a last resort in the expression of one's views, as well as in one's conduct.

The tough guy, cowboy, roughrider, football hero approach represents a miguided attempt to compensate for ill-concealed feelings of inferiority, especially in the bringing up of boys by their fathers. Tenderness and gentleness are considered feminine traits, but they should no less so be masculine ones. Such traits are not incompatible with being a good football player or player of any other game. And apropos of games, here an excellent opportunity presents itself for father to teach his children some fundamental character traits: that one plays the game not in order to win, but for the delight in the game itself and in the show of skill, in the skill of others, as well as of one's own; that one adheres to the rules; that one plays chivalrously; that one does one's best; that one never takes an unfair advantage of one's adversaries; and that being a good loser is as much part of the value of the experience of playing as being a good winner.

Considerateness, sympathy, appreciation, tact, discretion, the courage of one's convictions, and the ability to state and act on them—these all are qualities within the power of the father to teach his children.

The encouragement of that most wonderful of traits called curiosity represents a whole complex of experiences which the father can put to the most constructively educative and socializing uses. Originality, inventiveness, adventuresomeness, the ability to profit from one's mistakes, and the joy of making, creating, discovering, manipulating, and controlling —these all are learning experiences from which the child can profit when the father works together with him on various tasks. Working with father and given the responsibility for his share of the work, the child learns not only that he is needed but what cooperation, as well as much else, means.

One cannot too strongly urge the necessity of father's working together with his children on various projects. Patience, carefulness, resourcefulness, stick-to-itiveness, the unwillingness to settle for second-rate or shoddy work, the ability to take and seek advice, the control and mastery and putting to good use of frustration, the satisfaction yielded by the consciousness of a job well done *because one worked hard at it*—these all are invaluable lessons that the father can teach. Above all, he can teach the lesson that happiness is not something that comes to one by providential assignment or something one sets out to secure, but rather that it comes to one as a by-product of other things, principally as a by-product of work, hard work, and most often as a consequence of very hard and trying work, of struggle, turmoil, and torment.

The habit of hard and regular periods of work is one that should be inculcated by father in his children from an early age—five years of age is early enough. As soon as possible, regular study periods should be instituted and gradually extended in duration so that by the time the teens are reached, three hours of study at home after school should be an established habit. Household duties suitable to the sex and age of the child should be encouraged. He should thus be encouraged to feel that he is a contributing member of the household, one who gives, ungrudgingly, what he is able in return for what he receives, learning in this way that while his parents have duties toward him, he has duties toward them.

To be a good father is not easy, but it is the most rewarding responsibility a man can ever undertake and the most gratifyingly creative. It is worth putting all that one has into it.

Masculine expression of emotion

AMERICAN MEN don't cry because it is considered unmasculine to do so. Only sissies cry. Crying is a "weakness" characteristic of the female, and no American male wants to be identified with anything in the least weak or feminine. Crying, in our culture, is identified with childishness, with weakness and dependence. No one likes a crybaby, and we disapprove of crying even in children, discouraging it in them as early as possible. In a land so devoted to the pursuit of happiness as ours, crying really is rather un-American. Adults must learn not to cry in situations in which it is permissible for a child to cry. Women being the "weaker" and "dependent" sex, it is only natural that they should cry in certain emotional situations. In women, crying is excusable. But in men, crying is a mark of weakness. So goes the American credo with regard to crying.

"A little man," we impress on our male children, "never cries. Only sissies and crybabies do." And so we condition males in America not to cry whenever they feel like doing so. It is not that American males are unable to cry because of some biological time clock within them which causes them to run down in that capacity as they grow older, but that they are trained not to cry. No "little man" wants to be like that "inferior creature," the female. And the worst thing you can call him is a sissy or crybaby. And so the "little man" represses his desire to cry and goes on doing so until he is unable to cry even when he wants to. Thus do we produce a trained incapacity in the American male to cry. And this is bad. Why is it bad? Because crying is a natural function of the human organism which is designed to restore the emotionally disequilibrated person to a state of equilibrium. The return of the disequilibrated organ systems of the body to steady states or dynamic stability is known as homeostasis. Crying serves a homeostatic function for the organism as a whole. Any interference with homeostatic mechanisms is likely to be damaging to the organism. And there is good reason to believe that the American male's trained incapacity to cry is seriously damaging to him.

It is unnecessary to cry whenever one wants to cry, but one should be able to cry when one ought to cry—when one needs to cry. For to cry under certain emotionally disequilibrating conditions is necessary for the maintenance of health.

On these matters we are strangely confused in our culture. Consider, for example, the behavior of husband and wife when a sudden catastrophe or bereavement befalls the family. The wife is likely to be prostrated with grief, shedding virtual waterfalls of tears. Having consumed all the linen in the household and having resorted to the bathroom mat, in the attempt to stanch the flood, she will furtively glance out of the corner of her eye admiringly at the heroic creature she married. So different from herself! There he stands, godlike, strong, silent, and with stiff upper lip, puffing away intrepidly at his pipe, without betraying a sign of the inner turmoil which is so outwardly visible in herself. What a noble creature is the male!

There indeed he may stand, but the truth is that he isn't

standing the situation anywhere nearly as well as his wife is managing it horizontally. For in his marmoreal ineffectuality, not only is the male being useless to everyone for miles around, but he is also perhaps being most useless to himself. For while his wife is doing what she ought, weeping away and thus restoring herself to a state of equilibrium as soon as possible, her husband, being utterly incapable of expressing his emotions through tears, is nevertheless expressing his emotions in the manner to which he has been accustomed by those who have trained him in his incapacity to cry. He turns his emotions into his body. Instead of expressing them overtly, he expresses them covertly; he interiorizes them; he somatizes them—that is to say, he expresses them through his body. Instead of weeping through his lachrymal apparatus he now begins to weep vicariously, either through his skin in the form of some sort of dermatological eruption, such as urticaria, psoriasis, boils, and itching. Or he turns his emotions into his respiratory system and comes up with a variety of asthmatoid conditions and begins to wheeze and whine and cough. Or he expresses himself through his gastrointestinal tract in the form of peptic ulcers of the stomach or duodenum or hyperirritability of the intestines or inflammation of the colon. Or he may express himself by expediting his emotions into his upper story and there begin to develop bats in his belfry in the form of a nervous breakdown. Or it may all go into his cardiovascular system, and there he may begin to develop heart or hypertensive symptoms. And so on most unmerrily, not to say unprofitably—except, of course, to the medical profession.

And there lies his grief-stricken wife, peeping worshipfully out of the corner of a moist eye at her seemingly composed husband, admiring him and depreciating herself for all the wrong reasons in the world. For it is he who is doing the wrong thing and she who is doing the right. The male by his stolid behavior is succeeding in damaging himself further, while the female is succeeding in restoring herself to a state of equilibrium and to continuing health. And this, supposedly, is why women are the weaker vessels and men are strong and resilient! The very opposite is the truth.

Women, by virtue of the availability of such outlets as crying for the expression of pent-up emotion, are likely to suffer from fewer psychosomatic disturbances than men.

I know of no studies on the expression of the emotions in businesswomen. But the increase in psychosomatic disorders among women in recent years—for example, the rise in the peptic ulcer rate—suggests that women in business may be attempting to restrain the normal expression of their emotions. If so, I would say that this is not good. Women in business who believe that in order to succeed, they must imitate men are barking up the wrong tree.

I am not suggesting that every time the boss bawls one out or every time one runs into a major frustration, one ought to assume the supine position and have a good cry. I think this would be silly. Crying should be reserved for the appropriate situation, and that is whenever one's organism indicates the necessity. In this respect the American male has a great deal to learn from the American female—whether in business or out of it. In business the emotions that are likely to be called into play are not those which usually lead to the desire to cry. On the contrary, they tend to be the angry emotions, and crying is not a natural way of expressing such emotions, nor is it being suggested that they should—even if they could—be so expressed. Opportunities to blow off steam in ways appropriate to the occasion should be provided until such time as we have contrived to produce human beings who have learned to deal with their frustrations in a constructive manner.

It would be absurd to suggest that the psychosomatic disorders from which men suffer in America are the result of the fact that they do not cry. The inability to cry is but one reflection of many indicating that the American male has not been taught how to use his emotions efficiently, and it is this general inefficient use of his emotions, rather than one particular expression of them, that is principally at fault. Nevertheless, it is agreed by most authorities that crying is a beneficial means of relieving the person of tensions which seek expression in this particular manner. It is far better that the energies which seek release in such emotional expression find an outlet in weeping than that they should be pent up to seek adventitious expression through the body.

Tears have been likened to the clarifying and beneficent effects of the rain which comes after a thunderstorm on a sultry summer day. It was Charles Dickens, a man, who wrote: "Heaven knows we need never be ashamed of our tears, for they are rain upon the blinding dust of earth, overlying our hard hearts." Indeed, the evidence on all sides supports the view that under the conditions which call for it, a good cry is a wonderful restorative. Hence, it may be concluded that although crying would hardly be a solution to all the difficulties of the American male, it would certainly be a help in some.

Perhaps it would be helpful if instead of so wholeheartedly pursuing the ideals of life, liberty, and happiness, we modified our orientation in the direction of life, liberty, and the pursuit of homeostasis. Perhaps, also, the institution of the wailing wall is not such a bad idea. In any event, and quite seriatim, it is high time that parents realized that being a tender, gentle, warm, loving human being who can cry as well as laugh is not incompatible with being a man. The taboo on tenderness which is placed in the way of the American male's healthy development is something which we shall have to remove before American men are able to cry as and when they should. Italian and French men do not hesitate to cry whenever they feel like it, and I am sure that they are much the better off for being able to do so.

To be human is to weep. The human species is the only one in the whole of animated nature that sheds tears. The trained inability of any human being to weep is a lessening of his capacity to be human—a defect which usually goes deeper than the mere inability to cry. And this, among other things, is what American parents—with the best intentions in the world—have achieved for the American male. It is very sad. If we feel like it, let us all have a good cry—and clear our minds of those cobwebs of confusion which have for so long prevented us from understanding the ineluctable necessity of crying.

On the absence of public
conveniences

IN A PAMPHLET pleading for the establishment of public lavatories, Thomas Dolby in 1830 wrote, "By a simple concatenation of cause and effect the rapid extension of London rapidly increases the agony and urgency of natural exigencies. . . ." Not only of London but of all other cities is this true. The Romans and the Italians provided such comfort stations for their city dwellers, but it was not until the middle of the nineteenth century that London opened its first public lavatories. To this day a public lavatory does not exist in America. If one does, it is a rare exception to the rule.

Foreigners, used to public lavatories in their own countries, wander in agony in search of a public convenience, and many must be the tale of relief achieved in unpublishable ways until the discovery is made that a hotel, a private establishment, is the answer to the urogenital system's most pressing need, not to mention the gastrointestinal system's.

It is perhaps arguable that this public disregard of the citizen's comfort is a reflection of the low esteem in which the citizen is generally held by the guardians of the city's welfare.

I know of no other civilized land in which the elementary
needs of the citizen are so wantonly, so thoughtlessly, disregarded. The land of the outhouse, of Chick Sale, where
plumbing is regarded as one of the fine arts and the bathroom is often the most sumptuous room in the house, has no
public lavatories whatever. And by public conveniences I
mean lavatories that are situated in the streets. In England
the authorities often went to the trouble of digging holes in
the ground and placing the lavatories there. But many of
them are aboveground. In France cubicles which are situated
on the sidewalks are provided for men. In Italy there are such
outdoor luxuries as the *ritirata* situated against a wall and
shielded from view on each side by two short projections
jutting out from the wall. Ladies, alas, are not provided for
in this way.

It would be a great boon were our public authorities to
recognize the existence of certain basic needs and to provide
for them, instead of abandoning such services to hotels,
subway stations, railroad stations, and airports.

Secondhand bookstores

THE TRUE MEASURE of a civilization is the number of its secondhand bookstores. By that measure America fares very badly, for in this vast land there are fewer than 500 such stores, and most of them are within a range of 500 miles of New York City.

Secondhand bookstores are the second universities of the land, perhaps the first, for anyone seriously desiring an education can procure it by regularly frequenting the secondhand bookstores and from them building a working library.

For those who are interested in ideas and in books, there are few pleasures equal to that of wandering freely about a secondhand bookstore, scanning its shelves and stalls, like a hopeful mariner looking for a landfall and discovering the riches he never dreamed existed. Every secondhand bookstore is a perennially undiscovered land, full of new peaks to scale, watersheds to negotiate, and promising subterranean caves to explore. Every visit to the secondhand bookstore is an adventure and an excitement that never fail, an expedition into unexplored territory that is bound to turn up some new treasure—treasures one had never dreamed of, and what is more, would never have known existed had one not adventured into this exciting world of the mind of man. "Ask, and

it shall be given ye; seek, and ye shall find." The only place
in the world in which one can be certain that those two
injunctions stand a good chance of realization is in the
secondhand bookstore. It is a place of enchantment, full of
promises looking for fulfillment and finding fulfillment only
when you have made those promises your own. A book has
fulfilled its promise when it has been read and the promise it
held becomes part of the reader. That is what is so miracu-
lous about books: they can transfer the knowledge, the enthusiasm, the wisdom, the experience, the feelings, and the
very moods of the best minds of every time and place, and
books are capable of informing, enlarging, and ennobling.
How much of his lifeblood has the author put into his book,
the book that is his immortality. And there, arrayed on their
shelves, beckon these lives to you to share with them the
benisons of humanity. Christopher Morley wrote: "There are
some knightly souls who even go so far as to make their visits
to bookshops a kind of chivalrous errantry at large. They go
in not because they need any certain volume, but because
they feel that there may be some book that needs them." It is
the most highly rewarding of knight-errantries.

The bookstore selling new books, with their glossy shiny
covers, has its place, but it is as nothing compared with the
bookstore selling older books, mostly books that were printed
long before the invention of commercial dust jackets and in
whose bindings, therefore, the publisher took some pride.
They are books that have the loving patina of age, a patina
that is derived from being lovingly handled and that gives
the very covers a warmth and a glow that no fading back or
weakened spine can ever diminish. And then there is the
bouquet of old books, the like of which no scent of flower or
meadow or man (I will not say woman) can ever equal.
There is nothing quite like it in the whole world. This

fragrance is, I like to think, the exhalation of the spirit of the author, aged in the press as it were, making its presence felt so sensitively even before one has exchanged a thought with the author through the pages of his book.

There are many good new books, but not as many as there are old. And the old are much cheaper than the new unless, of course, they are rare editions and much sought after. Welcome as the paperback revolution is, even the best paperback bookstores do not come within light-years of comparing with the secondhand bookstore. For one thing, paperback publishers issue the books they believe will sell. They will not as a rule publish a book because it is good, but because it will earn money. Hence, innumerable good books, offbeat books, books hardly anyone has heard of—books capable of changing a life—are found only in secondhand bookstores. For another thing, only in the secondhand bookshop can you enjoy the visual and tactile excitement and variety of the shapes and sizes of beautifully made books. Here, too—and only here—lies the thrilling possibility of discovering a rare edition of a book or a book that will be uniquely meaningful to you. All these things count, and they are important or should be important in the experience of every individual.

Each time a secondhand bookstore is opened, there is rejoicing in heaven. And each time a secondhand bookstore is forced to close its doors, there is deep sorrow and mourning in heaven and rejoicing in hell. When the Nazis set out to destroy the best that had been said and done in the world, the first thing they did was burn the books, ransack the libraries, and close the bookstores. Quite rightly these enemies of humanity knew that they had everything to fear from books. For that reason the individual interested in learning the meaning of humanity and in making the best of himself will derive the greatest benefits from books. It is sad, therefore, to

have to record that in the United States during the last fifty
years more secondhand bookstores have been going out of
business than have been opening.

Why have secondhand bookstores fared so badly? The
reasons are many. One of them is that offender in so many
other respects: the automobile. People simply no longer walk
and certainly no longer leisurely amble. Where people do
walk, as in large cities (in New York and San Francisco
particularly) near their place of business, secondhand bookstores may occasionally be found. But these, as likely as not,
are located where they are, not because of the customers who
come in, but rather because of those who do not. This
paradox is soon resolved. Such bookstores do most of their
business by catalog, with special customers, with libraries,
and with other booksellers. Were such bookstores to depend
on the ambulatory customer, they could not exist. In the days
before the automobile, when the pace of life was much more
leisurely, cheap magazines and digests were not as available as
they are today and when there were neither movies, radio,
nor television, the secondhand bookstore provided a pleasant
and rewarding means of entertainment—an entertainment,
part of which one could purchase, carry away, and make a
permanent part of one's life, unlike the fleeting and ephemeral
entertainments provided by the mass media. The mass media,
the enormous increase in mobility caused by the automobile,
the spread to the suburbs, the proliferation of magazines, and
the paperback revolution—all have combined to work against
the continued existence of the secondhand bookstore.

Secondhand booksellers are the dispensers of civilized values. As such, they should be subsidized by the state.

Static and the cocktail party

It is seldom conversation, but what the communications people call static or noise. At the cocktail party speech often becomes a barrier to communication—sound and fury, meaning, most of the time, absolutely nothing. The purpose of speech is to put and keep people in touch with one another. It has an almost cutaneous quality, as the word "touch" implies. And perhaps this is the secret of the cocktail party, for the crush of the usual cocktail party makes contact between epidermises, it is true, through layers of clothes, hardly avoidable. Man is a gregarious animal, who battens on communication. And even though it may be little more than noise, the noise is nevertheless reassuring. It is the adult equivalent of the lullaby. And cocktails have a way of warming the cockles of the heart.

The cocktail party satisfies not only the need for sociality and communication, but also the need to lose oneself occasionally in the crowd. "I live in the crowds of jollity," remarked Dr. Johnson, "not so much to enjoy company as to shun myself." Whatever else it may satisfy, the cocktail party certainly satisfies the need of the host to give a party. That need may have different motivations. It may be the need to pay off accumulated debts to others for similar parties, or it

[255

may be the need to deduct trade or professional entertainment expenses from income tax. Whatever the need or the pretext, the guests come largely because the drinks are free and often for reasons even less elevating than that. Were one to offer tea instead of drinks, there would be lots of open space at such parties.

In a tension-ridden society, liquor is quicker than tea or other such innocuous beverages. Those who attend cocktail parties for the most part do so for reasons which, whatever the rationalization, add up to a hope and expectation of relief from tension. That certainly is a principal attraction for many, but anthropologically the cocktail party is much more interesting than that.

Not only does the cocktail party minister to the need for tension reduction, but there is a kind of magic about it which holds forth the promise of good things to come. Who can tell whom one may not meet here? A beautiful girl? A desirable man? One's destiny? Someone who may change the whole course of one's life? An unexpected assignment or assignation? A windfall? A contract? A commission? A new job? It is exciting, and like the postman's knock, who knows what unanticipated benisons it may not bring? One not only may establish a contact, but may even connect. So climb aboard that taxi, and hie yourself to that promise of alcoholic bliss. A hangover will be a small price to pay for that providential experience.

Stamps, mailboxes, and postal deliveries

IT MAY SEEM trivial, but it is in fact a great annoyance to those of us who write many letters and use many stamps that American stamps should be so tearable—tearable across the face of the stamp, instead of across the perforations which are presumably provided for the purpose of readily separating each stamp from its companion. In England I detached stamps across their perforations for years without ever tearing a stamp. In America I found I could hardly ever detach a stamp from a sheet or from a single other stamp without tearing the stamp itself. At first I thought the cause might be the poor paper on which the stamps were printed. Upon closer inspection I found the explanation. American stamps have fewer perforations than those of any other country whose stamps I have examined. The standard number of perforations for the size of the five-cent stamp is twelve, whereas the same size stamp in Belgium, England, France, India, Italy, and Japan has eighteen perforations. Count them and check for yourself.

Why can't we have eighteen perforations on our stamps? Must we Americans, who pride ourselves on our efficiency, have the most inefficient stamps in the world? How much time is wasted each year pasting torn stamps together again? How many millions of hours are lost this way each year? Let us discontinue the antiquated twelve-perforation stamp, and do what other countries have done for years and put eighteen perforations into our stamps. And interestingly enough, they improve esthetically.

Mailboxes

Mailboxes are yet another Post Office mistake. In every country with which I am familiar, putting mail into a mailbox requires the use of no more than one hand. In the United States two hands are necessary. This is often a great inconvenience, especially when one is carrying other things or when one is attempting to perform the operation from a car. Can there be any possible reason for continuing this antediluvian piece of inefficiency? Cannot we have single-handed mailboxes?

Mail Delivery

Mail delivery in the United States is anarchic. The mail may arrive hours after the time it is scheduled to be delivered, and there is only one delivery a day in most places. It often takes several days for a letter mailed in a large city to reach another address in the same town. Third- and fourth-class mail may take several weeks to reach another town fifty miles away! They order these things better in other countries.

The United States Post Office has been operating at a loss ever since its founding. Are not the mails consequential enough to be worthy of more government support than they have been receiving? The Post Office clearly needs more money with which to operate; it is in need of more personnel; it is in need of encouragement to do a better job.

With the handicaps under which it has been functioning, the Post Office has done an excellent job, but it will not be able to do much better unless it receives the support it requires, and this must come from the electorate.

New York bus drivers

THE RUDENESS of New York bus drivers is proverbial. I here put in a defense, not of the bus driver's rudeness, but of his right to be rude. The New York bus driver's own defense against the assaults on his integrity that he has to meet during his working hours is that very rudeness of which others complain. A civilized man should never be deliberately rude —the bus driver isn't. He's undeliberately rude. His rudeness is the effect of a spontaneous combustion, an escape valve for the accumulated pressure, in the absence of which he would burst. As it is, it is probable that the peptic ulcer rate among New York city bus drivers is high and that the cardiovascular, hypertension, and early death rates are also high.

If passengers were a little more understanding and considerate of the bus driver, the latter might be encouraged to respond with a little more loving-kindness than he is normally provoked to do. If only passengers would reflect on the fact that the bus driver is a really quite remarkable creature, worthy of a great deal more respect and consideration than they are usually inclined to give him, travel by bus would become much less painful than it is at present.

The New York bus driver drives a clumsy vehicle in the midst of the worst traffic conditions in the world. This in itself is problem enough, but in addition, he has to contend with all sorts of men and especially with eccentric women; make change while keeping his vehicle moving; watch the lights, the jaywalkers, the weaving out-of-town automobilists; answer innumerable questions; see to it that all passengers are on or off the bus before he closes the doors; and keep passengers moving to the back of the bus. Worst of all, he must deal with women who get on the bus, begin searching in the Stygian darkness and hopeless confusion of their bags for the change they seldom seem to have, and then produce a ten-dollar bill, which the driver cannot accept. Would it be too much to expect of such women that they have the change ready before boarding the bus? Perhaps this particular problem could be solved by resorting to tokens, as on subways. Then there are the people who get on the wrong bus and somehow manage to convince themselves that this is the fault of the driver. The bus companies could help here, as they do in England, and have signboards at various stops giving the route number for each bus. This would be a great help and would incidentally help expedite traffic.

To do all the things the bus driver is called on to do in addition to driving the bus—and everyone will surely agree that New York bus drivers are very good drivers—requires not only great skill, but also the patience of Job. I think then that a moratorium ought to be declared on the criticism of bus drivers. If passengers would only put themselves in the bus driver's place, they might be persuaded that his rudeness is not as awful as it seems. It might even occur to some New Yorkers that if they want consideration shown to them, they might well begin by showing it to others.

The blackout

AT 5:18 P.M. ON TUESDAY, November 9, 1965, the
electric power suddenly failed and plunged an area of some
80,000 square miles of the most densely inhabited region of
the world in complete darkness until the next morning.
Thousands of people were trapped in elevators, in subways,
and in the upper stories of skyscrapers. The blackout involved the states of New York, Massachusetts, Maine, and
New Jersey. Because the blackout affected the largest and
busiest city in the United States at an hour when millions of
workers were about to leave for home, the power failure was
everywhere immediately labeled "The New York Blackout."

Planes were unable to land because the airports were
blacked out and were therefore sent from New York to other
airports as far away as Bermuda and Puerto Rico. Travelers
by train were unable to depart, services of all kinds were cut
off, and the business losses ran into the millions. A great
disaster was miraculously averted. The cause of the failure
was apparently an overloaded cable to Canada. A circuit
breaker which should have opened failed to do so, and a
surge of excess current produced an oscillation which drained
away the power from functioning electric systems. No one
knows why the circuit breaker failed to open, and I don't

know whether or not the system is automated. If it is, then the computer should not draw its power from the sources it is supposed to inform and regulate, for if they fail, the computer will also fail. I hope that this sort of stupidity was not involved, but I shouldn't be surprised to learn that it was.

Until the actual cause of the failure was announced, some six days later, it was rumored all over the United States that sabotage was involved. For people who are always looking for Reds under their beds, this was, of course, the "natural" explanation. It must, according to them, have surely been the bogeyman, and everyone knows what color *he* is—not black, but red. Anything so crass as a technical failure, such as an overloaded cable, would hardly be likely to occur to such people. Vain is the hope that they might draw a lesson from this experience and conclude that not all difficult or threatening situations are due to Reds.

The wry comment that was making the rounds on the blackout was the appropriate one—namely, that while we were engaging in a tremendous effort to send men to the moon and conquer outer space, we couldn't even keep the lights on in our cities.

Clearly, the lesson to be learned and applied is that no city should ever depend on a single source for its power supply. Every town and every important installation should have several auxiliary sources of power supply, which can take over should the main supply fail. Each of these auxiliary sources should be independent of the others. Such auxiliary sources need not stand idle waiting for a power failure to occur but should be put into service in any number of ways.

The moral to be learned from "The New York Blackout" is that Americans would be well advised to cease looking for Reds under their beds and begin bestowing attention where it is most needed, such as in those areas of conduct, thinking, and organization in which we are defective and which, unattended, greatly increase the dangers to ourselves, not from without, but from within. If Americans would do what they ought in attending to their internal weaknesses and recognize these as the dangers that they are, they might discover that they need not worry so much about the dangers from without—and be much better prepared to meet any of the latter, should they ever materialize.

The hysteria and panic that might have developed during the blackout in the absence of any information on its cause were in large part averted by the reassuring voices of battery-powered auto radios, which gave a running account of the true story. This was very comforting. With a sigh of relief, people everywhere, with laughter and in a holiday mood, joined in a camaraderie which was one of the happiest consequences of one of the biggest snafus of our time. Men walked women from their offices to their homes, people helped one another in innumerable ways, and the whole experience was treated with the sense of humor and grace that reflected something of the deeper sources of man's basic cooperativeness and involvement in the welfare of his fellowman. That, too, is a lesson worth learning.

One of the unforeseen consequences of the blackout was the great surge of babies born nine lunar months after the event—yet another evidence of cooperation in crisis.

Has education failed?

No ONE CAN LOOK about him in our time and come to any conclusion other than that the human enterprise has massively failed in the task of providing human beings with an opportunity to fulfill themselves. Have educators contributed to this failure? I think it is a question that all educators must ask themselves. I believe that educators have certainly been major contributors to the failure. This is not said censoriously. Like most other human beings, educators have meant well. But what they have, in fact, been doing has been to maintain the *status quo* and very largely to smooth the way for the more efficient progression of those personal and social disasters which we are today witnessing being enacted upon the stage of international hostilities.

I have repeatedly stated that I regard the teacher of the young as the most important member of the community. I am, of course, well aware of the fact that the community does not agree with me. But here I believe it is the community that is in error, not I. Parents and teachers stand at the very center of humanity because it is they who make humanity, and where parents fail, it should be the task of the teacher to make the necessary repairs and to provide the necessary training and direction. Such a statement, I discover, induces a considerable amount of anxiety in some teachers, who respond by saying, "You are putting too much responsibility on our shoulders, but we are only one segment, one small part, of a large and complex society in which there are many other forces at work which contribute to the making of human beings and which often nullify our best efforts. Don't make us carry a load heavier than that with which we are already overburdened."

Of course, it is true that the classroom is one thing and the world outside quite another. But what I am pleading for is that the classroom should not continue to be part of the same problem that the outside world presents, but that the classroom should become the place where the major part of the solution to the world's problems is determined. Teachers must take a good look at themselves and realize that they do indeed stand at the very center of humanity, that their task is no less than the making of humanity, and that there can scarcely be a more responsible work than this. Those who feel that such a job is too much of a responsibility for them will have my complete sympathy, and I should encourage them to look for some other employment. I want to see teachers who genuinely understand the nature of the critically important relation in which they stand to the world of humanity, and I should like to see them conducting themselves as if they believed this.

It is my considered view, as a student of the origin and evolution of man and his cultures, that man has an evolutionary destiny and that this destiny is the realization of his humane potentialities. I think it can now be as satisfactorily demonstrated as it will ever be that the traits which have been at the highest premium in the evolution of man and which through the action of natural selection have always been characterized by the highest adaptive value have been the traits of love and cooperation; furthermore, that mental health consists of the ability to love and the ability to work; and that insofar as the individual is deprived of his birthright, which is the development of his capacity to love and work, to that extent will he fail in his ability to relate himself in a healthy manner to other human beings and to his work. On the firm groundwork of the biological capacities with which he is already endowed at birth, it seems to me, it is the function of parents and of teachers to educate the child—that is, to nourish and to cause to grow (which is exactly what the word *educare* in its original Latin means) his capacities for relating himself to other human beings in such a manner that he is increasingly enabled to confer survival benefits in a creatively enlarging manner on others, while fulfilling his own potentialities as nearly as possible to the optimum. *This* is what I think education should be, and anything that is not this is, in my view, not education. The three *R*'s represent instruction, not education. The three *R*'s properly should constitute the secondary skills, the techniques, which should more efficiently enable the person to realize his capacities and potentialities for being a warm, loving human being and for maximizing the capacities of others to do likewise.

It is what man makes of man that, as we all can surely see today more clearly and more challengingly than ever before, makes the difference between a fully realized life or no life at all. And, as I cannot too often repeat, it is the teachers of the young, the parents, and those who stand *in loco parentis* to the young who are the makers of man. And as man is made, so does he make the world.

Intimations of impending doom are all about us. But at the very edge of doom there is still time to turn back and begin again. It is not more light that we are in want of. No one ever died from lack of light, but many have perished from lack of warmth. It is quite possible that the whole human species may vanish from a lack of warmth in a blast of light. It will be a pity, for those who have understood the necessity of warmth will go down, carried to perdition by those who did not. The fact is that we have had far too much light, and it has blinded us to the need for warmth. I am making a plea for the rediscovery of warmth, for the revaluation of education as the art of human relations, and the reorganization of our minds and our so-called educational institutions as the means by which we shall return to that humanity from which we have so dangerously departed.

College presidents and administrators

THE AMERICAN COLLEGE president has an average life in that office of about five years. It is often five years too long. There are some excellent appointments, but too frequently appointments are made for the worst of all possible reasons. College presidents are usually appointed because they have displayed administrative ability and perhaps some capacity to attract funds. What else would one expect of a group of businessmen, the trustees, who generally determine what kind of president they want? Not what the university needs, but what they want. Some of our largest institutions have disgraced themselves by appointing former generals and similarly distinguished people presidents of their ivy-mantled towers. Such individuals have seldom done any harm. Perhaps as is the case with England's constitutional monarchs, the more mediocre they are, the less difficult they are to manage.

It is in the colleges of no great renown that real damage is done by the appointment of an individual, too often with only a diploma in education, who has had some experience as a school principal or superintendent, to so critically delicate a post.

Educators are the unacknowledged legislators of the world. I know of no group of people I find so congenial, so deeply interested in their work and in doing a better job. Yet I know of no group so unprepared to do that job as educators. Whatever it is that goes on in a school of education, it simply fails to prepare its products for the creative work of which they should be capable, the forming of human minds. Those who have passed through courses in schools of education or elsewhere have usually not emerged as either educated or cultivated individuals sensitized to the needs of the young. Such individuals are not qualified to teach, and least of all are they qualified to be the directing influences, the heads, of colleges.

The "educators" selected by so many of our colleges to be presidents are usually not educators at all, but administrators. They really have no notion of what education is for, what it is, or how one should go about it.

It seems to be the pattern that, once appointed, they must at once set about planning for the erection of more buildings, enlargement of the faculty, and continuing maintenance and rigidifying of the *status quo*. Typically something of their view of the faculty may be gathered from the fact that on several campuses where I have spoken, the faculty is required to pay admission to public lectures that are free to everyone else on campus. Where I have encountered this particular barbarity, the president is not very popular with the faculty. How any man could even have contemplated instituting such a degrading regulation is difficult to understand—unless he has the mind of an administrator and not that of an educator. That anyone should be capable of thinking of a college faculty in such a manner should, one would have thought, automatically have disqualified him from holding any educational post whatever. On the other hand, the fact that he is capable of such conduct recommends him most highly to the trustees! He is a good administrator, and that is what they want.

Altogether apart from the fact that every faculty member should enjoy the *right* to attend any public or intramural lecture as a fringe benefit, such events should be regarded as an opportunity for the continuing education of the faculty.

It ought to be mandatory, but certainly not a hidebound rule, that a college president be selected from the ranks of the humanities and that such a man should be a scholar—*not* a scientist. A scholar works in the library, a scientist in the laboratory. Scientists are, on the whole, too narrow and much too inclined to believe that the scientific method can be extended to the solution of all problems—even to human beings. This is not quite so. The difficulty with the scientist is that he is likely to be too narrow in his vision, not humanist enough. This is much less likely to be so in the case of the scholar. I would not care one bit whether such a man had administrative ability or not. What I would be interested in was whether he understood what education is and what it is for—whether he was interested in human beings.

As for administration, I would abolish the administration altogether. An administration as such is wholly unnecessary in a college or university except, of course, for janitors, plumbers, and keepers of the grounds and buildings. For the rest, educational institutions should be run by educators, and their secretaries should do all the work of putting the right forms in the right envelopes. As in England, there can be a secretary of the college who oversees all the organizational work in cooperation with the faculty. This has been the practice for hundreds of years in England, and it works most successfully. Administrators assert that they free the faculty for academic work by assuming the labor of administration.

But faculties do not feel this way. They would rather administer the college themselves, for they know what a college is for and administrators seldom do. Administrators frequently operate the college for what seems to be the benefit of the administration. In some institutions I know the administration decides what textbooks shall be used in what courses!

A college, of course, should be run for the benefit of the students and faculty, and all administration should be directed toward that end. And equally, of course, trustees should be appointed from the ranks of scholars and genuine educators and not from the ranks of businessmen.

Christmas

THE SECULARIZATION of Christmas has proceeded so far in America that it has virtually ceased to be a religious holiday, as witnessed by the frenzied participation in it of non-Christian Americans. It has, for the most part, become a bacchanalian celebration, a compulsive shopping spree (very good for and in a major way therefore encouraged by business), gift giving, ritual card sending, Lucullan feasts, overeating, overdrinking, all in a Dionysian frenzy, capped by the offering, over the weekend, of hundreds of devotional victims sacrificed on the public highways to the spirit of Christmas. Physicians and proctologists experience a great increase in the number of patients suffering from congestion of the liver and back pressures in the portal system, consequences of the unaccustomed quantities of alcohol consumed, often also reflected in outcroppings of hemorrhoids of the most discomforting kind.

For large numbers, far from being a period of good cheer, Christmas has become an exhausting chore. It is hardest on the women, upon whom the burden falls of doing most of the menial work, added to the customary load with which they are already saddled. For many women Christmas is a four-letter word. The shopping, the crowding, the rushing, the

crushing, the selection of gifts, the wrapping with the appropriately decorated papers and string, the filling of stockings,
the cooking, the table arrangements, the decoration of the
tree, the maintenance of good temper, the writing and mailing of cards, and the endless standing in queues at the post
office constitute a trying annual experience. Self-immolation
is a widespread custom, and there is, I suppose, no reason why
it should not be practiced in America.

From scenes of Bethlehem, the birth of the Christ Child,
the Holy Family, and the Wise Men of the East, the artwork
in Christmas cards has shifted to portraits of the unholy
family and other less intimate and more profane subjects.
The most obscene comments have been evoked on the receipt
of these productions. Such expletives have been uttered not
alone by those who repudiate Christmas as a pagan celebration but also by those who do not. There are others who
feel that it's a free country and that everyone has a right to
celebrate Christmas in his own way, even if it means celebrating one's own family rather than the family of Christ. The
intention is good. It is to keep distant friends informed of the
progress of the family, while conveying intimations of good-
will and the fact that they have not been forgotten. It is, in
many cases, as perfunctory as that. And in a busy world it
serves a useful social function. Many people maintain long
lists, often containing hundreds of names, representing those
to whom Christmas cards must be sent—and sent they are.
Would not most of the recipients of such ritually dispatched
cards prefer a personal note written at some less frantic time
of the year and not associated with the traditional period of
ritualized reciprocal civilities? Most people would. But most
people will not themselves do what is humanly desirable, and
so they welcome Christmas as the period during which they
can pretend to themselves and to others that they are being

what they ought to be. Hence, as a useful social institution, Christmas serves many self-gratifying functions.

Christmas cards should look expensive, bearing the evidence of conspicuous consumption and, hence, of success. As for gifts, this is one of the more iniquitous aspects of Christmas. It is generally considered not sufficient to offer each member of the family a few gifts; each must receive a quantity of gifts. The gifts should be piled so high around the tree that everyone will be sure to receive an adequate number. The number is important. The disappointment that would follow from receiving a few gifts would be equated with a withholding of love, for from their earliest days American children have been showered with unnecessary gifts, only too often as a substitute for love. Hence, very few parents have the courage to reduce to a reasonable number the gifts they make their children at Christmas. In any event, the competitiveness, the jealousies, and the disappointments that are frequently associated with the distribution of gifts, although they may be concealed, are often very real. No matter what the quantity of material gifts at Christmas, they cannot compensate for the intangible ones that have not been forthcoming during the earlier part of the year. But that is precisely what this frenzied gift giving is designed to compensate for.

Ritual gift giving at Christmas need not be the abhorrent practice it has become were it held within reasonable limits. Children are taught to value quantity as an evidence of esteem rather than to value the quality of the esteem in which they are held. The latter has no connection whatever with quantity, with things, or with celebrations, but only with one thing, the one thing Christmas is designed or supposed to be designed to celebrate—namely, the quality of love.

Terms of reference and address

AMERICANS ARE VERY confused about the proper appellations to apply to different people. For example, a woman is often referred to as a lady, when in most cases, whatever else she may be, she is quite obviously no lady. A lady is a woman of gentle breeding, of graceful manners. A lady is a special species of woman, not a synonym for all women, any more than the term "gentleman" constitutes a synonym for all men. "Lady" in the wrong context is an illitericism, and that is the long and the short of it.

The misuse of the term "sir" is yet another example. A man of menial status and occupation will frequently be addressed as sir by a person of superior status and station. This is, without in any way appealing to the snobbish, to debase the usage of an honored term. A menial is not a sir. The term should be reserved for a man of breeding, otherwise a man is a mister, and a woman a miss, a missus, or a madam.

"Ladies and gentlemen" as a form of address at the opening of a speech or meeting is a perfectly legitimate convention, even though most of the members of the audience may be anything but. It is terribly confusing when, cheek by jowl with each other, one door of a toilet will read "Ladies" and

the other "Men." What the meaning of this discrimination
may be I have not yet been able to determine. Perhaps the
explanation is economic: it takes more paint to put "Gentlemen" on the door.

Another abject confusion is the term "gentlemen." The
term applies not simply to a person by virtue of the fact that
he is of the male sex, but because he is a man of genteel
manners. To apply the term as incongruously as it is applied
to individuals who are anything but gentlemen is to render
the term ridiculous, not to mention those who misapply it
and to whom it is misapplied.

Such misuses of language blunt the fine sense of distinction
for which words have been created and which serve to render
communication as easy and as correct as it should be. There is
really little point to a word if it is going to be used to apply
to several things for which the appropriate word is already
available.

I am reminded in this connection of one of the most
charming men I have ever met—indeed, one of the finest
examples of a gentleman I have ever known. He was of an
indefinite age, but I was told that at the time I met him, he
was well over seventy. His father had been a slave, and he
himself had spent the greater part of his life in the South.
There he had got into the habit of addressing all white men
as "Yes sah." But what amused me when I first heard it—and
about which he and I had many a good laugh—was his habit
of addressing ladies as "Yes sah, ma'm." There was not the
least confusion in his mind about what he was doing. "It just
makes things go around more smoothly," he said. He had,
with those words, grasped the function of terms of address,
which most Americans have not.

Possibly while I haven't been looking, the terms "lady"
and "sir" have been undergoing linguistic change. If so, I

shall continue to resist the change and shall decline to call a nondescript woman a lady and a man who has not risen to the occasion sir.

In the area of what anthropologists call classificatory relationships there are some strange lacunae and even stranger ways of filling those lacunae in the form of terms of address. For example, there is no formal term for one's spouse's parents. They are parents-in-law, mother-in-law and father-in-law. But when one addresses one's parents-in-law one doesn't call them Mother-in-law and Father-in-law. The terms by which one addresses one's in-laws depend on such factors as age differences, personality, class, religion, and the like. In nonliterate cultures there are definite terms of address for such relationships, but not in ours. Things get very confused when people call their parents-in-law by the same terms that the grandchildren call them—"Granny" and "Gran'pa," or "Nanna" and "Nampa," or whatever similar terms they may be called by. Yet this is frequently done. It is very confusing to children if to no one else.

It is, I think, a great mistake for young people to call their parents-in-law by their first names. It should no more be done than one should permit one's own children to call one by one's first name. Such a practice confuses the meaning of age differences, statuses, and roles and diminishes the significance and the value of the role that each generation has to play in relation to the other. Age grade differences and statuses are important, among other things because they help clarify the socially expected behaviors. For want of such terms in our culture we obscure and lose much of value in the process of living. Classificatory terms incorporate the forms of behavior. It is not to be wondered at that in our fragmented society, in which no such terms exist, that the relations between in-laws, especially parents-in-law and the spouses of their children, should be so ambivalent.

And what do parents-in-law call their own children's parents-in-law? Again, we have no terms of reference or of address for such relatives by marriage. First names are often resorted to, and these will do for direct address; but since terms of reference are wholly lacking for such relationships, we are forced to such statements as "My offspring's parents-in-law." It is quite unsatisfactory.

Members of the lower classes in America are especially confused in their usage of terms of address and will apply such terms as "Buster," "Bud," and the like indiscriminately.

In a democracy, in which everyone is allegedly the equal of everyone else, it is not surprising that there is a widespread confusion concerning the meaning of roles and statuses, especially among those who desire to be at least as "equal" as others; hence, the anarchic condition of terms of address of various sorts. It is also considered a mark of good-fellowship to call people by their first names. It is also an evidence of friendliness and is always well intentioned. But the way to undisillusioned confusion is paved with such good conventions. In many cases the first-name psychosis reflects a basic lack of respect both for oneself and for the other. It requires a peculiar kind of insensitivity, a certain thick-skinnedness, not to understand that an individual's name is an essential part of him and that one should be no more free to take it than one should be with respect to any other part of his person. A person's first name is his private possession, and one should not unseemingly invade that privacy. It is not a matter of snobbery or stuffed-shirtedness, but purely and simply a matter of good manners. A surname is one's public name. One's given name is one's private name. An acquaintance is welcome to shake you by the hand, but in general you do not want him to become physically more intimate, especially when he is of the backslapping variety or shoulder-embracing type. On an occasion, which shall not be of more particular record, a backslapper greeted his victim, "Hello, George. Remember me?" The victim replied, "The manner is familiar. The face is not." Undue familiarity constitutes a lack of respect, a lessening of the dignity of the human situation. Dr. Johnson defined a gentleman as one who refrains.

In England, when I was a youth, it was the custom, at school and at college, to call one's friends by their surnames. Given names were generally reserved for use by one's intimates. Quite often one varied the names, and frequently, of course, nicknames, contractions, and diminutives were used.

The English tend to be more reserved and also more assured than Americans and in their reserve often go to the opposite extreme. But English reserve is generally a respect for the other person's rights, and we could do with more of that reserve and respect in the United States. Human behavior matters, and civilized behavior is essentially respect and consideration for the other. Unwarranted first-name calling constitutes, in my view, yet another evidence of the breakdown in our understanding of human worth.

"Run a mile to see a fire"

A CHILD IS A promise seeking fulfillment. It is or should be the function of adults to promote that fulfillment, to provide the conditions in which it may best be achieved. But in America adults customarily act as if it were their purpose to frustrate the fulfillment of the child—and this in the apparently most permissive ambience for children to be found anywhere in the world. Americans like children, but they don't respect them. They tend to think of children as inferior beings, who must be commanded so that they learn to obey, who must be ordered and told what to do and what not to do, for whom others make decisions, and who are maintained in dependent relationship to the adult world far beyond what is either necessary or desirable.

Instead of helping the child to fulfill himself as a person who is interested in neither commanding nor obeying, but in doing what is right by the measure of those universal standards of right which he should have been taught by adults, as well as by other children—for children learn at least as much from their peers as they do from their elders—he is from the beginning made to feel his subservience to adults and the omnipotence of the "word." "What did I say?" and "What did I tell you to do?" are frequent phrases on the lips of

[281

parents. But it is what parents themselves do, not so much what they say, that constitutes the model on which children form themselves. And the model that is most frequently presented to children is their own inconsistency so that children learn that it is quite compatible with human logic to say one thing and do another.

Adults set absurd standards for children, expecting them to be better than they themselves are. They make too many of the wrong demands on children and an insufficient number of the right ones. The manner in which these demands are usually made tends to be destructive. Parents, especially mothers, make these demands in a context of conditional love. "Do as mother wishes and she will love you. Disobey mother and she won't love you." The one thing in the world that should be completely unconditional, unreservedly given, is converted into a commodity which is used as a bargaining point, whose advantage is all on the side of the vendor. In this marketing approach the child learns two things: he learns the art of repression, by internalizing energies which would otherwise have been expressed and which would have benefited the child by being expressed, and he learns that love is a commodity with which one can bargain. Both these lessons are very damaging to the developing human being. They are damaging because the repressions accumulate a store of frustrations which become readily available for expression in the form of aggressiveness and hostility and because they disturb the individual's ability to love.

Firmness is one thing, and frustration quite another. Frustration should not be mistaken for repressiveness. American parents are not repressive, but they tend to be frustrating— not deliberately so, but unwittingly, most of the time. Frustration is the thwarting of expected satisfaction. A certain amount of frustration is inevitable and even desirable in the socialization of every human being. Children, especially, need to learn the art of postponing immediate satisfactions for long-term goals. But this is a very different thing from the constant frustration to which children are exposed. At the same time a great deal of permissiveness is allowed the American child. The combination of permissiveness and frustration is very confusing and disorienting to the child and tends to make him insecure and unsure of adults, for he cannot depend on them from one moment to another for anything resembling consistent behavior. Hence, as an adolescent, be begins to look elsewhere for security and individuals on whom he can depend—his peers.

The inconsistencies and irreconcilable values that adults exhibit and the demands they make on him to be like themselves give children little confidence in their elders, and in adolescence the disenchantment with adult values is such that they tend to reject them altogether. The adolescent comes to regard adults with something less than respect, and observing what they have made of the world, he grows inclined to look on them with something between derision and contempt. In rejecting the world of adults, a world he never made, he throws in his lot with others who, like himself, are bent on making their own world.

Possibly for the first time in history teen-agers have formed a subculture of their own within the larger culture in which they live. The adolescents of America—not all of them, of course—function as an autonomous culture distinct from that of their elders. They like it that way. And almost anything that can be regarded as rebellion against the values of the adult world they will embrace with an all-consuming passion. Observing the inadequacies of adults and how much adults, especially their parents, fear them, the world has become their oyster, and there are no days in the month in which they do not find it palatable. The movement is worldwide, but while elsewhere in the world youth is still cowed by its elders, in America youth considers that elders are strictly for the birds. Beatle hairdos, fright-wig haircuts, blue jeans, the cult of ugliness among girls, with their pale faces, lipstickless lips, lank horsetail hair, high boots, and black capes, constitute but a few of the most obstreperously ostentatious evidences of revolt. But the revolt is far deeper and more extensive than the external evidences alone would suggest. The significant aspect of the revolt is ideological, not in the sense that there has been a shift in interest from Moscow to Peking, from Hungary to Havana, but in the sense that there has been a shift from dependence for one's guidance on parents and the parental generation to dependence on one's own revolutionary judgment and that of all other youth supporters.

Not surprisingly, support, in a major way, for the revolt of youth has come from an unexpected quarter (unexpected only to those who had not given the matter much thought)—namely, big business. Since almost half of all Americans alive now are under twenty-five, and they do the most hectic kind of buying, big business increasingly directs its attention to the multibillion dollar a year market they represent. And it is not kid stuff and acne lotions, alone, but the modern form of the love potions that medieval witches and sorcerers used to brew. The appeal to youth is made on the basis of love, sex, attractiveness, worldly success, and independence. The volume of advertising that is directed at the under-twenty-five part of the population exceeds, by many times, that which is aimed at any other age group. Youth is made to feel that the rest of the population scarcely counts. And youth, indeed, soon discovers that the world is made for it.

Time was when parents made it quite clear to their children that in old age they expected their children to support them. Times have changed. Children now expect their parents to support them into old age. And parents contribute to this notion by encouraging their children to think in terms of independence and uninvolvement with themselves, the parents. With all the agencies of their culture thus conspiring to remove them from involvement with their elders, it is hardly surprising that youth should take the leap it has into the wild blue yonder of freedom from the adult world to enter into the newfound freedom of the world of self-conscious youth.

After World War II youth began to wake up to the fact that while the adults were doing the lying, it was youth that was doing the dying, and this being the case, they were going to have a say about things for themselves. The leaders of the world were for the most part finks who had led it to disaster. It should not happen again. Hence, the earnestness of youth in search of a new faith, and the destruction of the empty shrines at which their elders had for so long and so hypocritically burnt the smoke of incense.

Youth and age never were able to live together. The rift between them today seems deeper than ever. Parents on the whole behave as if they have completely forgotten what it was like to be a child, an adolescent, a young man or a young woman: "Now when I was a boy" or "When I was a girl." Yes, when you were a boy and you were a girl, dear parents, times were different. Your children are not living in the age when you were children. Not only have times changed, but the changes have also proceeded at a speed which has constantly accelerated, far more rapidly than at any previous period in the history of humanity. Ideas have changed on politics, religion, the relations between the sexes, parents and children, and a thousand and one other things.

Children are biologically the offspring of their parents, but socially they are the children of their time. Children stand, as it were, on the shoulders of the parental generation and are therefore able to see much farther ahead and to take in a much broader horizon. "I don't know what the younger generation is coming to." It is an old refrain. What the younger generation is coming to is the development of those ideological differences for which their elders provided the foundations. This seems difficult for parents to understand. Could they but think occasionally on Robert Louis Stevenson's words, it might be helpful: "Prudence is not a deity to cultivate in youth. Youth is the time to go flashing from one end of the world to the other both in mind and body; to try the manners of different nations; to hear the chimes at midnight; to see the sunrise in town and country; to be converted at a revival; to circumnavigate the metaphysics, write halting verse, run a mile to see a fire."

Santo Domingo

WITH THE INVASION of Santo Domingo the United States lost the few shreds of whatever reputation for political decency it had left. The ruthlessness of American foreign policy has been revealed in all its naked ugliness for all the world to see. The unabashed lying of the President of the United States—that we were in Santo Domingo in order to remove United States citizens and, at the request of their governments, the nationals of other countries—was soon revealed for what it was.

As many predicted when they heard the announcement of the invasion over the radio, we would soon be hearing announcements that the revolution, whether instigated by others or not, was in danger of being taken over by the Communists. And that, as the whole world now knows, is exactly what occurred. The President blithely proceeded to inform us that we did not want another Cuba in Santo Domingo, and so the United States forces, from the moment of their arrival in Santo Domingo, proceeded to supply and support the reactionary militarists against the people—the rebels. The President and the State Department have done all they could to deceive the American public about what was really going on in Santo Domingo, and it is now transparently clear that the shortsighted and misguided policy of the United States in Santo Domingo has produced the very conditions that policy sought to avoid. As everywhere else in the world where the United States has interfered in the internal affairs of a country, it is the reactionaries we have sought out and to whom we have given our support. The myopia of our government, especially of our State Department, is so great that it is unable to see the consequences of dealing with such persons, and that such a policy invariably plays right into the hands of the Communists. The history of the last fifty years is full of tragic instances of this. And it is not as if these tragic instances involved a few small countries that could soon and easily be forgotten, for several of these instances represent the two largest nations in the world, the U.S.S.R. and China. But the concern, memory, and understanding of most people appear to be limited; hence, human beings learn very little, if anything, from history.

The Russian Revolution was a revolt of the Russian people against the corruption, inefficiency, and tyranny of the tsarist regime. It was the spontaneous expression and uprising of the people, in the towns, the villages, and the armed forces. The Russian Revolution was not the doing of the Communists. It was not a Communist revolution, and the Communists had nothing whatever to do with it. But what helped make that popular revolution of the people fall like a ripe fruit into the outstretched hands of the Communists, was the policy of the Allied forces—the American, English, and French—and of the Germans. This statement generally startles most people who hear it. But it is only too tragically true. The Germans wanted to do everything in their power to keep the Russians from continuing in the war on the eastern front, for this meant that they would then be able to transfer all the divisions fighting on that front to the western front. The popularly elected Kerensky government was resolved to keep Russia in the fight on the side of the Allies against the Germans. It was, therefore, to the interest of the Germans to see that the Kerensky government was destroyed. To this end they sent the Communist agitator Lenin in a sealed armored train into Russia in the hope that he might bring the Kerensky government down and negotiate a separate peace with the Germans. This is exactly what Lenin accomplished for the Germans. The peace was signed at Brest-Litovsk on March 3, 1918. Meanwhile, the Allies—America, England, and France—maintained forces in northern Russia, which were misused to fight the Russian forces. This gave the Communists the rallying cry they needed. Whereas, previously, there might have been a chance that the Communists would have failed to unify their forces, Trotsky now found it comparatively easy to consolidate the divergent revolutionary elements against the common enemy, the "Imperialist-Capitalist Armies," bent on destroying the "People's Revolution." From 1917 to 1922 the Allied Powers kept their small and ineffectual forces on Russian soil, affording the Communists everything they required for their propaganda "in the struggle of the liberated masses against the common enemy, the Imperialist-Capitalists." In this way, if there were ever any doubt about the direction of the Russian Revolution and its successful capture by the Communists, the Allied Powers by their misbegotten conduct did everything possible to assure the ultimate victory of the Communists.

Those who find this difficult to believe should read the two authoritative books on the subject: the first, by Professor E. M. Halliday, *The Ignorant Armies* (New York, Harper, 1960), and the second, by George F. Kennan, *The Decision to Intervene* (Princeton, Princeton University Press, 1958). Halliday's book to some extent constitutes a more accurate account of what actually took place than Kennan's. The whole sorry story, especially the disastrous role played in this debacle by the American Ambassador, David R. Francis, has to be read to be believed. But its reading should be obligatory for all Americans so that they may be able to judge for themselves what the decision to intervene in the affairs of other nations, in the manner in which we usually do, leads to.

It was another American Ambassador, William Tapley Bennett, Jr., Ambassador to the Dominican Republic, who recommended the landing of United States Marines in that country on the ground that a take-over by the Communists was imminent. This was utterly false. As a reward for his services, in April, 1966, Mr. Bennett was appointed Ambassador to Portugal—where he will, no doubt, feel very much more at ease since there is not even the suspicion of a Communist in that country.

By the manner of our intervention in Santo Domingo we have created in that country conditions that are ripe for the Communists and dislike and hostility toward ourselves throughout the length and breadth of Latin America. Everywhere throughout Latin America we have done the same. Castro would not have been possible in Cuba had we not supported reactionaries like Batista and thus created the conditions in Cuba for a Communist take-over. Had we not trained and supported the monstrous Trujillo in the Dominican Republic, there would have been no Santo Domingo. Had we supported the democratic elements in China instead of the reactionary Chiang Kai-shek, we should now have 600,000,000 friends rather than 600,000,000 enemies in China, and there would have been no Korean and no Vietnamese conflicts.

When will such follies cease? I do not know. But I should like to see men of wisdom elected to political office, rather than the kinds of creatures who now find their way into politics in such dominantly large numbers.

Americans and Spain

FOR MANY YEARS Spain has been a repressive dictatorship of the worst kind. Generalissimo Franco has been an open friend and supporter of Nazi and Fascist movements everywhere in the world. During World War II he served as a listening post for our enemies and regularly transmitted information to Hitler and Mussolini that was designed to be damaging to the American and Allied cause. Freedom of speech in Spain died with the dictatorship of Franco, and no dissident opinion is permitted. All criticism is sternly repressed with heavy fines, loss of property, and imprisonment. Franco has been a calamity for Spain. The dictator stands for virtually everything to which Americans are opposed. Nevertheless, the American government and American tourists have been pouring millions into Franco's coffers for years.

The American government believes it must have bases in Spain; hence, Franco must be paid millions for the privilege. But there exists no such excuse for the thousands of American tourists who thoughtlessly and irresponsibly help fill Franco's treasury with gold. By spending their money in this way in Sapin, Americans help ensure the continuance of the dictatorship in Spain.

Are these American tourists political Adams? So innocent

of any understanding of the consequences of their conduct
that they know not what they do? That is, no doubt, the
charitable view to take of their conduct, but it is no less
inexcusable. Voluntary ignorance is no excuse, either in law
or in ethics.

Each time an American spends a dollar in Spain, that
money delays the joining of Spain in the community of
nations and assists Franco to suppress the humane and creative spirits of the land he so cruelly polices. The arts,
literature, the humanities, and the sciences all are in fetters
in Spain, virtually moribund, and its great men are dispersed
over the face of the earth. The few intellectuals who are not
in jail are permitted a limited freedom at the price of silence.
The poor suffer in quiet and hopeless desperation, while
Spain is crucified on a Calvary which Americans joyously pay
admission to support.

The scientist

THE SCIENTIST, the god not alone of the common man's but of everyone's idolatry, may yet prove to be the most destructive of our deities. And this threat constitutes the principal reason why the humanities should always receive the major priority in the education of everyone. For if the potential scientist had been humanized before he entered on his scientific activities, he could never become as insensitive as the modern scientist generally is to the needs of humanity.

The condition which may cause the scientist, unwittingly, to put a term to the existence of man is his training as a scientist, training which essentially serves to put him out of touch with humanity, to dehumanize him. I cannot flatter myself that there will be any kind of commotion at this statement; I wish there were, but it is either true or it is not that most scientists are, as a result of their training nothing more than glorified technicians with a Ph.D. degree. The specialized training that most scientists receive narrows their vision to a tiny area on the retinas of their minds.

And the more the scientist comes to focus on his small area of knowledge, the more constricted become his intellectual horizons. Of course, there are notable exceptions, and while they are many, I am sure they are not nearly as numerous as the narrow specialists. It is a real question whether the danger of the specialized scientist will be recognized in time and something done to avert the disaster into which these trained automata may yet lead us. And therein lies the tragedy of the automated, unwitting scientist, for he has become an unwitting instrument of the aims and purposes of others.

There are among us too many scientists who assume a handwashing indifference to the consequences of their work. They are scientists, they say; their job is to work, and what anyone chooses to do with their work is no concern of theirs. This is, in my view, an utterly reprehensible and worse than irresponsible position to take—and a morally indefensible one. Anyone asked to do anything that will be put to evil uses should decline to do it. Was it not Herr Eichmann who claimed that he had never killed a single Jew? He had not. All that he had done, he claimed, was to obey orders. What else, said he, could a soldier do? He could, of course, have disobeyed orders. But that never occurred to him, just as it never occurs to some scientists that they can decline to work on areas which they well know are going to be put to evil uses. It is as simple as that. The scientist who, in the light of such knowledge, proceeds with his work is guilty of evil, as guilty of evil as he who puts that work to evil use. It is not enough after the act to exclaim, "We have known sin." It is much more important to recognize the sinfulness of an act before it becomes sinful and to prevent the sin from being committed than to look back and recognize and acknowledge the sin when it is too late.

Because of the narrowness of vision of so many scientists, science has become far too important and dangerous an activity to leave to the scientists. Just as war is too important to leave to the generals and it is therefore necessary that they be under the control of the Secretary of the Army, so, until they can take care of themselves, scientists should be under the control of a Secretary for Humanity, who sees to it that their work is not misused. Of course, the best protection for the scientist, and for us all, is a basic education of everyone, including the would-be scientists, in the humanities, in *humanitas*.

The American Indian

A CENTURY OF DISHONOR: *A Sketch of the United States Government's Dealings With Some of the Indian Tribes,* by Helen Hunt Jackson, was published in 1881 and ceased to be in print in the year of her death, 1885. Her novel *Ramona,* dealing with the same subject, has been reprinted more than 300 times! Such is the superiority of imaginative over historic literature. The history elicited nowhere nearly as much interest as the novel, the novel being read for pleasure, the history being relegated to the archives. And this, indeed, has been the fate of the American Indian, to be treated as a novelistic figure rather than as a historic living accusing reality. Mrs. Jackson's *Century of Dishonor* presented a devastating account of the mistreatment of the American Indian by the government of the United States during the century preceding the publication of the book. There have been other books of a similar sort on the subject, but all of them have suffered the same fate, for they seem to have had very little effect on whatever it is that serves most Americans for a conscience.

The treatment of the American Indian by American whites is a story, not only of dishonor, but also of infamy. The treachery, murder, dispossession, disfranchisement, genocide, destruction, robbery, cruelty, exile, and injustice which the American Indian has suffered at the hands of American whites constitute one of the blackest records in the history of the relations between peoples. Whole tribes exterminated, pledges, promises, treaties broken, dispossession and forced migrations from his native lands, forced to live on reservations as wards of the United States government under the rule of venal agents, without voting rights or representation, abandoned, disregarded, and often brutally hunted down and murdered in a spirit of sheer wantonness, the American Indian constitutes the shame of the American people.

In the name of making the world safe for democracy or self-determination, we intrude with armed force or the threat of it or with money or food or matériel in the internal affairs of other nations but neglect to secure the benefits of democracy to the original inhabitants of the United States, the original inhabitants who welcomed the first white men to their land with love, friendship, and admiration.

The discoverer of America, Christopher Columbus, described the American Indians as "a loving, uncovetous people, so docile in all things that there is no better people or better country. . . . They loved their neighbors as themselves and they had the sweetest and gentlest way of speaking in the world, and always with a smile."

In 1584 the Englishman Captain Arthur Barlowe wrote Sir Walter Raleigh about the Indians encountered on the Carolina coast: "We were entertained with all love and kindness, and with as much bounty as they could possibly devise. We found the people most gentle, loving, and faithful, void of all guile and treason, and such as live after the manner of the golden age."

Little, alas, did these innocents know that in return for

their friendship, these creatures from another world would steal their lands and property, destroy their way of life, and turn them into refugees and beggars in their own country— and then, for attempting to resist the inhuman incursions on them, be branded as fierce savages, who must be subdued or unmercifully destroyed. With the logic that is the rule in such matters, the American Indian was saddled with the crimes committed against him. For example, history and folklore tell us that the American Indian scalped his victims. What is not told us is that this practice was taught the American Indian by the invading whites, who offered a bounty for every Indian scalp taken.

Those who commit atrocities against others are shocked and outraged when their victims rise up and retaliate in kind and then, of course, proceed to condemn them for being what their teachers have taught them to become. As I have mentioned on an earlier page, even in the Declaration of Independence, in spite of the fact that American Indians had in innumerable ways greatly assisted the Revolutionary forces in their struggle for freedom, it is stated that the King of Great Britain "has excited domestic insurrections amongst us, and has endeavoured to bring on the inhabitants of our frontiers, the merciless Indian Savages, whose known rule of warfare is an undistinguished destruction of all ages, sexes and conditions."

Thus was the myth of the savage American Indian enshrined and perpetuated in the most important and basic of all historic American documents.

The crimes and cruelties committed against the American Indian can no longer be shrugged off by continuing to subscribe to the mythology that was created to justify white infamy, nor can they be evaded by pretending that the American Indian will soon cease to exist. The birthrate of the American Indian is among the highest in the land, but so, owing to the depressed conditions under which these once free people are forced to live, are their sickness and death rates. Let Americans of the "Not So Great Society" shed their hypocrisies for making the world safe for democracy abroad and devote some attention to making it safe at home for all Americans—and who has a greater claim to the title of American than the American Indian? Americans owe an incalculable debt to the American Indian. It is time they began making some attempt to repay that debt.

China and America

HAVING SUBSTANTIALLY assisted to convert the Chinese people to Communism and having done everything in our power since to harden them in their Communism, we are rapidly engaged in turning the Chinese people into our Number One Bogeyman. Throughout our relations with China, from 1784 to the present day, America has done virtually everything to convince the Chinese that we are nothing but capitalist imperialist exploiters. Americans trafficked cruelly in opium, coolies, and arms, while diplomatically siding with the French and the English in their Opium Wars. Chinese laborers in the United States were grossly mistreated, massacred, robbed, and expelled. The Exclusion Act of 1882 finally, officially intimated to the Chinese people what the American people thought of them.* Communist propagandists in China have not neglected any of this and use it to good effect. In the 1940's, instead of supporting the democratic elements, the American government chose to support the reactionary Chiang Kai-shek.

* For an account of Chinese-American relations giving the facts, see Kwang-ching Liu, *Americans and Chinese* (Cambridge, Harvard University Press, 1963). See also A. T. Steele, *The American People and China* (New York, McGraw-Hill, 1966). Also Lisa Hobbs, *I Saw Red China* (New York, McGraw-Hill, 1966).

When, by 1950, Chiang had been driven from the mainland of China by the Communists, whom we greatly assisted by our support of Chiang, we continued to support Chiang, as we do to this day on the fortress of Formosa. Here an alien ruler, Chiang, was imposed as dictator on the people of Formosa. From this base, supported by American arms and the American Seventh Fleet, Chiang has continually threatened to invade the mainland of China and "liberate" its people. All this has provided most effective grist for the propaganda mill of the Chinese Communists. Our policy-makers in Washington are worth billions to the Communist propagandists. We give them exactly what they want, free and for nothing. Chiang is a godsend to the Communists, this enemy on their doorstep, oppressing the unhappy Formosans, and made possible by that other gift of the great minds in Washington, who dictate the policy of support for Chiang. The Chinese know that the American Seventh Fleet is always within shelling distance of their coast. The Chinese people know that the one great power that has prevented them from being invited to join the United Nations is the United States. The Chinese also know, in spite of American denials and equivocations, that American planes have "wandered" over Chinese territory. And, finally, the disaster that is Vietnam has given them the incontrovertible proof of America's hostility toward them. For in spite of the American pretext of fighting a war to ensure free elections in Vietnam, what America is in fact fighting is a war of containment, as it thinks, against the Chinese Communists.

The stupidity and shortsightedness of American foreign policy everywhere are exceeded only by the immorality of that policy. This policy has been motivated first by greed, for which the customary euphemism is "The American Way of Life," and second, as in the case of Russian and Chinese

Communism, by an obsessional fear of the bogeyman—"the Communists"—who is envisaged as the monster that will destroy "the American way of life" unless we contain, if not destroy, him. We know that we cannot destroy him, but if we can contain him, many Americans persuade themselves that maybe somehow the bogeyman will go away. But the bogeyman will not go away until we cease treating him as a bogeyman, for he is a creature of our own creation. Creatures of the imagination can be very much more frightening than creatures of reality, and the unreal can be very much more real than the real. Chinese Communism is reality enough to deal with without investing it with all those myths that in our anxiety we have come to build up about it. It is a reality with which we had better learn to live, and of all the myths and misunderstandings, the fears and anxieties, it is a reality with which we can live, yes, even in amity rather than in enmity and even with some sympathy and friendship. Communism cannot remain unchanged but must, as conditions improve, develop toward a more democratic form of government. The Russians have not yet got that far, but if we will leave them alone—or even if we won't—they will get there. It would be to everyone's advantage if we would help all peoples who have shaken off their oppressors realize the goals, the long-term goals, of their revolutions.

We Americans made a revolution and succeeded in unburdening ourselves of a tyrannical rule. Following that, after a great struggle, we succeeded in achieving a semblance of democracy. In the face of such a history it is remarkable that we cannot allow other peoples their revolutionary uprisings against oppressive rulers or cannot assist them to achieve their liberties.

Fear, jitteriness, and anxiety have a way of displacing reason and sense. It is hard for those so afflicted to behave rationally, and therein lies the greatest of all dangers. But it is not too late perhaps for such people to acknowledge that spying, bad faith, ideological and military threats, and open hostility have not served to improve conditions and that indeed things have gone from bad to worse. Might it not be worth trying sincerity, good faith, cooperation, mutual aid, honesty, and friendliness in our relations with other peoples? We might give it a go for a few years and see where we get.

We could begin by sponsoring the admission of Communist China into the United Nations. Simultaneously we might abolish the C.I.A. We could institute trade and cultural exchange programs with China, and by giving the Chinese people all the aid we reasonably can, prove to them by action, not by words, that we are on the side of the human race, no matter what its political organization may temporarily be.

Vietnam

In 1955 AND 1956 the United States declined to be involved in the military action of the French in Vietnam or to assist the French in any way. Ten years after the disastrous defeat and withdrawal of the French from Vietnam, the President of the United States suddenly discovered that America must continue the conflict in Vietnam in order to keep the North Vietnamese out of South Vietnam. No war has ever been declared by the Congress on North Vietnam, and the President first sent American soldiers to South Vietnam as "advisers." The American people were told that it would all be over in a "few months; by Christmas," Secretary McNamara said. Now McNamara's band plays a different tune. From nonescalation McNamara has proceeded to escalation, from 50,000 "advisers" to more than 350,000 soldiers, not to mention naval personnel, from a short action to a long-drawn-out war. Billions of dollars are being poured into this war, and many thousands have already died and been maimed, on both sides, in this war. All to what purpose?

Our stated purpose is to prevent the forceful conquest of South Vietnam by North Vietnam. That is what the President says. But it is not true. Americans have been committed to a war in Vietnam in order to make it clear to the Communists everywhere that the government of the United States will not permit them to take over Asia by either force or political chicanery. In other words, the United States in Vietnam is engaged in a preventive war, a preventive war that will preclude the possibility of the Asian nations from falling like so many dominoes into the orbit of Communist domination.

Such reasoning constitutes the most abject folly. I do not think there is anything to be said in favor of the Communists. I think they are wrong on virtually every major aspect of human affairs, and I should be very distressed to see them take over any people by any means whatsoever. For this reason I should like to see all foreign troops removed from Vietnam and the United Nations step in. The presence of foreign troops on Vietnamese soil simply hardens the determination of the North Vietnamese and their Communist supporters to continue the fight to the end. In any event, the Vietnamese situation is not a problem that any one nation can take it on itself to solve unilaterally, even though it has the token support of other nations. And even if it could be done—and it cannot—it would be undesirable for any one nation to take it on itself to put the internal affairs of another where it thinks they ought to be. If political and social justice, autonomy, and the right to maintain its separateness are being threatened, then this should be a matter for action by the United Nations, an organization which was created for just such a purpose.

Had the Chinese Communists and the North Vietnamese been admitted to membership in the United Nations years ago, it is quite possible that the struggle now proceeding in Vietnam might have been averted. If some powerful nations, particularly the United States, will insist on excluding other nations from membership in the United Nations when it suits their purposes to do so, there can be no adequate debate or discussion. And such excluded nations can only resort to other means to make their points. Furthermore, if member nations persist in expediently bypassing the United Nations and acting unilaterally, they are much more likely to exacerbate the situation than to improve it.

The United States has no right whatever to be in Vietnam, and being there is in direct violation of the Geneva Agreement of 1954. No nation has a right to elect itself policeman of the world, especially when an international policing body, the United Nations, is already in existence. Each time the United Nations is slighted in this way, its authority is weakened.

In South Vietnam we have supported one corrupt government after another. Our man in Vietnam, as I write, is General Ky, a man who has declared his hero to be no less a person than Adolf Hitler. There is little doubt that General Ky will not last long—the popular opposition against him is too great—and were it not for the support given him by the United States, he would have fallen long ago. Why is it that our government is so often involved in supporting the wrong people? We have apparently learned absolutely nothing from the tragedy of supporting Chiang Kai-shek in China instead of the democratic elements and then compounding the felony by proceeding to support the same man in his virtual dictatorship of Formosa.

Increasingly the people of South Vietnam are staging anti-American demonstrations. This is a peculiar way in which to exhibit gratitude to one's defenders. Can it be that the people of South Vietnam do not look on Americans as their saviors, but as foreign intruders who are fighting a war in Vietnam that they do not want? Can it be that the Vietnamese peasants do not appreciate having their crops destroyed, their homes burned down, their menfolk killed and maimed, themselves attacked with napalm bombs, and visited with every other sort of iniquity in order to make America safe for democracy?

If the freedom to choose its own form of government is to be made safe for any people anywhere in the world, it will not be by such means, but by the efforts of the United Nations to ensure every people the right to enjoy its own self-determination. The United States has no right to be in Vietnam, and it has no right to interfere in the internal affairs of other peoples.

This is a war the United States cannot win. It can win this war neither militarily nor politically, and were it to win militarily, it would almost certainly lose politically. Either way the United States will lose. It is a futile war, which, if continued, will bleed America to such a state of weakness that the very end it seeks to defeat will be rendered all the more easy for the Communists to accomplish. Why cannot those in the government see this? Senators Morse, Fulbright, Gruening, and several others do see this, but they are in a small minority. Alas, the government seems to attract the kind of people who are largely without vision, who cannot see beyond the immediate issues, and who are scared to death of the bogeyman of Communism.

Mr. Johnson is conducting this unpopular war as if it were a political campaign, his own private war, in which at all costs he must succeed. But he cannot succeed; he can only fail.

It is utter nonsense to talk, as Vice-President Humphrey and others have been talking of no cease-fire in Vietnam until North Vietnam guarantees free general elections in South Vietnam. Such statements betray how ill-informed are our highest officials in government on matters Vietnamese. The

Vietnamese villagers do not understand free elections on a national level. On a village level elections are possible, but on a national level they will not be for some time. Vietnam is not a political democracy, and it is rather unrealistic to expect that the Vietnamese can be made ready, as it were, overnight. They cannot. A national election would mean very little, if anything, at the present stage of political development of the Vietnamese. It is either the sheerest nonsense or the most abysmal ignorance or both to talk of a free national election in Vietnam. The Johnson Administration has muddied the issues in Vietnam long enough. Why continue to render them more turgid?

There is an old Chinese saying that when one is astride a tiger, it is difficult to dismount gracefully. It is better to dismount ungracefully than to be disgracefully thrown. What will happen when the United States finds that it is engaged in a war that the Vietnamese people do not want, and it loses its principal excuse for being in Vietnam at all? Will the American generals take over and maintain a puppet government in Saigon, or will Washington discover some new rationalization for continuing the conflict?

There is yet another saying, this time Greek; it is that those whom the gods wish to destroy they first drive mad.

Hotels

AMERICA HAS SOME of the finest hotels in the world and some of the worst—the newest ones, especially. I have lived in the country for many years and greatly enjoy its quietude. Hence, the new hotels, with their thin walls, wholly uninsulated, which transmit the voices of the guests on the other side of them, the crackling of TV and radio, the telephone, are not for the likes of me. Worst of all are the flushing toilets. These are enough to disturb one's sleep and give one nightmares, for when a toilet is flushed, it sounds like the combined thunders of the cataracts of the Nile and the Victoria and Niagara Falls—louder, in fact, for water seems to be rushing straight through the walls aiming for one's prone body about to be engulfed. What single-mindlessness it must have taken to have planned such comforts for the hotelier's guests? One wonders whether an architect was ever involved or whether it wasn't all left to the plumber to do the planning?

Windows do not seem to be constructed with any thought of shutting out the street noises and traffic. And where, in older establishments, air-conditioning units have been placed in the windows, it is quite impossible to open or close the window, and only too often one is forced to suffer the noises of the air-conditioning motors.

I find such noises particularly difficult in motels in which the air-conditioning noises originate from a central system about which it is impossible to do anything. I prefer motels, in general, to hotels because in the former there are generally no bellhops. I have nothing against bellhops; they are very helpful people. It is simply that I don't need their help, and I resent having it thrust on me. It is really quite amazing how well guests manage in a motel without a bellhop. Most hotels insist that their guests, having checked into a hotel, must be shown to their rooms by a bellhop. When I have inquired why it is not possible for a guest to let himself into his own room without the offices of a bellhop, I have been told, "It is a house rule." Having pressed for a further explanation, while waiting for a bellhop, I have been informed, "The bellhop must see that everything is in order." When I have replied that I considered myself quite capable of making such an inspection, I have been told once again, "It is a house rule."

I don't think it is a good rule. It should not be mandatory, but at the discretion of the guest, whether he should have a bellhop or not. What has annoyed me most about this business is that I have often had to wait an unconscionable time, especially when I was in a hurry, for a bellhop—as long as fifteen minutes. And usually, since I travel lightly, I have not had the slightest need for a bellhop. But "It's a house rule," and hence, I, with numberless others, must continue to be victimized by utterly indefensible and stupid rules which contribute to the guest's discomfort.

It seems to me also that during rush hours there ought to be some more speedy means of both checking in and checking out. Here, too, there is often much waste of the guest's time and much room for improvement.

I wish that lamps in hotel rooms had switches or buttons

that were in accessible places, instead of where they often are, in the most inaccessible of places.

I wish that hotel doors were constructed in such a manner that it would be impossible to slam them and possible only to close them noiselessly. The noises originating from this cause alone are usually amplified by the poor construction of the corridors on which they open.

I wish that maids would be encouraged to make up rooms rather nearer lunchtime than breakfasttime, when one is often awakened by their opening and closing of doors, frequently disturbing one's best sleep.

I wish that when one asked for a quiet room, one were given one.

I wish that distinguishing marks were put on bath mats so that they would not be confused with towels.

The South

THE SOUTH IS a disaster area, a human blight—a region where inhumanity and injustice have been endemic for more than two centuries; where, indeed, inhumanity is a way of life; where the murder of Negroes and of anyone who offers them aid, is not only condoned by white juries, "twelve good men and true," but widely applauded; where law enforcement agencies exist to perpetuate the endemic inhumanity and injustice; and where the law itself exists to defend the Southern way of life.

The white Southerner is a very sick man. His sickness is so widespread in the South that as a way of life it is considered both normal and healthy. Anything, therefore, that threatens that way of life is condemned as abnormal, unhealthy, undesirable, and to be mercilessly repressed. Hence, Negroes who become "uppity"—that is, who demand the right to be treated as full citizens and as human beings—receive short shrift. Brutal beatings and murders of Negroes, their homes and churches burned down and bombed—the calendar of crimes against the Negro is endless. The record is a terrible one, and before the bar of humanity the South stands roundly condemned.

All classes of white society in the South are equally guilty of crimes against the Negro. If anything, it is the upper rather than the lower-class elements that are to be held chiefly responsible for the degradation of the Negro, for attitudes toward the Negro have been transmitted from those above to those below. To this day the so-called educated classes, the professions, especially the one profession, the law, from which one might have hoped for some worthy example, have remained shamefully silent. The Church has remained equally unconcerned. But, then, the Church in the South is not a house of God, but a denominational institution devoted to the service of the *status quo*—each denomination being exclusive of the other and, with few exceptions, each excluding the Negro. Indeed, for the last two centuries the Church in the South has been among the most segregated of institutions.

By degrading the Negro, the South has degraded itself. The South is in every way the most impoverished region in America, educationally, culturally, spiritually, socially, and politically. And this is entirely the South's own doing, in spite of the fact that the Negro and the North are the rationalizations which are employed to explain the problems of the South. If only Northerners would not interfere and leave the problems of the South to those who understand them and who, of course, understand the Negro, all would be well. Whites and Negroes would get along beautifully, as they always have! It is an incredible psychosis, a schizophrenic flight from reality, which has spread like a contagion throughout the South.

The chief problem, of course, is the Negro problem. But there is no Negro problem. What there is is a Southern white problem, and until the problem of the Southern white man is solved, none of the significant problems of the South stands the slightest chance of solution.

The Negro needs all the help he can be given, but neither the Negro nor the white will be much benefited until the white Southerner has undergone a fundamental reeducation as a human being. A change of heart is indicated perhaps more than anything else. Being human, Southerners are, I believe, capable of making such a change, and I am convinced that they will. And who will help them most effectively to achieve it? The Southern Negro.

Racism

RACISM HAS BEEN endemic in America ever since twenty Negroes were purchased from a Portuguese man-of-war by the citizens of Roanoke in 1619. The doctrine of racism as such was not born until much later, at the beginning of the nineteenth century, but discrimination of one sort or another against the Negro goes back to the very beginning of the seventeenth century.

For three and a half centuries the American Negro has been exploited, degraded, and deformed. Treated as a second-rate human being and as a second-class citizen, his struggles to better his lot, when they have not been harshly repressed, have met with very little encouragement. It is a widespread and deep sickness, this racism with which Americans are infected, and it has been terribly damaging to everyone who has come within the reach of this contagion. As Booker T. Washington said, one cannot hold a man down in the gutter without coming up dirty oneself.

The Negro has for so long been the white man's scapegoat that it is difficult for him to be seen as anything else: an inferior and contemptible creature who must be kept in his proper place. That crippled and weak personalities find it rewarding to indulge in racism is understandable. That

[315

racism is basically nonsense is apparently not understandable to those who believe in it. There are many millions of Americans who honestly believe that Negroes are inferior people and that they must therefore be treated as such. That, at any rate, is the phrase. But it is the most arrant hypocrisy, the most abject of rationalizations. It is, this way—or any other, for the matter of that—the easiest thing in the world to be a racist. All that one requires is a capacity for feeling inferior and the ability to project that feeling on others. If, in addition to this, one can develop some skill in deducing facts from assumptions, one has at one's disposal all that is required to qualify as a person who honestly believes that Negroes are inferior and must therefore be treated as such.

There is not the slightest evidence that Negroes are in any way inferior to whites, in spite of the numerous attempts that have been made to find such evidence, but let us for a moment suppose that any group of people were found to be inferior to another. How then does one treat inferior people? Does one behave toward them in such a manner that one depresses their quality even further, or does one afford them every possible opportunity to develop within whatever limitations their genes may place upon them? The inequalities in endowment that may exist among individuals surely call for behavior designed to meet the requirements of those inequalities rather than discrimination against them. The real question is not what hereditary differences may exist between persons, but whether, as human beings, they have a right to their birthright—that is, to the development of their potentialities, whatever those potentialities may be.

He who stands in the way of another human being's fulfillment commits the greatest of crimes against the human spirit, against the individual, and against humanity, for he deprives each person of the unique gifts that one is capable of bestowing upon his fellowmen. No matter how modest or how generous those gifts or whatever the limitations with which human beings are born, every individual should enjoy the right to the optimum development of his potentialities. As Carlyle put it, "The great law of culture is: Let each become all that he was created capable of being; expand, if possible, to his full growth; and show himself at length in his own shape and stature, be these what they may." This is the right secured to every American—by the book. But in reality it is quite another thing. The Negro's birthright in America is frustration, degradation, and exclusion from the community of his "fellow" Americans. Yes, some progress has been made, but it is little compared with what requires to be made. Meanwhile, millions of Negroes are forced to live under the most appalling conditions. Read Claude Brown's *Manchild in the Promised Land* (New York, Macmillan, 1965), *The Autobiography of Malcolm X* (New York, Grove, 1965), and Mary Greene and Orletta Ryan's *The Schoolchildren* (New York, Pantheon, 1965) for devastating accounts of the manner in which "loving" white Americans contrive to crush the spirit of the American Negro.

America as a power in the world will either stand or fall on what it does during the next two decades to rectify the wrongs it has done against the Negro. But that is not the point. What *is* the point is simple justice for the Negro and massive indemnification for the past wrongs done him. The Germans have attempted to make some sort of restitution to the surviving Jews for the wrongs committed against them by the Third Reich. The United States could, perhaps, be expected to do no less for its Negroes, whom it has grievously wronged for three and a half centuries.

The indemnification should take the form of the necessary number of billions of dollars devoted to special rehabilitation programs, not undertaken in the perfunctory manner in which these things have been done in the past, but on a large and generous scale, with the very best people involved at every level. Education of Negroes should receive the most intensive and careful attention. Residential schools and colleges should be established throughout the land and staffed with faculties specially trained to give Negroes the very best possible education, so that they may be prepared to cooperate and compete with whites at an equal level. This kind of residential education should receive the highest priority, for lack of education in the past has been the greatest weakness of the American Negro in attempting to compete with white Americans. Subsidized housing and employment and large cash subsidies designed to raise the standard of living of Negroes are all urgent desiderata. What is needed is a federal restitution project, which will make restitution not alone to Negroes, but to all American citizens who have been abandoned by their government—and the time is now.

The automobile disaster

NEXT TO THE PROBLEM of overpopulation, the
greatest disaster of the twentieth century is the automobile.
People and automobiles come into being for pretty much the
same reasons—or rather, lack of them. People enjoy sex, and
they enjoy the equivalents or substitutes of sex, and there is a
sort of feedback interaction between them. The more people,
the more cars, and the more cars, the more people, for
mobility itself adds to the possibilities of multiplying human
beings.

Here are some raw statistics. In the United States:

98,000,000 persons hold drivers' licenses.
85,000,000 cars are on the road.
2,000,000,000 miles are driven each day.
30,000 drive-ins are scattered along the road to minister to the
  drivers' needs.
11,000,000 car accidents occur each year.
55,000 persons are killed each year.
1,750,000 persons are injured each year.
50 popular magazines are devoted exclusively to cars.
One-seventh of the total labor force of the United States is
  employed in industries connected with the manufacture of
  cars.
Smog pollution of large cities, such as Los Angeles, San Fran-

[319

cisco, Chicago, New York, and many others, is largely due to
the gases spewed forth from automobile exhausts.
More than 50 percent of fatal automobile accidents are caused
by drunken drivers.
Large numbers of drivers are psychotic, paranoid, violent, sui-
cidal, or depressed.
In several states it is possible to obtain a driver's license merely
by writing for it.
In one state (Kansas) a blind person may hold a driver's license.

The automobile explosion, paralleling the population explosion, constitutes a disaster of major proportions. In
America it has already irreversibly destroyed and lacerated
vast areas of natural beauty, replacing the meadowlands, the
trees, and the grasses with highways and roads and freeways
and interchanges and bridges, with tollgates, service stations,
drive-in movies, junkyards, hamburger stands, and other
forms of ghastliness.

When the first horseless carriage necessitated the removal
of a single tree, the rape of the land by the automobile began,
and it has proceeded at an accelerating pace since. But what's
a tree? Mayor Daley of Chicago said in answer to that question, "You can't stop progress." Only God, it has been said,
can make a tree. But, of course, man can make cars much
faster than God appears to be willing to make trees, or so it
would appear. For the trees vanish as the cars increase. In the
folly that leads him to perpetrate such disasters, man fails to
perceive that there is a vital connection, affecting his own
welfare, between the number of trees and the number of cars.
For it is mainly our leafy trees which, by photosynthesis, give
us our oxygen. Hence, when we kill trees, we reduce our
sources of oxygen supply, for with the exhausts from our cars
and the pollutants we empty into the atmosphere from other
sources, we are depositing in the atmosphere a layer of

carbon which cuts down the necessary sunlight and which, together with the already reduced foliage available, further reduces the process of photosynthesis. Instead of cutting down trees, we should be planting them. For every automobile put on the road there should be 10 trees planted; for every truck, 100 trees planted; and for every jet, 1,000 trees planted. It is not commonly known that when a jet takes off, it puts as much pollution into the air as 3,500 six-cylinder automobile engines idling for one minute. Plants wilt, their lower surfaces coated and glazed with a silvery sheen so often seen on the undersides of leaves; livestock sickens, and meat and dairy products are affected; stone, paint, and mortar are eaten away from our buildings, monuments, and bridges; and metal is corroded. And as for ourselves, well, there are so many of us that *we* are expendable. What these poisons in the air do to our eyes, mucous membranes, throats, and lungs, not to mention other organs, is damaging enough, but how many people know that one of these poisons (in the form of nitrogen dioxide) also puts runs into nylons? And there lies the hope for the future. For once women's vested interests are threatened in this way, something may yet be done about the reduction of pollutants in the air.

There are some 6,000 communities in the United States which are seriously affected by atmospheric pollution. The U. S. Public Health Service has estimated that in various ways this pollution costs the American people the staggering sum of 11,000,000,000 dollars a year. And most of this pollution has its source in automobiles. It has been estimated that every 1,000 automobiles operating in an urban community discharge daily into the atmosphere 3.2 tons of carbon monoxide, 400 to 800 pounds of hydrocarbon gases, 100 to 300 pounds of nitrous oxides, and smaller amounts of sulfur and other irritants. Additional damaging products of the disastrous automobile, scarcely ever mentioned, are the solid particles, some so small they cannot be seen by the naked eye, such as bits of pulverized rock, ground metal filings, particles of rubber, residues of carbon, ash, lead, and carbohydrates. Then there are the droplets of oil, grease, and tar that drift suspended in air currents. Since I have had to have such metal particles extracted from my eye, I can speak with feeling, as well as with authority, on the subject.

Aware of the health problem presented by the increasing pollution, our government makes occasional noises and promises to do something about it, but the net result so far is that of the 6,000 communities already seriously affected, only a little more than 100 have air-pollution control projects with full-time staffs. The automobile industry, whose sole purpose is to make money, is not interested in the welfare of its customers. This is a shortsighted policy, for even so thick-skinned an industry ought to be able to see that the more healthy customers they have, the more cars they will sell. But there is no hope from that quarter, for what is good for the automobile industry has from the beginning turned out to be generally bad for the land and for the people. The health menace from the automobile continues. In 1961 the then Secretary of Health, Education, and Welfare, Abraham A. Ribicoff, asked the automobile industry to install pollution-reducing devices as standard equipment in all 1964 cars. For some reason the automobile industry has not yet seen fit to do so. In at least one state, California, where the pollution problem is so serious, since June, 1965, these devices have become mandatory on all new cars.

In the Bay Area alone 6,400 tons of pollutants are daily pumped by automobiles into the air. In Los Angeles, a city engulfed by automobiles, 7,500,000 gallons of gasoline are burned every day. More than two-thirds of the land surface is given over to the automobile, in streets, access roads, freeways, interchanges, parking lots, and service stations. In 1965 the state government of California spent more than 1,250,000,000 dollars on highways and other direct costs of the automobile—not including the tremendous costs in loss of life, injury, and damage to property.

What California shows, as it were, in high relief is the pattern of conditions which exist in every large community in the United States—where wealth accumulates and men decay. The deadly killer, by 1,000 fatal injuries a week (not to mention the 23,000 incapacitating injuries a week), without reference to the probable fatalities induced by automobile pollution, has produced other disastrous consequences.

A city was, until the advent of the automobile, a place where people met, exchanged ideas, enjoyed themselves, and engaged in trade. These were the traditional values of the city, and these are the values which the automobile is successfully destroying. Where this may be observed in its extreme form is, of course, in Los Angeles. Here no one walks, there is hardly any public transportation and so everyone moves by car, and there is no such thing as a community or a neighborhood, for everyone lives in isolated units traumatically displaced from their neighbors. Instead of a public transportation system, Los Angeles has a private transportation chaos, contributed for the most part by cars with a single passenger, the driver. This is idiot man disporting himself at his acerebral worst. Not only in Los Angeles, but everywhere else, motor transport, the privately driven automobile, should supplement, *not* supplant, other modes of public transportation. Private transportation is in every way extremely wasteful, uneconomic, inefficient, and damaging. Public transportation can carry vastly greater numbers of people much more rapidly and at considerably lower cost than private cars. In Manhattan in 1911 a horse-drawn vehicle could speed through city streets at a rate of eleven miles an hour. In the year of grace 1966 an automobile can do an average of six miles an hour when crossing Manhattan. Such is progress! However, on California freeways it is inviting an accident to do less than seventy-five miles an hour. If someone is suddenly forced to stop—that is unfortunate. Under such conditions as many as 126 cars have been known to pile up against one another!

Foresight, alas, is the last of the gifts granted by the gods to man. If men had behaved sensibly and not reproduced as irresponsibly as they have, the invention of the internal-combustion engine would not have proved such a double-edged disaster. A smaller population would have required a smaller number of engines. Today the exploding populations of the earth look to ever-increasing numbers of engines for the power they need. At the moment there are already hundreds of millions of engines in use. This, of course, includes not only automobile engines, but also engines used for every other kind of purpose. Add to the gases they produce the exhausts of diesel and jet engines, and we arrive at the staggering fact that there must be well over a billion such engines spewing their poisons into the air and progressively polluting it. It may well be that if we continue to pay as little attention to this problem as we are bestowing on it today, we shall poison ourselves out of existence long before we shall have managed to crowd or atomize ourselves into oblivion.

The problem of automobile pollution could be easily overcome by substituting the fuel cell electric motor for the internal-combustion engine. The fuel cell utilizes alcohol or similar substances, and its exhaust is nitrogen, a harmless gas. Our space capsules are successfully operated by fuel cell systems. Such systems could be even more readily adapted to providing the energy to drive automobiles. With one such fuel system in each wheel, efficiency, safety, sound levels, economy all would greatly improve, and pollution from automobile exhausts would be reduced to the vanishing point. The fuel cell engine in automobiles is perfectly practical now. If the consumer would demand it, he would get such cars. I rather expect, however, that the demand will have to come from the federal government, for the consumer doesn't appear to be interested enough in his own welfare to do anything about such matters—alas!

The competition between people and the automobile for space is one which people are losing at an accelerating pace to the automobile. The chaos and congestion created by the automobile in our cities, the clogging of vital arteries, the snuffing out of the community, the exchange of meaningful and interesting city life for the increasing monotony and boredom of enforced automobility, the traumatic displacement from neighborhood to high-rise buildings, the breakup of the extended family into atomized families separated from one another by great distances—all are conditions directly traceable to the effects of the automobile.

What began as freedom of movement has terminated in the necessity to keep on moving. The automobile continues to give the illusion of freedom and power, while proclaiming the driver's private ego. No hope, therefore, is to be looked for from that quarter. If the strangulation of our cities is to be arrested, the federal government will have to act. And one of its first acts might well be the outlawing of most cars from the vital centers of our cities.

The Big American Car

Glitter, glitter, monstrous car,
I don't wonder what you are.
You're the chromium and the essence
Of tinny, inbuilt obsolescence.
You're a thing of bits and patches,
Which alone but one thing matches:
The fate, oft told, alas no more,
Of giant extinct dinosaur.
His brain grew small, his body big;
He couldn't park; he couldn't twig.
His wits unable to exploit,
They're now most treasured in Detroit.

Among the populations of some Pacific islands it is a mark of high status to secure for oneself a stone of monetary value so large that no one can move it. In the United States it is an evidence of status when one can acquire a movable object of glittering metal, embellished with the maker's symbol of costliness, which by the very fact of its unnecessary size declares its owner's putative opulence. The American status symbol, beyond all others, is the American big car—the juggernaut of the masses.

The American big car is, of course, only one of many status symbols. The house in which one lives, for example, has become among the most conspicuously valued of status symbols. But a house is, after all, sessile, stationary, fixed, whereas when one is living in an ethos of conspicuous consumption or keeping up with the Joneses, a house on wheels is the thing, short of a trailer, with all the comforts of home, and, indeed, taken all in all, rather more impressive than home.

The psychological appeal of the big car, altogether apart from the opportunities it provides for the expression of aggression and the vicarious demonstration of virility, constitutes a fascinating study in motivation.

It is only in a monarchic or an aristocratic society that one encounters sizable numbers of levelers or revolutionaries who want equality for everyone. In a democracy, in which everyone is supposed to be equal, no one wants to be. People don't want to be equal; they want to be different, to be recognized, at any rate, as in some way distinguishably themselves. And this is precisely as it should be, for one of the healthiest things about a democracy is that it maximizes the opportunities for being different. This desire to be different is one of the reasons, I believe, why Americans have become such perfervid status seekers, seekers after the symbols which will bring them the satisfaction of knowing and advertising to others that they are different. And different, of course, by the measure of the greatest of all American values: dollar-volume success.

Ministering to many needs, the big car is a most ingeniously designed device, calculated to meet the American's need for inequality, for status, for self-substantiation, and that feeling of luxury that only a well-appointed car can give.

In a highly competitive society in which titles and other undemocratic modes of distinction are constitutionally disallowed, the need for distinctiveness and social recognition becomes very pressing indeed. Other societies provide socially sanctioned outlets for such needs. Americans have to create and secure them for themselves. This is one of the reasons why Americans are such joiners, why Phi Beta Kappa keys and symbols to wear on the lapels of one's coat are so highly valued among us. Any Georgian sheepherder's sons, calling themselves princes, can be sure of the richest women throwing themselves at their feet, for Americans dearly love a title.

It is or should be clear that when a society fails to provide the symbols that confer status on its members, the members of that society will secure them for themselves. You may not become a Grand Klaxon or a member of the Order of the John Birch Society or other similar imbecilities, but a big car will succeed where all else fails. Americans are perhaps the only people in the world among whom bigness itself has become a value. We have the biggest buildings, the biggest roads, the biggest ships, the biggest annual per capita income, the biggest— In short, our biggest is bigger than anyone else's. Bigness itself is taken to confer status. It would naturally follow that one of our commonest objects of conspicuous consumption would have to be big.

It is not that the citizens of other countries are not also to some extent status seekers or that Americans are really more interested in status than other people. All human beings are interested in status, and if a status is not assigned to them, they grow anxious about acquiring one. In other countries the big car is no less a status symbol than it is here, but fewer individuals abroad can afford a big car, and in any event, the roads being much narrower in general in Europe and elsewhere, a small car has considerable advantages over a large one. Even so, Europeans admire and sigh over a large car. This is probably nothing new. Ancient men probably gaped at the man in the large coracle and thought him distinguished for owning so enviable an instrument of aquatic bliss. Ancient Romans are known to have vied with one another over the appearance of their chariots and, of course, their magnitude. Certainly down to the very commencement of the twentieth century the coach was used not only as a means of conveyance, but also as a vehicle for the display of status.

Some years ago George Romney, then president of American Motors, predicted that by 1963 small car sales would reach 300,000,000 units. In his view the end of the big car domination of the American market was close at hand. At first it looked as if Mr. Romney's prediction would turn out to be right. But the American car owner having tried the small car, which has enormous advantages over the large car, eventually turned it in for the big car. The small car simply reduced him to size, and he did not like that. The big car made him look big, and *that* he liked. In spite of the fact that the Rambler, Mr. Romney's own car, is a very good car, it hasn't been doing nearly as well as the monsters turned out by General Motors and Chrysler and Ford. The best car ever made in America, the Franklin, was scorned by the American car buyer because it didn't look tinselly enough. It was a car of quality, and that is a commodity the average American doesn't care much about. After all, it is appearances that count.

In addition to the fact that it is both less expensive to purchase and to maintain and easier to park, the small car has an appeal of its own. It is the appeal of inverse snobbery, as those geniuses who advertise Volkswagen are well aware. When most people drive a big car and you drive a small one, that makes *you* remarkable and *them* unremarkable. But for obvious reasons, inverse snobbery has a limited appeal, for it takes a genuine snob to carry off inverse snobbery successfully, and the genuine article among snobs is very rare.

The dominance of the big car may be disputed for a while by the little car, but it is improbable that the small car will ever even so much as reach parity with the big car. The big car does too much for one's ego.

The psychology of the big car is fascinating. In one of its widely distributed advertisements one of the big car manufacturers prints the emblem associated with its car and above this a necklace of the most beautiful precious jewels, courtesy of course of the appropriate house, and above this there is the word "Prestige." The copy then states that when you drive up before your neighbor's house in such a car, this car in particular, he doesn't have to *ask* who you are; he *knows* who you are! A great success, of course.

As illustrative of this psychology, I can quote from personal experience. Some years ago in a small town in Virginia, one of its half-dozen surgeons told me that he was finally forced to purchase a big car because all five of his colleagues were driving prestige cars, and he could no longer afford to hold out because people might think he was not as good a surgeon as the others!

There are innumerable other motivations underlying the addiction to the big car. In addition to what it does for his ego by way of pride in the possession of so eminent a mark of distinction, the driver feels, as he sits behind the wheel, very like a god in his machine—omnipotent, for a car grants one the power to move effortlessly in whatever direction one chooses and at whatever time one wills. The driver not only proposes, but, like a god, disposes. He commands, and the genie obeys. Indeed, where wife and children and other human beings of all sorts and kinds may fail him, the car seldom does. One opens the door, sits down, turns on the ignition as the accelerator (or as one man I recently overheard so charmingly and illuminatingly put it, the "exhilarator") is depressed, and the genie comes to life, thereafter doing exactly what it is told. The consciousness that this power is in his hands and that he is able to command it contributes further to the driver's feeling of omnipotence. In the car he has the feeling that he can triumphantly, at last, do everything—and, unfortunately, only too often he does!

A big car compensates for the weaknesses of the driver while endowing him with power that he can obtain in no other way. Both the driver and the observer often feel that the power of the car has, without metamorphosis, been transferred to the driver-owner (if he is merely a chauffeur, it doesn't so much matter, for a chauffeur is considered to be only a part of the machine).

In spite of the fact that we call ourselves civilized and live in the twentieth century, magical ways of thought are still very much with us. But instead of accepting these magical ways of thought for what they are, today we rationalize our magic and say, "Well, a man with a powerful car must be powerful to afford such a car. And he *is*, in any event, powerful because he is now in fact in command of such great power." We may not put it into so many words, but this is too often what we subliminally think.

In addition to the halo effect of prestige, there is then the power of bigness and the feeling of omnipotence associated with it. While the former may be operative in the case of women, the latter is of little or no concern to them as drivers. This brings us to the factor of sex.

The big car as a symbol of the male's sexual prowess, a mechanical or dynamic equivalent of sexual potency, is undoubtedly a factor in its appeal. It is closely allied to the feeling of generalized power, of the omnipotence to which reference has already been made. Sexual potency is highly valued in a culture in which, as Dr. Edmond Ferris tells us, "only about 40 percent of men are capable of fertilization most of the time during the peak of their reproductive lives." The capacity to become a father is, however, by no means the principal value of which sexual potency is considered to be the expression. Sexual potency is identified with manliness, with strength, with power. Put strength and power into a car, and you have produced an unbeatable combination of symbolic representations, dynamic equivalents, of sexual power and manliness.

Ever since the advent of the automobile, it has ceased to be necessary to be a football hero if one wishes to make a hit with the beautiful girls. It can be done much more efficiently with a big powerful car. This combination of conditions was perhaps most perfectly realized in the Roaring Twenties, when a real he-man, with surefire instinct, donned a raccoon coat and went apicking up the Daisys in a Bear-Cat Stutz—a powerful car if there ever was one! After all, man *is* a symbol-using animal, and he is as accomplished in the use of those he realizes unconsciously as he is in the use of those he creates consciously. The powerful car enhances the male's sex appeal, and he feels enhanced by it—the powerful car.

People enjoy sex, and they enjoy the power substitutes for sex. That is one of the less obvious great secrets of the success of the automobile. For the sexually inadequate or unsatisfied, a car, especially a big car, is a wonderful way of experiencing a feeling of orgiastic power, of holding the very power of life and death in one's hands, the excitement and the thrills incident to the climactic perils of driving.

Finally, the car is not merely a vehicle, but a means of self-expression.

Teen-agers and the Automobile

One of the reasons why teen-agers drive as dangerously as they do is not merely that they relish to its fullest the novelty of a new experience, but also that they find stepping on the accelerator an exhilarating experience, a substitute for their inhibited sex drives. Exceeding the behavioral speed limit, free of the cramping inhibiting effects of one's elders, is the ultimate expression of freedom for the teen-ager. And if nothing goes on in the back of the car or stops short of the real thing, what goes on in the front of the car is almost the best of all substitutes. Anyway, it is experienced as the next best thing.

The uninhibited teen-ager, driving his car with careless abandon, is irresistibly appealing to the teen-age girl. She can experience the substitute for the forbidden thrills in the front, as well as in the back, of the car. It is a perfect arrangement, what with roadstands, drive-ins, and drive-in movies. Not missing a trick, the Ford Motor Company, in selling its Mustang in 1965, seriously considered, in appealing to the younger generation, using the advertising come-on "Make out in a Mustang." But at the last moment the idea was, for the time being, dropped.

The status symbol of the car is not limited to adults. The juggernaut represents even more of a status symbol for the young—a rite of passage celebrating the transition from supervised disciplined childhood to the uninhibited freedom of independence. And that the young are not uninfluenced by the prestige of the car as a symbol affecting their own status was forcibly brought in on me some years ago. I had been addressing a parents' study group in a New York suburb, in which, I was informed, the average income was in the vicinity of $100,000 a year. During the discussion period the first person to ask me a question was a woman. This was the question: "We have a problem with which I think you could be of help. We have a sixteen-year-old son. Six months ago we bought him a Thunderbird; now all his friends are driving a Jaguar. What should we do?"

The question left me speechless. If anyone had told me such a story, I confess, I would have experienced some difficulty in believing it. But there I was hearing it with my own ears. The woman had a problem, and it was as real to her as the most serious of problems could be to anyone. She never obtained an answer from me, for although I asked her to come see me at the conclusion of the meeting, we never did meet, I suppose because I was quickly whisked away. I suspect her little boy got his Jaguar and was thereafter able to hold his own among his peers. Poor chap, he will probably end up driving his car four hours a day to and from his place of work, supporting the girl he got pregnant in the back seat of the car and their subsequent unplanned offspring.

Has anyone ever considered what a contribution the automobile has made to the population explosion? To the illegitimacy rate? To early marriages? For many teen-agers, the automobile has, among other things, become a bedroom on wheels. In many parts of the country, teen-agers now drive to and from school. School parking lots are now designed for student cars. Possibly someday school curricula will also be designed to teach driver education which will include some reference to population control.

Putting the teen-ager into possession of an automobile, we put him into possession not only of a substitute for sex but also of an instrument that leads to and facilitates it. Whether it does or not, both the vicarious thrill and the promise of the real thing are there to more than sustain him. Alas, for the carless teen-ager who is forced to find other outlets frequently, shall we say, less profitable to the automobile industry!

Twenty-five percent of teen-agers admit to having driven more than 90 miles an hour, and not surprisingly teen-agers are the main cause of automobile accidents. In certain localities more than 75 percent of high school teen-agers have their own car. And if this is the way their doting parents want it, this is the way they shall have it.

Automakers, Safety, and Responsibility

The automakers are in business to make money, and nothing else. The fact that they make cars is only secondary to their purpose. If they could make as much money making sardine cans, they'd make sardine cans. Not that their cars don't frequently resemble sardine cans. In order to get in or out of most of them, more than one user has remarked that a sardine-can opener would be helpful. The automakers are in business for profits, and they make lots of them. The main consideration in the manufacture of a car appears to be the appeal of the features that will make it salable. Such features, the automakers have learned, are exclusively, or almost exclusively, those that will catch the eye. Hence, the stylist reigns supreme, and the public gets what it wants. In accordance with the principle that the customer should be given what he wants without any consideration for what he needs, the automakers are right up there in the front line with the rest of big business, not only giving the public what it wants, but also causing it to want what it does not need.

But when a commodity is involved that may be damaging to life and limb, it is surely the right of every consumer to expect—nay, his obligation to demand—that the manufacturer will do everything possible to reduce the hazards. The Food and Drug Administration regulates the standards of the drugs that are offered by the manufacturers, and the Federal Aviation Agency regulates the safety standards for airplanes. Surely, the time has arrived for the regulation of safety standards designed to safeguard the lives of automobile users.

The automakers have resisted every kind of regulation. A congressional inquiry into the safety of automobiles, headed by Senator Abraham A. Ribicoff, designed to strengthen the administration bill that would give the federal government discretionary authority to establish and enforce minimum safety standards for new passenger cars, has revealed that the automakers are as opposed as ever to such governmental regulation.

When a principal critic of the automakers' lack of responsibility put his criticisms into a book, *Unsafe at Any Speed* (New York, Grossman, 1965), General Motors instituted an undercover investigation into the personal life of the author, Ralph Nader. When Mr. Nader brought this matter to the attention of the congressional committee, Mr. James M. Roche, president of General Motors, publicly apologized to Mr. Nader for subjecting this public-spirited young lawyer to such unseemly harassment. Mr. Nader's sex life, his political views, his past history—all were the subject of investigation by private detectives. Sex lures were thrown in Mr. Nader's way, all this, as General Motors hypocritically announced, as part of "a routine investigation." It was a shocking performance, not one whit mitigated by the public eating of crow by the president of General Motors. But then, General Motors can always repair its tarnished "image" by putting some extra chrome on its cars.

The fact is that the automakers are interested only in the consumer's money and not in the least in his welfare or in dealing with him in any way whatever, except through sexual lures in advertising. It is the dealer who is left to deal with the customer, and it is the dealer's responsibility to make good any defects that may exist in the cars he sells. Anyone who has attempted the fruitless task of attempting to persuade the automaker to assume responsibility for manufacturing faults and not make the dealer liable for these will know how rapidly one gets nowhere with the manufacturer. The consumer is politely informed that the automaker sells his cars to the dealer, and thenceforward all responsibility for defects is assumed by the dealer—at least, that is what the Chrysler Corporation told me when I endeavored to persuade its officers to take back the lemon of lemons that they had manufactured and that I had in good faith purchased on the assumption that it would behave reasonably well as a motor vehicle. There was so much wrong with this new car, a Plymouth station wagon, that I felt very strongly that the dealer should not be held responsible, but that the manufacturer should. The dealer could not give me another car; the manufacturer could. I had paid for a new car and got a private and public danger instead. But the Chrysler Corporation declined to see it that way. Reasoning that after both the gearshift lever and the emergency brake came away in my wife's hand, and a leak developed in the transmission, and the paint began to flake off the steering wheel, the probability was high that more serious defects were likely to show up, as indeed they did—among them, the breaking of the piston rings, requiring a whole new transmission—I asked for either a new car or my money back. I got neither. After three months of agonizing experiences with the car and steadily getting nowhere with the Chrysler Corporation, I turned in the lemon for a Ford, which served us well, and I have never since touched a Chrysler product. This doesn't seem to have worried the Chrysler Corporation very much, but then, as Sir Edward Coke wrote in 1612, "Corporations cannot commit treason, nor be outlawed, nor excommunicated, for they have no souls." At no time would the Chrysler officials with whom I corresponded admit that its product was defective, and, indeed, in response to my describing the misfortune I had acquired as a lemon, it was specifically asserted that the Chrysler Corporation had "never manufactured a lemon." This refusal to admit the possibility of defects in workmanship, not to mention the threat to life that these defects presented, seems to be the invariable establishment position of the automakers. It is an irresponsible and an indecent posture, and it cries out for correction. The irresponsibility and indecency will continue so long as the stylist is at the top and the safety engineer at the bottom of the Detroit power structure. The fact that several automakers have recently acknowledged defects on certain models, Chrysler, among them, with a faulty throttle link capable of stepping up creepage, strongly indicates the need for federally regulated safety and inspection standards.

Safety Last: An Indictment of the Auto Industry, by Jeffrey O'Connell and Arthur Myers (New York, Random House, 1966), is the title of yet another critical examination of the auto industry's failure to concern itself seriously with the problem of safety in its products. It is quite clear from such works and more than fifty years of experience that until the federal government regulates the standards for safety in automobile design, Detroit will do very little about the matter.*

Minimal safety standards should require that all projecting parts, both in the interior and on the exterior of the car, shall be entirely eliminated wherever possible; that handles be inset; and that all knobs be replaced by buttons in such a manner that they are flush with the surfaces of which they form a part. Doors should be of the sliding variety. The steering wheel and the steering column should be collapsible, and the head of the steering column heavily padded, as, of course, the dashboard should be. All blind spots should be eliminated, and the greatest possible visibility for the driver and his passengers achieved.

Detroit takes the view that the chief cause of accidents is

---

* On September 9, 1966, President Johnson signed the bill requiring automobile manufacturers to manufacture safer cars.

careless driving and, occasionally, poor highways. This is the chant that the automakers and their Washington lobbyists ritually repeat on every possible occasion. But accidents need not cause injuries. And supposing what the automakers say were true, would not this constitute all the more reason for improving the safety features of all cars?

Certainly more careful driver selection is necessary. There are large numbers of people who are constitutionally unfit for driving; these and other inadequates should not be permitted to drive cars. Various studies have shown that at least half the number of people driving suffer from a classifiable mental illness. Alcoholics drive cars; pathologically aggressive individuals drive cars; sheer incompetents drive cars. Indeed, there exists no device that enables an individual to express his frustrated aggressive feelings as effectively as a car. And as Dr. Melvin L. Selzer of the University of Michigan Medical School, has stated:

> The automobile lends itself admirably to attempts at self-destruction because of the frequency of its use, the generally accepted inherent hazards of driving, and the fact that it offers the individual an opportunity to imperil or end his life without consciously confronting himself with his suicidal intent.
>
> The automobile presented the depressed and frustrated individual with an opportunity to end his life in what he may perceive as a burst of glory. The automobile may also constitute a special enticement to the aggressive and vengeful feelings present in any would-be suicides (*The New York Times*, December 24, 1965).

This is an aspect of the automobile age which will require serious attention on the part of the states and the federal government, and the sooner, the better. But none of this will ever relieve the automakers of the responsibility of making the commodities they sell as safe as possible.

Envoi

MORE THAN a century and a half ago De Witt Clinton wrote of America: "Can there be a country in the world better calculated than ours to exercise and to exalt the imagination?" It is a question that may be even more pointedly asked today than when it was originally posed. For America today, more than ever, stands before the world of humanity, in an arena of competing political ideologies, as the Great Experiment, the democratic enterprise in the new dispensation of man.

How has that experiment fared? I believe that most objective critics agree that, on the whole, the experiment has succeeded admirably. It remains an experiment, and the hope is that it will continue so, for that essentially is the nature of democracy: government by trial and error.

Innumerable errors have been made in the government of this land, and some of these errors have become strongly entrenched in the thought and conduct of many Americans. That is unfortunate; but in a democracy the chances for the correction of such errors are greater than in any other form of society, and the whole of American post-Revolutionary history testifies to the fact that error, wrong, injustice, and abuses of every kind may be corrected if only the individual citizen will take it upon himself to see that they are rectified.

The American way of life renders it not only desirable but

feasible for every American to participate in the great experiment we call the United States of America. Whether this last best hope of earth will be nobly saved or meanly lost, I have been trying to say in this book, will ultimately depend on how the citizens of this great land respond to the privilege of being American.

Index